The Wildlife Gardener's Guide to
HUMMINGBIRDS
and Songbirds from the Tropics

HarperCollins books may be purchased for educational,
business, or sales promotional use. For information
please write: Special Markets Department, HarperCollins
Publishers Inc., 10 East 53rd Street, New York, NY
10022.

FIRST EDITION

Designed by Stuart L. Silberman

Library of Congress Cataloging-in-Publication Data

Day, Susan.
The wildlife gardener's guide to hummingbirds and
songbirds from the tropics / by Susan Day, Ron
Rovansek, and Jack Griggs. – 1st ed.
p. cm.
ISBN 0-06-273742-2
1. Gardening to attract birds–United States. 2. Songbirds–
Summering–United States. 3. Songbirds–Feeding and
feeds–United States. 4. Hummingbirds–Feeding and
feeds–United States. I. Rovansek, Ron. II. Griggs, Jack L.
III. Title.

QL676.55 .D29 2003
639.9'788'0973–dc21

2002027289

03 04 05 06 07 (PE) 10 9 8 7 6 5 4 3 2 1

The Wildlife Gardener's Guide to HUMMINGBIRDS

and Songbirds from the Tropics

by Susan Day, Ron Rovansek, and Jack Griggs

HarperResource
An Imprint of HarperCollinsPublishers

Acknowledgments

PRODUCTION AND LAYOUT
Jack Griggs

INTERIOR DESIGN
Stuart L. Silberman

PREPRESS
John E. Griggs
U.S. Color

COPY EDITOR
Virginia Croft

PROOFREADER
Helen Garfinkle

ILLUSTRATOR
Victoria Ackerman

COVER DESIGN
Robin Bilardello

CONSULTANTS
Miriam Davey
Dennis K. Demcheck
Howard Williams

COVER AND TITLE PAGE PHOTOGRAPHS
Front Cover: A male ruby-throated hummingbird hovers dramatically in front of a columbine. Photograph by Richard Day/Daybreak Imagery.

Back Cover: A Baltimore oriole stretches to feed from an orange half. Photograph by Richard Day/Daybreak Imagery.

Title Page: A female rufous hummingbird displays her rufous underparts and distinctive tail while drinking nectar from a fire pink (*Silene* spp.). Photograph by Ralph Paonessa

PHOTOGRAPHERS
Names of photographers are followed by the page number on which their work appears. L = left, R = right, T = top, B = bottom.

Aspects, Inc.: 12, 16L, 17L
Wm. P. Bergen: 42, 88L, 109, 112T
Mary Lynn Cervantes: 34, 36T
Kathy Adams Clark/KAC Productions: 64L, 64R
Marion Davey: 73L, 89L
Richard Day/Daybreak Imagery: 15R, 23L, 25, 26L, 28, 30, 43, 44L, 44R, 45, 46L, 46R, 47L, 47R, 55, 66, 72, 93R, 102, 103L, 103R, 104, 107
Susan Day/Daybreak Imagery: 52, 58, 106
Larry Ditto/KAC Productions: 100R
Bill Duyck: 7R, 26R
Roger Eriksson: 23R
Jeanine Falk: 49, 50
Todd Fink/Daybreak Imagery: 11, 120L

Carol Foil: 48L, 48R
Jesse M. Harris: 59L, 59R, 60, 78, 79, 87L, 87R, 90R, 91, 96L
Dona Hilkey: 15L
Sharon Kirkendoll: 32, 33
Arlene Koch: 37, 38
Glen Lee: 36B, 63. 75T, 81TR, 81B
Jim Manhart: 73R
Steve and Dave Maslowski: 10, 92, 114
Robert McCaw: 7L. 9T, 24T, 29R, 121L
Joe McDonald: 112B, 115L
Charles W. Melton: 9R, 14, 16R, 17R, 71. 75B, 76T, 95T, 95B, 108, 113L, 117R
Anthony Mercieca: 19, 20, 115R, 122
National Wildlife Federation: 8
Ralph Paonessa: 3, 6, 62, 110L, 110R, 119T
Marie Read: 5, 121R
James H. Robinson: 18, 24B, 111
Brian E. Small: 31, 113R, 116R, 118, 120R
Hugh P. Smith, Jr.: 22L, 22R, 86, 97, 116L, 117L, 119B
Connie Toops: 51, 53, 56T, 56B, 57, 61, 65, 67, 68, 69, 70, 74, 76B, 77, 80, 81TL, 82TL, 82TR, 83, 84, 85, 88R, 89R, 90L, 93L, 94, 96R, 98T, 98B, 100L
Sandy Vanderbrug: 39T, 39B, 40
Tom Vezo: 21, 29L
Michael Wiegand: 41
Scott Wright: 13, 35T, 35B

SPECIAL THANKS TO
John W. Fitzpatrick
    Louis Agassiz Fuertes Director
    Cornell Lab of Ornithology
Allison Childs Wells
    Director, Communications and Outreach
    Cornell Lab of Ornithology
Miyoko Chu
    Science Editor
    Cornell Laboratory of Ornithology
David Mizejewski
    Manager, Backyard Wildlife Habitat Program
    National Wildlife Federation
Megan Newman
    Editor in Chief, HarperResource
Matthew Benjamin
    Editor, HarperResource

VERY SPECIAL THANKS TO
All the participants in NWF's Backyard Wildlife Habitat Program who generously shared their experiences and knowledge to make this book possible.

The Wildlife Gardener's Guide to **HUMMINGBIRDS**
and Songbirds from the Tropics

CONTENTS

An adult male rose-breasted grosbeak displays its mating finery amidst apple blossoms.

The Birds of Summer —
The Miracle of Migration

Backyard birders often think of hummingbirds, warblers, orioles, and the other birds of summer as native species that go south for winter, much like the farmer in Michigan or shopkeeper in New England who shuts down the family business and heads to balmy southern Florida to escape the snow. Ornithologists, on the other hand, see these birds as tropical natives seeking to escape the competition in their homelands for nest sites and food supplies.

Billions of tropical birds wing their way north to the relatively uncrowded expanses of North America each spring. They are greeted by an emerging crop of insects, fruit, and nectar-bearing flowers. Their only competitors for the bounty are the winter-hardened resident birds, mostly seedeaters. Neotropical migrants, neotrops for short, are what scientists call the summer visitors; "neo" referring to the "New" World tropics of the Americas.

For some backyard birders, such as John Barnum, of Stillwater, Minnesota, the brief time that neotrops spend in the yard is the most rewarding of the year. He says, "The bird that got me interested in feeding and looking at birds was my first rose-breasted grosbeak, thirty years ago. Apparently they come back on the same flight as the orioles, because both birds arrive in my yard at the same time each year." Barnum, who owns The Bird House, a wild bird specialty store, adds, "We have a greater variety of birds in the winter, pine siskins, redpolls, purple finches, and juncos, but

A male rufous hummer hangs suspended in midair. Rufous hummers — at least the northernmost nesters — migrate farther than any other hummingbird. The color of the gorget (throat feathers) depends on the positions of the sun and the viewer relative to the gorget feathers.

summer is my favorite time because that's when I see the colorful orioles, grosbeaks, and hummers in their brilliant plumage."

Whether the birds of summer are at home here or in the tropics is of little real importance. What is remarkable is that in order to lay their eggs, raise their young, and perpetuate their species, birds whose weight is measured in ounces or less embark on journeys whose distances, in some cases, are measured in thousands of miles.

And if that doesn't make your jaw go a little slack when you think about it, consider the young birds that must make the return trip. A ruby-throated hummer fledged, say, in the forests of southern Ontario doesn't have adults to guide it home in fall. Mom kicks the kid out on its own about a month after fledging, as soon as she teaches it basic survival skills. The young ruby-throat is alone 2,000 miles or more away from its home in Central America, with no conscious knowl-edge of how to get there or even where it's going. My, won't the Gulf of Mexico be a surprise?

The map of the way home is one of the thou-sands of hummingbird secrets encoded in the pea-sized egg of the ruby-throat before the bird even starts to develop. The right time to leave its birth-place and head home is also written in the bird's genes. But how a hummingbird, with a brain the size of a BB, navigates the daunting distance is not yet clearly understood. The sun, the stars, and magnetic fields all appear to play a part for different bird species. Birds can also remember and follow visual clues.

The seeming impossibility of a ruby-throated hummingbird, just a few months out of its nest and weighing only a fraction of an ounce, being able to make the long journey home alone is at the root of the popular myth that hummers migrate by hitching rides on the backs of geese. Compared to the truth of the matter, the goose explanation seems positively rational.

For some songbirds, the migration journey is much longer than the 2,000 or so miles that ruby-throated hummers travel. Swainson's thrush and the bobolink migrate the farthest, as much as 6,000 or 7,000 miles each way. Both species winter as far south as northern Argentina. The bobolink migrates north as far as southern Canada, and some Swain-son's thrushes travel all the way to western Alaska.

The extent and timing of migration of different species can be determined by ground observers. In daytime, observers can bird-watch with binoculars, and on nights with a full moon, they can watch through a telescope and see the silhouettes of migrants passing across the face of the moon. Until the mid-1900s, about all that was known about bird migration came from ground observers and from banding records.

A **male ruby-throated hummingbird** drinks sap from holes or wells drilled by a yellow-bellied sapsucker. Early migrants may depend on sap instead of nectar until flowers bloom, especially in northern regions.

A **pair of hooded warblers** (male, left; female, right) feed four two-day-old nestlings. Hooded warblers are one of many warblers and other neotropical migrants that cross the Gulf of Mexico in large numbers. Hooded wablers usually build their nests near the ground in patches of shrubs in deciduous woods or at their edges.

The advent of radar permitted a far greater understanding of the magnitude and dynamics of bird migration (see sidebar). It was radar in the 1960s that first revealed the enormity of the night migration across the Gulf of Mexico, and in the years since, it has been radar that has documented the major decline of migrants across the Gulf.

A sensitive new generation of weather radar, NEXRAD, installed throughout the U.S. in the early 1990s, reveals bird migration patterns in great detail. NEXRAD, optimized for sensing small water droplets, easily detects flocks of songbirds, even swarms of insects and clouds of pollen.

Because of NEXRAD's usefulness in tracking bird migration, Clemson University established The Radar Ornithology Laboratory in 1990. The Radar Ornithology Lab uses data collected by radar and satellite imagery to relate bird migration to topography and weather. It also develops migration maps and identifies important migration stopovers.

The information about bird migration provided by radar and ground observers cannot, by itself, affect the future of the migrants. **Reversing the decline of neotropical migrants** requires action, and the task is daunting because of its scope. The survival of the birds must be addressed in their tropical homes, at their North American nesting grounds, and everywhere along their migration routes.

Recognizing the scope of the problem, the National Fish and Wildlife Foundation, created by Congress in 1984, launched Partners In Flight in 1990. Partners In Flight was founded as a hemispheric partnership of all parties concerned with

conserving neotropical migrants and has since widened its scope to include nearly all landbirds. Governmental agencies, philanthropies, conservation and academic groups, industry, and private individuals all participate in Partners In Flight. Any individual interested in bird conservation can attend a Partners In Flight meeting. (Check the Resources section for contact information to find out about meetings.)

There are a number of other ways that an individual can benefit migrant songbirds. Does fieldwork inspire you? Check the "citizen-science" programs developed by the Cornell Lab of Ornithology, a

Bird Blips on a Radar Screen

Radar reveals that most birds migrate at night. Hummingbirds are daytime migrants, although ruby-throats usually wait for a favorable night before attempting to cross the Gulf in spring. Bird blips on a radar screen start becoming numerous 30 to 45 minutes after sunset on a typical night of migration. Two or three hours later, the screen is brightest. If weather conditions remain favorable, birds may fly until one or two hours before sunrise before choosing a spot to settle.

Migrants travel on a broad front with some clustering. Most birds fly independently even though they may be surrounded by many others of their species. The largest concentration of night migrants is typically around 1,500 feet above the ground, but some birds reach altitudes of 15,000 or even 20,000 feet, especially when crossing the Gulf.

Migrants are constantly making judgments about when to fly and when to lay over. They prefer clear, bright night skies for flying so they can see the terrain below, and they wait for tailwinds to speed them along. They avoid flying in rain or storms, although in the East, they will often bunch up just in front of a weather system in spring or just behind one in fall.

participant in Partners In Flight. Citizen science is a powerful but simple research concept employed by the Lab. Thousands of volunteers — ordinary citizens — collect data that scientists at the Lab use to provide answers to important ornithological questions. Some citizen-science programs are continuing; others are short-term; all are satisfying to people who want to make a difference. Check with the Lab (see Resources) for current programs that use citizen-science volunteers.

At this writing, a Cornell Lab citizen-science program dubbed BirdCast is morphing into a new program, eBird. Both programs use the Internet to transfer information. BirdCast was a fascinating experiment that attempted to forecast bird migration with radar the same way weather is forecasted. The citizen-science volunteers ground-proofed the forecast by reporting the migrants they recorded at a given location. "The bird migration forecasts proved to be about as accurate as the weather forecasts," says ornithologist Steve Kelling, of the Cornell Lab of Ornithology.

The Lab recognized that the lists of birds that citizen scientists supplied for BirdCast had many potential research uses beyond forecasting migration. Any list of birds seen at a specific time and place provides valuable data for science when combined with thousands of other such lists. "eBird provides the means for birders to attach specific coordinates with their list and contribute it to a comprehensive North American database on birds," says Kelling.

If you would like to have your yard certified as a Backyard Wildlife Habitat (and we hope you will), turn to the application form on the last page of this book.

One of the most rewarding things you can do for migrating birds is to improve your own backyard habitat for them. You not only help the birds by doing so, but you have the satisfaction of seeing them visit. Ornithologist Ken Rosenberg, at the Cornell Lab of Ornithology, says, "In areas with high levels of disturbed or developed land, it helps to preserve or restore even the smallest fragment of natural habitat to provide helpful stopover sites for neotropical migrants."

The participants in the National Wildlife Federation's Backyard Wildlife Habitat Program agree that even small urban yards that offer bird-friendly habitat can serve as busy hubs for migrating hummingbirds and songbirds.

The NWF established its Backyard Wildlife Habitat Program to provide a way for individuals to become active in conservation without attending meetings, writing letters, or marching on Capitol Hill. "It's a form of personal activism that affects people's own lives and spaces," says David Mizejewski, Program Manager. Over 31,000 yards have been certified since the inception of the program in 1973.

"Those yards with their little certification signs do so much for educating the public," says BWH participant Charlotte Seidenberg, of New Orleans, Louisiana. Charlotte was one of many program participants who told us how neighbors were inspired to follow their lead and begin planting for wildlife.

Ginny Widrick, from northern Illinois, says certification helped her family sell their property when they relocated. "We advertised our house as a certified wildlife habitat and we had two offers in five hours! Both potential buyers wanted it because the landscaping was designed and already established for wildlife. We were thrilled that our birds would continue to be fed and cared for without us."

Applicants to the Backyard Wildlife Habitat Program can order a Starter Kit containing graph paper, a landscape stencil, and a 48-page planning guide. Some of the other goodies currently in the kit are a poster with kids' nature activities, habitat tip sheets, and plans for a birdhouse.

The Backyard Wildlife Habitat Program is intended to benefit all wildlife, not just migrating birds, but many of the participants find birds — especially hummingbirds — among their most satisfying visitors. As a result, some of them focus their gardening on attracting birds. A few have gone on to create incredible bird gardens and have become experts on the subject.

The gardens they create are not your grandmother's garden. They are adorned not only with blossoms but also with birds and butterflies. In the pages of this book, the BWH experts will share with you what they have learned about creating backyards for the beautiful birds of summer, the neotropical migrants.

Craig Tufts, Chief Naturalist with the National Wildlife Federation, has been helping wildlife enthusiasts create habitat in their backyards for over 25 years.

A mature male orchard oriole pauses among the blossoms of a cherry tree during spring migration. Orchard orioles are the smallest of the North American orioles. They nest in much of the East, often in rural or suburban areas with scattered trees.

Does Your Yard Have What It Takes to Attract the Birds of Summer?

Bill Hilton, Jr., owns an 11-acre patch of the Piedmont in South Carolina. In the early 1980s, he says, "It was easy to look from one end of the property to the other. There were a few big trees, but no understory." Like much of the Piedmont, Bill's land had been clear-cut long ago, and for more than 100 years, it had supported agriculture — cattle grazing and crop growing.

Today Bill's acreage supports wildlife, including numerous migrating orioles, warblers, and hummingbirds. A total of 164 species has been recorded, including ruby-throated hummingbirds by the dozens.

The hummingbirds and songbirds from the tropics don't show up at Bill's place by accident, and very few of them come to the seed and suet feeders he provides for the resident birds. To attract the summer birds, Bill learned how to provide for their special needs — a place to pause and refresh as they journey north or a spot to nest.

Thousands of people like Bill have made the effort to provide for the special needs of migrating hummers and songbirds. Some are motivated by concern over the diminishing numbers of migrant songbirds; many are equally as interested in bring- ing the birds in close for a good look.

The beautiful warblers are a delight to behold, and nearly everyone is enchanted by humming- birds. Many people, including Lanny Lincoln in Iowa, even remember their first hummer encounter.

"When I was little," Lanny reminisces, "I used to pick wildflower bouquets of columbines, phlox, and wild violets for my mother. One day when I stopped to rest on my way home from the woods, a hum- mingbird nectared at my bundle of flowers. From that moment on, I was hooked on hummers!"

Lanny and most backyard birders can attract hummers to their yards with a nectar feeder. If there's a hummer in the neighborhood, chances are good the little gem will find it. Dale Turner, of Honeoye Falls, New York, will vouch for that: "I just started feeding ruby-throats last year, and they

A male Anna's hummingbird sips from a nectar feeder, opting not to use the perch provided. Hummingbirds are the easiest of the birds of summer for most people to attract; all it takes is a nectar feeder.

really came in quickly. I put out my first feeder in the summer when I saw one flying by the flowers in the front yard. Then I put up a second feeder and had three or four at a time. It was amazing!"

Nectar feeders for hummers are inexpensive, and if you get the right kind, they are easy to use and care for. In Chapter 1, our Backyard Wildlife Habitat experts tell you the brands that they prefer and why. They also explain where to hang feeders so that hummers will use them and tell you everything else you need to know about foods and feeders for hummers and the other birds of summer.

Although most people can have the same success as Dale Turner attracting hummers to feeders, some need to add habitat to their yards or modify it before hummers will find and use their feeders. One birder told us, "I know a person with one large pine tree in the middle of a mowed lawn. That's it. Each year she hangs a hummer feeder under the tree, and the hummers never come."

To best attract hummers and to see almost any of the gorgeous songbirds from the tropics, you need to provide the habitat — trees, shrubs, vines, and other plants — that they prefer and, if possible, lots of it.

In Chapter 2, the Backyard Wildlife Habitat experts and several landscaping professionals describe exactly what good habitat for birds consists of. They will help you determine the potential of your backyard for attracting the birds of summer and advise you how to realize that potential. Some yards are situated where they will attract more

hummers and summer songbirds than others, but nearly all yards can be improved.

When they find a yard with habitat they like, many summer migrants, including hummingbirds, return year after year. There is at least one nesting hummingbird species in nearly all the populated parts of North America. Rufous hummingbirds migrate all the way to southern Alaska.

Hummingbirds are so widespread and fascinating that gardening for them is becoming increasingly popular. Even gardeners unconcerned with most wildlife may have a section of their garden devoted to plants for hummers, and a few wildlife gardeners plant almost exclusively for hummers and butterflies.

It is not hard to find a list of names and photographs of "good" hummingbird plants. There are countless such lists in books and on the Internet, but much more than a name and a picture are needed if you are to select the right "hummplant" for your specific situation.

In Chapter 3, Ron Rovansek, a well-traveled expert on flowers for hummingbirds, provides a complete profile of the plants he recommends, and he describes how you can select the right ones for your circumstances. He tells you which plants are the top choices of hummingbirds, and for hummer aficionados new to gardening, he explains step-by-step just how easy it is to plant a "hummgarden."

To find out more about the birds of summer themselves, check Chapter 4. In addition to information on identification, Jack Griggs provides fascinating accounts of their lives in the wild.

A rare albino ruby-throated hummingbird female sips nectar from a feeder. Partial albinos with patches of white and with normal eye and bill color are seen more often than full albinos with pink eyes and bill.

Using FEEDERS

to Attract the Birds of Summer

by Susan Day

A male ruby-throated hummingbird pulls away from a Perky-Pet Four Fountains feeder to check over his shoulder.

Setting Out Feeders for Hummers — For Our Pleasure and Their Satisfaction

People feed hummingbirds for their own enjoyment, and it is expected that you will **place feeders where you can easily see them.** For most of the Backyard Wildlife Habitat (BWH) experts I spoke with, that meant not too far from a window, but there are other places that people commonly place hummingbird feeders, such as on decks and patios near container gardens of hummingbird plants. I put some of mine on poles in flower beds because I enjoy the hummers' company while I'm weeding and caring for their plants.

Lanny Lincoln, in Iowa, spends a lot of time in his workshop, so he mounts a feeder on his garage window. "I can watch them from my workbench," he says. "Their feet look like tiny little wires!"

Because hummers are so small, Pricilla Trudell, of rural New Hampshire, prefers feeders that attach directly to windows. "I can get a really good look at the birds," she says, "and I can can also tell when the feeders need to be cleaned or refilled."

Pricilla, Lanny, and the many other BWH experts I heard from provide habitat for their hummingbirds. They have yards full of trees and shrubs near their feeders that provide perches and safety for them. If you hang your feeder in a spot surrounded by expanses of lawn or under an isolated tree, hummers will be unlikely to visit it.

It is important to **make sure that hummers can find your feeder.** Not surprisingly, I heard that if hummers don't see a feeder, they won't come to it. Some hummers might not recognize a feeder as a food source even if they do see it (picture, p. 19).

Billy Snider, of Harlingen, Texas, suspected that many hummers simply didn't see the feeders in his small urban backyard. He and his wife, Sue, had

5 or 10 ruby-throats at a time visiting feeders during fall migration, but he suspected there were many more passing migrants that he wasn't attracting.

Billy wondered if the reason he didn't have more hummers was because most of his feeders were under the eaves of his house or in trees, where they weren't easily visible from the air. To see if that was true, Billy placed a feeder at the edge of his property in a spot where it would be visible from above for nearly a mile in three out of four directions.

"Within days of setting up this 'Open' sign, we had 20 ruby-throats at our feeders," Billy reports. "They stayed for three or four days before moving on." More waves of ruby-throats followed, and during peak migration, the Sniders estimated there were between 50 and 75 hummers in their yard at a time.

A hummer enthusiast in western Colorado says, "In spring I put out orange fluorescent flagging tape in bushes and trees. Since hummers are attracted to orange and red, they make a beeline to the tape." He believes that hummers see each other when they're foraging for food and "birds attract more birds."

Pricilla Trudell says, "The way to attract hummingbirds is to hang red clothes in all the windows each spring." On the outside of each window, Pricilla hangs a feeder. "If I don't get hummers when they first arrive, they'll go somewhere else to nest. If they stop here, some will stay for the season," she says.

By placing feeders near red flowers, you'll greatly increase your odds of having hummers find them. Even though most feeders have red plastic blossoms on them to attract the inquisitive little snoops, the first place hummers look for food is real flowers. Some hummgardeners snatch the first blooming plants of the season at their local nurseries to have something blooming when their hummers return. If hummers arrive before your first flowers bloom, try "planting" pots or beds of artificial red flowers near your feeders. The larger the red target, the better.

No one I spoke with still adds red food color to nectar to create a beckoning splash of red. While it's not been proven that red dyes are harmful to hummingbirds, the universal attitude is why take a chance? You can just as easily tie a red ribbon to the feeder to get a hummer's attention.

There are other considerations in the placement of nectar feeders besides making them easy for hummers and their hosts to see. **Hummers have several specific concerns about feeder placement,** the most important of which is their safety from ambush. Have you ever noticed a hummer pull its bill out of a feeder or flower and back away momentarily while feeding? It's checking to see that nothing is zeroing in on it. A hummer feels safest where it is able to see the surroundings without anything blocking the view and where it has a clear path to nearby cover.

Hummers also care a great deal about whether they have to sit in the sun and drink heated nectar

A window-mounted nectar feeder, Aspects' Nectar-bar, attracts a male broad-tailed hummingbird. Hummers are not reluctant to approach a window to feed.

or lounge in the shade and sip nectar at ambient temperature. They might visit a feeder hanging in the sun on a cool morning, but at midday, they will typically ignore a feeder in the sunshine in favor of one in the shade. Nectar heated by the sun also spoils much faster than cooler shaded nectar.

If there is no shade where you want to place your feeder, make your own, as Miriam Davey, of Baton Rouge, Louisiana, does. She fashions feeder hats from red plastic picnic plates, punching a hole in the center of them for the wire feeder hanger to slip through. "The hat helps with three things," Miriam explains. "First, it shades the feeder, which retards spoilage and prevents dripping (p. 17). Second, it helps keep rain off the feeder; and third, if the hat is bright red, it acts as a beacon to hummers."

Several companies include a built-in sunshade on some models of their hummingbird feeders.

Last but not least among concerns to hummers is to have a convenient perch on which to rest and guard the feeder between feeding bouts. Hummers will select a favorite perching spot, often a bare twig in a shady place above the feeder, and use it consistently. A feeder without a nearby perch may well be ignored for one with such a perch.

Hummers don't seem overly concerned about how high off the ground you place your feeders. "I have feeders at many different levels and all are swarmed by hummers," says Melissa Pappas, of Marietta, Georgia. Her hummers slurp nectar at feeders near ground level in her flower beds and from one more than 16 feet high next to a huge old trumpet creeper. Melissa cautions that there needs to be cover available at each level.

If you have cats roaming outdoors in your neighborhood, however, be advised that the height of a feeder from the ground is one of the **concerns that hummer hosts have with feeder placement.** Feeders need to be placed 6 feet from the ground in order to be beyond a cat's leap.

One of the major concerns hummer hosts have is placing feeders so that hummers can feed without fighting. If you have more than one hummingbird using a feeder, odds are good that they won't get along. Our charming little gems turn into dive-bombing rascals that mercilessly defend their food source whenever an interloper arrives on their turf.

People just starting to feed hummers may find their fighting upsetting and attribute it to mean spiritedness or some other character flaw, but hummers are merely acting in the way that nature intends — when they find a good nectar source, they defend it. An aggressive defense is part of what makes a good hummingbird.

Tracey Banowetz, in Louisiana, described this situation at her feeders: "The male hardly ever feeds from 'his' feeder but very aggressively defends it. Interestingly, the dozens of other birds seem to

A male ruby-throat attacks a young bird at a feeder. Most territorial fights for a feeder feature a noisy chase, but birds can come to blows.

respect the dominance of this single bird. They could clearly gang up and outnumber him but don't."

Gary Springer says he has experienced the same behavior at his feeders in Georgia. His solution is to "replace the feeder with a smaller one, then put another feeder where the bird cannot guard both from any single perch." In Gary's experience, adding more small feeders increases the number of hummingbirds in his yard, and he continues adding feeders as needed.

Hummingbird expert Nancy L. Newfield, co-author of *Hummingbird Gardens,* also recommends Gary's strategy when there are relatively few birds. But she says, "If you have lots of birds, place all the feeders in close proximity to each other so a single bird won't be able to defend against all of the others, and they will share — at least for a while." Many people move feeders about, grouping them close together or isolating them as the seasons and the number of hummers in their yards change.

How Important Are Feeders to Hummers?

Hummingbirds are rarely dependent upon feeders to survive. The numbers and ranges of some western species in particular seem to have been affected by feeders and the flowers we plant for them, but an individual is very unlikely to perish as a result of you removing your feeders and mowing your hummingbird flowers to the ground. The most notable exception would be hummers in winter or migrants in early spring that find themselves momentarily without any natural nectar sources.

So if you're planning a summer vacation and wondering if your hummers will be okay without their regular supply of nectar, they will; they'll just go elsewhere. You can make sure the birds are still at your feeders when you return by arranging to keep the feeders full. Many people employ house sitters, plant waterers, pet sitters, or house checkers while they're on vacation, so why not have someone feed the birds as well? All you have to do is prepare a supply of hummer juice ahead of time and leave it with the person taking care of your birds.

A young girl feeds a female broad-tailed hummingbird. This feeder with a tube port is the first model made by Perky-Pet. Old feeder models are seldom discontinued, and new ones are constantly being developed, making for a plethora of choices.

In places fortunate enough to have hummers year-round, feeders may be constantly shuttled around a yard, but most of us set them out in spring and take them down in fall. Exactly **when to put feeders up and take them down** is a question we have to consider.

The first hummers usually arrive by April 25 at my Illinois yard, so I have my feeders up by April 10. The arrival time varies a great deal with location. If you aren't sure when hummingbirds

Leave a Feeder Hanging

Frank Cantrill had never heard about the occasional rufous hummer overwintering at a backyard nectar feeder in the East and Midwest. When an adult male showed up at his hummer feeder in southwest Michigan on October 3, 2001, he didn't know what to think. "I thought it was a brown moth," Frank says. "I hadn't seen any hummers for two weeks, and this one was the wrong color."

Frank's rufous was one of hundreds reported in winter in the snowy states north of the Gulf in 2001–2002, including a celebrated pair of calliopes in New York City's Central Park. How it found Frank's yard is a mystery. Frank has a single small hummer feeder on a shepherd's hook about 3 feet from his dining room window. He suspects it was the splash of red from a modest patch of plants that caught the bird's attention. "I had a lot of salvias, some cosmos, and some geraniums," says Frank.

The rufous hummer stayed in Frank's yard one month, visiting the feeder almost hourly before moving on to who knows where. Before it left, Frank had notified people at the local nature center, who arranged to have it banded. If it returns next year, as these birds sometimes do, the identity of the bird will be known with certainty. "Next year I'll be sure to leave my feeder out long after the last ruby-throat has left — just in case," Frank says.

arrive in your area, you can find out at your local wild bird supply store.

Not everyone who puts up a feeder in spring can expect to see migrating hummers. Although they migrate on a broad front, they follow paths that they feel promise food and shelter. If there isn't good habitat for hummers in your yard or nearby, you may see very few spring migrants, and you definitely won't be having nesting hummers visiting your feeders.

It may not make sense for you to put out and maintain feeders until summer, when fledglings are beginning to explore the world and adult males are starting to migrate south. When fall migration peaks, hummers should find conspicuous feeders and gardens throughout the U.S. and southern Canada.

After fall migration, feeders can be removed. The rule of thumb I heard most often was to wait two weeks after the last bird was seen before bringing your feeder in for winter.

Many people believe that hummingbirds go south when flowers stop providing nectar, and they reason that their hummingbirds might not migrate when they are supposed to if full feeders remain available. When the first cold snap occurs and their hummers don't leave, they start to worry. Some take down their feeders while the birds are still present to make sure that they migrate on time.

The reasoning seems sensible, but it is not necessary to force your hummers to leave. Lanny Chambers, hummingbird expert in St. Louis, Missouri, advises, "A hummingbird migrates when it's stored enough fat for its journey and when the length of daylight shortens enough to trigger the internal urge to head south. Each bird's exact departure date may be a little different and will vary with latitude."

And the bird that won't leave is probably not what it seems to be. Banding efforts have revealed that the hummers you see at your feeders in fall are seldom the same birds returning day after day, but a succession of migrating birds, none of which stay for more than a few days. These birds may be doing their best to put on fat for their demanding journey. "Late stragglers will be the birds who will need the feeders most," Lanny warns.

A growing number of eastern hummer hosts are leaving one feeder out until winter, hoping to lure a wandering rufous or other western hummer. And some are succeeding (sidebars, left and p. 37).

Selecting Hummingbird Feeders — Saucer or Vacuum Style

Most hummingbird feeder manufacturers produce variations of two different feeder types. One type, such as the popular Perky-Pet pinch-waist design (picture, p. 11), features an inverted bottle or other container that drains into a reservoir with ports for feeding. A vacuum created at the top of the container when it is inverted keeps the nectar from flowing out the feeder ports.

The second type, such as Droll Yankees' Little Flyer (picture, below) or Aspects' HummZinger (picture, p. 17), is shaped like a covered saucer, with feeder ports in the cover.

Hummers use both styles, although birds used to a particular feeder may reject a different model when it is first set out (picture p. 19). "I use several brands of feeders, including Perky-Pet, Droll Yankees flying saucers, and a couple we got as gifts that we don't know who made," explains Charles Strait, whose certified Backyard Wildlife Habitat is in northern New York state. "Our hummingbirds use them all and don't prefer one over the other."

Michael Liebenstein reports that hummers fight for all the feeders in his northwestern Illinois yard. He says, "I keep three different kinds of feeders out — one model is mounted on a pole; another I hang on a clothesline. The one I stick in the ground is shaped like a sunflower."

The hummingbirds that visit Norm Helzer's hummer haven in Nebraska can dine from four different feeder models.

So if hummers aren't very fussy about feeders, **how do you select the best model** from the hundreds available? The BWH experts told us they look for models that are the right size for their traffic, transparent, easy to clean, and durable. Features that deter bees and other insects are also considered. Some people like the vacuum type better. Others prefer the saucer type.

Many people consider cleaning ease the most important feature of a hummingbird feeder. Glenn Swartz, of Corpus Christi, Texas, says, "If it's

not easy to clean, then it won't get cleaned. And if it doesn't get cleaned, you shouldn't put it up."

A midwestern woman described a handcrafted feeder that she received for Christmas. "It was a very pretty mobile with three 10-ounce red glass balls, but it was so hard to clean that after using it awhile, I put it away." A Louisiana hummer enthusiast agrees: "I've never seen an object d'art or glass-blown decorative feeder that I considered usable. Any feeder that doesn't easily come apart is going to be hard to clean."

Another common problem with handcrafted feeders is that the reservoir that holds the nectar is often not transparent. As Miriam Davey says, "Tinted syrup reservoirs can mask sour, cloudy water. Clear is much better."

Both saucer-type and vacuum-type feeders can be easy to clean or difficult. It depends upon the particular model. "The base is so hard to clean!" one woman said about the venerable Perky-Pet Four Fountains, a vacuum-type feeder. Beth Maniscalco, of Louisiana, feels the same way about her old Droll Yankees Little Flyers. "Those little suckers are hard to clean," she says. But she adds that her new Droll Yankees models are easier to care for and that even her old ones are still as good as new.

Dona Hilkey, who runs a high-volume hummingbird hangout in Colorado, uses several Perky-Pet vacuum-type models ranging from the 3-ounce Little Beginner (picture, p. 16) to the 96-ounce World's Largest (picture, below). "I've found them to be the easiest to clean, and the birds like them," she says.

Among the saucer types, the HummZinger models made by Aspects receive special praise for ease of cleaning. The designs have no sharp corners or areas that are difficult to get to. Aspects makes

In the West, a bossy rufous hummingbird may dominate all the ports on a large feeder even during fall migration when there are many hummers present. Dona Hilkey has a solution. "I hang a small feeder near the large feeder and a little higher. The rufous will usually guard the higher feeder and not be such a pest," she says.

This "World's Largest" feeder from Perky-Pet hangs in the backyard of Dona Hilky in Colorado. She calculates she has up to 2,500 hummers a day at peak.

This saucer-style feeder is being visited by hungry ruby-throated hummingbirds. Hummers typically do not fight at a feeder when there are so many of them that fighting is futile. This feeder is the Little Flyer by Droll Yankees.

A male Costa's hummer feeds from a HummZinger II. The raised flower petal design around the ports diverts rain, which would dilute the nectar if it entered the feeder.

A male Anna's hummingbird probes through a bee guard to find the nectar in a Perky-Pet Little Beginner.

You can recycle used 1-liter plastic bottles to make a hummingbird feeder. Kits that include a base and a hanger to connect to the used bottles are available. Plasticraft even provides a protective roof with their kit. However, the openings on plastic bottles are not all the same size. Some bottles may not screw into the base of an adapter kit properly.

feeders virtually identical to some HummZinger models for Wild Birds Unlimited, which markets them under their own brand name.

Ease of cleaning is so important that many of the BWH experts recommend that you disassemble any new feeder in the store before you buy it. Make sure it comes apart and can be put back together easily. Can you get into tight places with a brush to remove gunk? Are the perches sturdy enough for repeated scrubbings?

Both styles of feeders come in a range of sizes. There are models that hold 6 ounces or less and have only one or two ports, and others that hold a quart or more and have up to eight ports.

Smaller is usually better than larger when choosing a hummingbird feeder. You don't need a feeder that will hold more than a few days' supply of nectar, and if you have only one hummer feeding at a time, your feeder really only needs one feeding port. The big feeders are for people like Dona Hilkey who, at times, counts her hummers by the hundreds, and even Dona finds little feeders useful (sidebar, p. 15). Don't worry about needing a big feeder to attract a hummer; just tie a large red bow on a small feeder.

Veronica Welsh, of St. Francisville, Louisiana, initially scoffed at the Perky-Pet Little Beginners. "They seemed too small to me then, and they were only $2.50 at that time!" Could she really get something the hummers would like that cheaply, Veronica wondered. "Within two days these cheapies became my favorites — because of ease of cleaning and filling — and the hummers' favorites, though they haven't told me why."

Don Richardson, of Pearland, Texas, also likes the Little Beginners. "I have 12 and put out 6 at a time," he says. "I made a carrier, like the old carriers milkmen once used. I load it with 6 clean, full feeders and make my rounds, exchanging fresh feeders for the used ones. Then I clean up the used

feeders and let them dry in my carrier until it's time for the next changing."

Saucer feeders come in small sizes also and are very popular. Aspects makes a 6-ounce size that has a suction cup for attaching to windows (p. 12).

If you use a larger feeder than necessary, there is no need to fill it with more nectar than will be consumed in a few days. If you don't overfill, you know the nectar will be used before it spoils.

I like saucer-type feeders because my midwestern yard sits in flatland with few windbreaks. When the wind blows and the feeders sway, the nectar doesn't slosh out of a saucer feeder. A 20-year-old Droll Yankees Little Flyer that I use is still in perfect condition, other than a few scratches from my cleaning brush. It's pricey, but cheaper plastics don't hold up, particularly in hot sunny areas.

Most feeders are made of either plastic or glass, and both are popular. Some say glass is better than plastic because it's easier to clean, stays clear, and lasts longer. Others prefer plastic because it's lighter and doesn't break. In fact, a quality plastic can be as easy to clean and long lasting as glass, and hardened glass can be quite shatter resistant.

One small but interesting controversy among backyard hummer enthusiasts is whether feeders should have perches or not. Saucer-style feeders are typically designed with perches so birds can either perch or hover to sip nectar. Vacuum-style feeders may or may not have perches provided.

Hummers are used to eating on the fly. No flower provides a perch for them, so perches are clearly unnecessary. But hummers like to sit. They spend 80 percent of their time perched on twigs, wires, and other hummer-sized perches. There is no known harm in allowing them to sit to eat, and it gives us a chance to look at them longer.

Although HummZinger (Aspects), Perky-Pet, and Droll Yankees were the names our BWH experts mention most frequently, there are numerous other sources for hummingbird feeders, far too many for me to mention. In addition to feeders manufactured for hummingbirds, I heard from people who used chick waterers and waterers designed for hamsters.

Pam Perry, in Minnesota, says she likes her chick waterer because it attracts lots of different songbirds, as well as hummingbirds. "Orioles, warblers, and even nuthatches and chickadees will drink nectar from the chick waterer."

One important difference between vacuum- and saucer-type feeders is their propensity to drip. Vacuum-type feeders will drip as the day warms. The increasing temperature causes the contents of the feeder to heat and expand, forcing some nectar out the feeding ports, where **ants, bees, and wasps** can get to it.

Insects smell fragrances and can probably home in on the sweet smell of nectar. Supposedly, they are attracted to yellow the same way hummers are attracted to red, but as with hummers, the color doesn't matter as much as the reward. Flowers or feeders that offer sugar nectar will be found by bees and hummers alike, no matter what their color.

Feisty as hummers are, they feel threatened by stinging insects and avoid them. Joseph Kennedy, of West Houston, Texas, discovered that a swarm of bees at his feeders could be a threat to him as well. "The bees were agitated because they could not drink at the feeder all at once. That aggression was almost instantly transferred to me when I opened the door," Joe relates. He got back into the house without getting stung, but he warns, "Anyone with feeders should be a little careful if they get bees."

Vacuum-type feeders may have bee guards either built in or as an accessory. They typically prevent bees from getting to a leaky port, but they seldom keep them from getting to the leaking nectar. Some vacuum types are advertised as no-drip. These have the feeding level raised above the reservoir so that a hummingbird must thrust its bill well into the port to reach the nectar. They do resist dripping but might still drip with large temperature changes, and they definitely will drip if windblown.

Saucer-type feeders are inherently drip-proof. They can't drip unless held at an angle. For that reason, they won't attract a swarm of bees or wasps. If bees are a serious problem for you, the sure solution is to replace the drippy vacuum-style feeder with a saucer type. If your hummers reject it, you might need to "teach" them about it (picture, p. 19).

Using a saucer-style feeder doesn't mean that you are totally free of troublesome bees or wasps. The sweet smell of nectar will still attract some insects to explore the feeder, and if the feeding ports are large enough for an insect to crawl into, it will. "I have found bees on the inside of every feeder I own!" says an exasperated Sarah Driver, of Missouri.

The occasional bee around the feeder or swimming in the sauce won't discourage your hummers, but if your bee or wasp problem is severe, you'll want to investigate the HummZinger II. It includes flexible nectar guards made of soft plastic, which keep bugs out but allow a hummer to poke its bill through. Robert Bescherer, owner of Aspects, says it is not as popular with hummers as the other HummZinger feeders, but they do use it readily and it does solve the bee problem.

However, many hummer hosts prefer vacuum-type feeders, even with the drips. Sometimes the reason is aesthetics. More often, people believe that they attract more hummers with vacuum-type feeders. The people who use vacuum-type feeders have some ingenious ways of dealing with bees.

Some feeders include moats as part of their hangers, such as this HummZinger. You can also buy moats separately or make them from film canisters, spray paint can lids, or other containers.

The bee guards on the Perky-Pet Four Fountains feeder don't prevent bees or this Bullock's oriole from drinking the nectar that leaks from the feeding ports.

A ruby-throated hummer warily eyes a yellow jacket feeding from a Little Beginner without a bee guard. Most of the time, a hummer will carefully avoid one or two bees at a feeder and attempt to feed when it can, but it will abandon a feeder that attracts numerous bees or other stinging insects.

"Bumblebees on my hummfeeders have always been a big problem for me," says Pat Lanier, of Husser, Louisiana. "But when I diluted my solution just a bit, they became much less of a problem." The usual "bee-free" ratio is 1:5 — enough difference from the standard 1:4 to discourage insects sometimes but not enough to matter to hummers.

Often, however, serving a 1:5 ratio nectar doesn't discourage bees any more than it does hummers. Pat got back in touch to say that as the summer continued and the drought in her area deepened, the bees came back to the feeders. "Only in less stressful times does the dilute nectar seem to help," she concluded.

Some people make peace with the insects by luring them away from the hummer feeders to foods or feeders set out especially for them. Heidi Allen, of Milford, Michigan, discovered the ploy by accident. She explains, "One year when I was canning fresh peaches, I put the pits and bruises out for my night critters. I discovered that the pan became completely covered with bees and hornets to the point that there were none on the hummingbird feeders."

Heidi didn't decide to feed peaches to her bees on a regular basis to lure them away from the hummer feeders. The inspiration she took from discovering the concept was to "hang a second feeder, with bee guards removed, a few feet away from the hummer feeder. It's so easy to access that the bees don't bother with the hummer feeder."

Susan Orwig, from Houston, Texas, has a subtler technique for dealing with flying insects. "I have lots of honeybees at my feeders," she says. "I put Little Beginners in several locations and the bees gather only at those receiving sun." Since the feeders in direct sunlight are the ones that get hottest, they are the ones that leak the most, attracting the bees. "The one in the shade, next to my kitchen window, is the only one my rufous hummer uses," Susan says.

In Idaho, Michael Wiegand says he has big problems with yellow jackets. "When I fill my hummingbird feeders, I have to put out yellow jacket traps. They're small tube-shaped boxes with an attractant inside. The yellow jackets enter and get trapped. I don't like doing this because I want to be as natural as possible, but after getting stung seven times, I had to do something about them." Other people make traps by poking holes in the lid of a quart jar and putting spoiled food or very sweet nectar inside.

Ants are much easier to control than bees or other winged nectar raiders — just interrupt their path to the nectar ports. Installing moats (picture, p. 17) is one way it's done. Filled with water or oil, the moat provides a barrier that ants can't cross.

Moats have to be kept full of liquid to work. Hugh Smith, a hummingbird photographer and expert from California, found a way to avoid that chore. "I learned that you can smear a good thick layer of Vaseline or car grease inside the moat and then turn it upside down. When the ants crawl down the outside of the moat, they can't get to the hummer feeder, and if they continue up the inside, they get into the grease."

Moats are seldom used on pole-mounted feeders. Most of the BWH experts apply slippery substances to feeder poles to deter ants. Vaseline, Pam cooking oil spray, Avon Skin-So-Soft, and castor oil were all recommended.

The same substances can also be used on hanging wires. I like to thwart ants by placing a glob of shortening on the hanging wire. Others say they have stopped ants by hanging feeders from a monofilament line or from a string or pipe cleaner soaked in salad oil.

To discourage ants from window feeders, smear castor or another type of oil around the cups and where the feeder touches the window.

Louisiana hummer host Olga Clifton maintains 17 feeders in July and up to 40 in September during migration. **Keeping feeders clean** is a big job, she says. "I always tell people that if you don't have time to keep feeders clean, then don't put them out. Putting out feeders is a commitment, and some busy people just can't keep the commitment."

For those willing to go the distance, maintaining clean feeders is worth every ounce of effort just so they can be close to the charming little sprites. Rinse hummingbird feeders every time you change the nectar, and clean thoroughly at least once a week. Should you notice cloudy nectar in them — one of the first signs of spoilage — clean them immediately

The definition of clean is, to a degree, personal. Some people clean with boiling water, and others use hot tap water and a toothbrush. Still others have feeders they can put in a dishwasher. Then there's the bleach vs. no bleach groups. Some say bleach is necessary; others believe it damages plastic feeders or fear it might harm hummers. I've heard similar arguments about soap vs. no soap. And some people recommend a white vinegar rinse, while others swear that lemon juice is the way to go.

It is fair to say that if a feeder is clean enough for you to drink from, it is clean enough for your birds. If you wouldn't drink from it, you shouldn't put it out or leave it out.

When feeders aren't cleaned often enough, black scum (fungi) sometimes forms inside them and can be difficult to remove. There is no evidence that the scum is harmful to hummingbirds, although studies show that hummers prefer feeders without it.

Several feeder manufacturers make brushes for cleaning feeders. The Perky-Pet Cleaning Mop, a small foam mop with a wire handle, works well on their feeders. Droll Yankees offers two styles: the HummerPlus Brush — which can be swished inside a feeder — and their Perfect Little Brushes, which come in a set of three and are great for cleaning nectar ports. Duncraft sells three assorted brushes in their Hummingbird Feeder Brush Set. Significantly, Aspects doesn't make brushes for HummZingers.

A few people mentioned swirling rock salt inside feeders to remove black stuff. They recommend mixing equal portions of rock salt and water for best results. A hummer host in Mississippi suggested putting BBs in water and giving the feeder a good shake, and a feeder manufacturer told us you can get good results using dry, uncooked rice.

How We Make Nectar — Ambrosia for the Tiny Gods

Hummingbirds need a diet high in carbohydrates. To survive, they must engage in behaviors that require the expense of lots of energy. Darting from place to place, fearlessly investigating anything interesting, flycatching, indulging in utter promiscuity, and chasing and fighting each other all burn up lots of calories. (Except for the flycatching, don't those behaviors sound familiar?)

The formula we prepare for the little dynamos is merely a substitute for flower nectar. The accepted **recipe for hummer nectar** is simple: Stir ¼ cup white sugar into 1 cup of boiling water. Cool and serve. Any leftover nectar can be stored in the refrigerator for two weeks.

You can't go wrong with that 1:4 formula, but in the past, nectar was often prepared differently, and many knowledgeable people today routinely vary the ratio of sugar to water with circumstances.

The earliest recorded formula that I can locate — the first instance of a hummingbird being fed — was published in Alexander Wilson's early 19th-century *American Ornithology.* The formula is imprecise, to say the least. Wilson writes that in 1803 a woman he knew undertook to rescue a fledgling hummer in distress. She "dissolved a little sugar in her mouth, into which she thrust its bill, and it sucked with great avidity."

When the young hummer had been nursed back to health, Wilson writes, "I kept it upwards of three months, supplied it with loaf sugar dissolved in water, which it preferred to honey and water, and gave it fresh flowers every morning sprinkled with the liquid." So by 1803, if not earlier, people had discovered that hummers like sugar water better than honey (although they had odd ideas about what was an appropriate container).

Some people continued to make nectar with honey well into the 20th century, thinking it a more natural and complete food than refined sugar.

Hummingbirds have to learn how to use feeders. These young calliopes are being taught with a flower placed near the feeder port. Peggy Siegert, of Slidell, Louisiana, says she has had luck with feeder-challenged hummers by placing a single orange abutilon petal on the port. Hummers that are wise to a vacuum-style feeder may be confused by a saucer-style one, so Lanny Chambers, of St. Louis, Missouri, educates them. "During spring migration, I hang an empty Perky-Pet vacuum-style feeder next to a full HummZinger saucer-type. The Perky-Pet attracts the less-experienced birds. After finding nothing in any of the four ports, they nearly always go to the HummZinger and quickly figure out how to use it."

However, the sugar in flower nectar is primarily sucrose, like that in white sugar; the sugar in honey is mostly dextrose and levulose. Sucrose is absorbed into the bloodstream differently and much more quickly than the sugars in honey. More important, honey ferments easily, and fermented honey can produce a fungus that is fatal to hummingbirds.

Refined white sugar, either from beets or cane, is closer to the nectar in flowers and better for hummers than brown sugar, raw sugar, powdered sugar, invert sugar, or any other sugar. And of course, sugar substitutes, like Sweet 'n Low, Equal, or Nutrasweet, are more than useless; they could be harmful to hummingbirds.

While experts are unanimous that hummingbird nectar should be made only from white sugar and water, a few have opinions about the best source of water — tap, bottle, or well. The considerations for hummingbirds are similar to the ones for humans. Other experts question the need to boil the water used in nectar, pointing out that boiled water is only sterile until the moment the first hummer sticks its tongue into it. "I personally pour a cup of sugar into a 1-quart water bottle, fill with hot water, and shake," says Dave Patton, of Lafayette, Louisiana.

Note that Dave Patton's method of making nectar does not produce a 1:4 solution. With 1 cup of sugar already in his quart container, it takes only about 3 cups of water to fill it. As to **the best proportions of sugar and water,** there is rational argument. Early recommendations vary considerably. The original Droll Yankees Little Flyer feeder had a recipe of one part sugar to eight parts water molded into the top. In his 1953 book, *Songbirds in Your Garden,* John K. Terres also recommends a 1:8 solution or weaker. In the same book, he describes a woman in Massachusetts feeding a 1:2 solution.

While most hummer hosts usually provide a 1:4 solution, some increase the concentration to 1:3 or even 1:2 in cold weather and may reduce it to 1:5 in very warm weather. Some also use a 1:5 solution when insects become a problem, feeling that they tend to reject the weaker solution (p. 18).

Adding 1 cup of sugar to 4 cups of water results in 5 cups of nectar. One-fifth, or 20 percent, of the nectar is sugar. Similarly, a 1:3 ratio of sugar to water is a 25 percent solution, not a 33 percent solution. Moms making Kool-Aid or nectar can be content with this explanation, but a beer maker will point out that it is the weight of the ingredients that must be compared, not the volume. A chemist will scoff at the whole concept of "total percent sugar," which ignores the critical fact that sugar and water molecules have different atomic weights. A refractometer measures a 1:4 solution as being 18.6 percent sugar.

A female Anna's hummingbird drinks water dripping from a faucet. Hummers typically get all their water from nectar but will drink plain water if they need it.

High sugar concentrations are offered in cold weather in the belief that hummers need more energy to survive low temperatures. Of course, the birds could simply drink more of a 1:4 solution to get their sugar fix. Dilute solutions are offered in hot weather in the belief that hummers need the additional water to keep from dehydrating, although this is questionable.

One person told us he uses a 1:3 ratio in some feeders and a 1:4 ratio in others. His theory is that plants have different concentrations, and he wants to give his birds the same choices that plants do.

Dennis Demcheck, of Baton Rouge, Louisiana, uses a refractometer to measure the sugar content of flower nectar. He's made hundreds of tests and finds that many plants do have sugar concentrations in the vicinity of 1:4, but the plants hummingbirds like best are the ones that offer the most sugar. "The sugar content of plants in the gardens of hummer fanatics averages around 27 to 30 percent [between a 1:3 and 1:2 ratio]," Demcheck says, "and some salvias favored by hummingbirds have sugar concentrations greater than 1:2."

Experiments by C. R. Blem with rufous hummingbirds in 2000 confirmed that, given a choice, they preferred high sugar concentrations. They had no trouble discriminating between concentrations that differed by 10 percent, and they preferred a 50 percent concentration (approximately 1:1).

Hummers definitely prefer higher concentrations of sugar than most plants offer. Are the plants offering less sugar than is best for hummers, perhaps just enough to attract them, or are the hummers being little pigs with wings when they search out plants with the highest sugar concentrations? To pose the question in a more useful form, should the

Living on Sugar Water

How can a hummingbird survive on a substance as nutritionally lacking as refined white sugar? It can't, as John James Audubon discovered and reported in his epic Birds of North America (1840–1844). About the ruby-throated hummingbird, he writes, "I have seen many of these birds kept in partial confinement, when they were supplied with artificial flowers made for the purpose, in the corollas of which water with honey or sugar dissolved in it was placed. The birds were fed on these substances exclusively, but seldom lived many months, and on being examined after death, were found to be extremely emaciated."

On the other hand, Audubon observed that hummers thrived when kept where they could capture insects as well as drink nectar. He concluded, "Their food consists principally of insects...the nectar or honey which they sip from the different flowers, being of itself insufficient to support them." Modern ornithologists agree.

nectar we use in our feeders emulate the dilute solutions that the average plant offers or the rich concentrations that the very best plants produce and that hummers prefer?

It is a question that science does not yet answer. Hummer researcher Christopher N. Lotz says that high sugar concentrations would seem to be best for the birds physiologically. He cites the stress on the kidneys and the loss of minerals involved in excreting large amounts of water, in addition to the energy wasted warming excess amounts of cold water to body temperature.

In summer, there is really no doubt that a 1:4 solution is at least adequate. Birds that drink it remain healthy and return to the same feeder to suck up more of it year after year. But if you host a hummer in cold weather, Lotz says, "I think that the chances of survival would be greatly increased by offering them more concentrated nectar."

Miriam Davey says she serves her winter hummers in Louisiana a syrup with over 40 percent sugar when the weather is freezing, "because the hummers prefer it, and because higher sugar content lowers the syrup's freezing point." She adds, "No research has shown that syrup with a high sugar content is harmful to hummingbirds. Existing research shows hummingbirds are able to digest sugar in ways humans can only wish for in their wildest sugar-plum fairy dreams!"

Nearly all experts agree that purchased nectar offers no advantages over homemade sugar water. If the purchased product is liquid, it probably contains preservatives that hummers aren't used to consuming. If it's dry, it will need the same amount of preparation as white sugar and water.

Some commercial nectars are fortified to provide all the necessary nutrients a hummer needs. Fortified nectar is useful only for hummers in captivity, and even then, some experts question whether it adequately compensates for the insects and spiders that are a normal part of a hummer's diet.

Feeders and Foods — For Summer Songbirds

Summer songbirds from the tropics are primarily attracted to our yards because of habitat, but there are foods that will bring them in close where you can easily see them.

If you have set out a feeder for hummingbirds, you have probably discovered that **many songbirds like nectar** as much as hummers do. More than 50 species of birds have been known to sip the sweet stuff, including orioles, tanagers, woodpeckers, and a number of different warblers.

You'll have to remove any bee guards on your hummer feeders to let songbirds drink from them, although some feeders leak enough that it is not necessary. Julie Lundstead's orioles in Missouri have

learned how to remove the bee guards themselves. "We're always picking up the bee guards that they knock to the ground," she says.

Hugh Smith, in California, says his orioles didn't pay any attention to his oriole feeders, but "they loved the hummer feeders and removed the flowerets themselves." On the other hand, Sandy Vanderbrug's orioles and hummers in Toronto, Canada, share the same orange Perky-Pet vacuum-style oriole feeder.

Ginny Widrick, in northern Illinois, uses a Perky-Pet vacuum-style hummer feeder with four perches. "Orioles, woodpeckers, and hummers eat out of it all the time. Scarlet tanagers really like it!" she reports.

A Minnesota expert, Pam Perry, uses chick waterers for nectar feeders and has seen Baltimore orioles, hummingbirds, white-breasted nuthatches, chickadees, and scarlet tanagers using them. She says, "One year we had four male scarlet tanagers and an assortment of females. It was amazing!

"Probably my favorite," she continues, "was the Cape May warbler that came in one cold spring day in May. It ate oranges, grape jelly, and sugar water and took turns with the tanagers. People came over here for days to see those birds!"

Holes in saucer-style hummer feeders may be too small for orioles to use. Benito Trevino, in Texas, solved that problem with a ⅛-inch drill bit, but before you head for the workshop, John Barnum, of Stillwater, Minnesota, cautions that "when the opening is big enough for the oriole to insert its beak, bees can get in too."

Bees can be a big problem with oriole feeders. Feeder manufacturers have recently started tackling the problem, coming up with some innovative designs. In one, the weight of a songbird on the perch causes the feeding port to open. Otherwise it stays open only wide enough for hummers to use.

Nectar will stay liquid even below 32° F because of its sugar content. The more sugar, the lower the nectar's freezing point. To keep nectar liquid at very cold temperatures, try the warming techniques described for wintering Anna's on page 116.

A male orchard oriole feeds from a port of a Perky-Pet Four Fountains feeder with a missing bee guard while a male Baltimore oriole impatiently waits.

A male Bullock's oriole investigates an apple half.

A male western tanager tries a taste of orange.

The HummZinger II has soft plastic port protectors that keep insects out but allow birds to push their bills through.

Many **summer songbirds eat a variety of fruit.** Oranges, apples, grapes, raisins, watermelon, kiwi, blueberries, cherries, figs, plums, grapefruit, strawberries, guavas, bananas, and prickly pear cactus fruits (tunas) are all consumed by birds in our experts' yards.

Oranges are most birds' favorite, but fruit preferences depend upon what a particular bird recognizes and is used to eating. "At first our birds didn't know how to eat oranges — even the orioles," says Benito Trevino, from Texas. "It took a long time before any bird even touched them. The curved-billed thrashers and cactus wrens were the first, and they showed the orioles that it was really good stuff!"

Billy and Sue Snider, also from Texas, tried putting an assortment of old fruit on a tray. "We found that we were attracting butterflies but not that many birds," says Sue. "Then we tried guava fruit, which the woodpeckers like to pull seeds from. Other favorites are ripe prickly pear 'tunas' and bunches of grapes that we hang in the trees."

The 'tunas' are so sweet that hummingbirds feed from them, Billy says. "The hummers knock holes in the fruit, pull the liquid out, and are stained purple in the process. We have a lot of hummers with purple faces — it's comical to see!" The sweet fruit also attracts insects, and some birds are as interested in the insects as they are the tunas, Billy says.

Pat Culbertson also hangs clusters of grapes in her bushes and trees in upstate New York. She says catbirds, orioles, and other summer birds eat them.

Our experts place fruits in trees, on trays, or on the ground. "To get the maximum amount of use out of your feeders, you have to feed at the height the birds are comfortable with," advises Dave Ahlgren, in Minnesota. "You can put an apple on a high feeder and probably nothing will touch it, but if you put that same apple on the ground, where the ground-feeders are comfortable, they'll eat it and come back for more." Hermit thrushes, robins, catbirds, and cardinals eat apples at Dave's place.

Dave spears orange halves at different heights on the branch tips of bushes in his yard. In Colorado, Dona Hilkey drives nails in trees on which she hangs orange halves and watermelon slices. Western tanagers, Bullock's orioles, hairy woodpeckers, and red-naped sapsuckers are regulars at the oranges, she says. Sapsuckers and hairy woodpeckers snack on the watermelon.

There are also commercial feeders designed to hold oranges and other fruits. Some include a reservoir for nectar and/or places to serve grape jelly.

Choice Materials for "Feathering" a Nest

Many BWH experts offer nesting material for birds in spring, items such as sheep's wool, pet hair, hair from their own brushes, short strips of yarn or bailing twine, small twigs, toothpicks, pieces of dried grasses and plant fibers, sphagnum moss, thread, and scraps of string. Everything is cut in 4- to 6-inch sections because birds can get tangled in longer pieces. I collect snakeskins that I find and cut them in 5-inch pieces that I toss on the ground for our great-crested flycatchers. They swoop down and collect them as soon as I leave. Don't use materials such as cotton that retain moisture or items that won't biodegrade. Avoid putting out fishing line, which can get wrapped around birds' feet.

Putting out nesting material in a basket for the birds is a great way to help locate their nests. Watch where the birds go after they leave with the goods. It's critical to avoid disturbing a nest, so use binoculars to watch nesting progress. You can get closer looks when the nestlings visit your summer buffet.

Grape jelly is a popular food with several summer songbirds, especially orioles. "I find that orioles come to oranges in the spring and prefer grape jelly in the fall," says Alicia Craig, who manages nature education for Wild Birds Unlimited. Doug Ahlgren, in Minnesota, agrees. "They eat oranges when they first return. Then we put out grape jelly next to the oranges, and when they start eating the grape jelly, we know they'll stay for the summer."

Julie Lundsted, in Missouri, serves grape jelly and oranges on a platform feeder outside her living room window. "I'm so fortunate to have Baltimore orioles," she says. "They bring their young to the feeders next to the front window. Sometimes the male will sit there and sing, and if the window is open, it just fills the house up with such heaven!"

When traffic peaks, she says, they go through 2 cups of grape jelly a day, as well as a dozen or so orange halves. "We discovered the catbirds eating orange halves on the ground, and now a catbird comes to the feeder at my front window and eats the grape jelly, Julie says. "Every once in a while I can hear him *meow* at me!"

Jack and Leona Tutt, from Kinmundy, Illinois, typically host five pairs of Baltimore orioles each summer. "They come here for the Smucker's jelly," says Jack. When the Tutts discovered they had orioles in their yard, they set out nectar feeders and all kinds of fruit, but their orioles were interested only in grape jelly. "If they run out of jelly, they let me know," adds Jack. "They make a certain rattle noise and sit in the pine tree until I go out and feed them. Before I get back into the house, they're back at the jelly. They're worse than kids!"

Anything that will hold grape jelly works as a container. Jack Tutt uses plastic plates fixed in flower pot hangers. Others fill orange halves with jelly after birds have eaten the fruit. Norma Zier, in Missouri, made a wooden feeder that holds oranges and two cooking ramekins of grape jelly. "My orioles eat oranges but dearly love that grape jelly," she says. "They bring their babies here each summer."

Pricilla Trudell offers grape jelly in recycled plastic bowls. She places them on her deck and on supports in her garden, where they attract ants as well as birds. "I get a lot of customers at my grape jelly because of ants," she says. "I've seen robins, downy and hairy woodpeckers, yellow-bellied sapsuckers, orioles, and grosbeaks picking ants out of the jelly."

In my own yard, I have discovered that some birds love grape jelly juice. I mix 1 cup of grape jelly with 2 cups water and pour it into a saucer-type feeder. I don't put the top back on, so the feeder is just a saucer hanging on a hook or mounted on a post. Catbirds, mockingbirds, and cardinals sit on the side of the saucer and drink the purple nectar.

Since most of the summer songbirds are bug-eaters, **mealworms are a favorite food.** Even most seedeaters feed insects to their young, so many of our BWH experts place mealworms where nesting birds can find them as a source of fast food for hungry nestlings. When cedar waxwings nested in a pine tree near his garage door, Dale Turner, in New York, said, "The birds gave me heck when I went in and out that door. After I put a few mealworms nearby, they accepted me."

Shelly DuCharme, in Alabama, started buying mealworms because she'd heard they would attract bluebirds. They did, and they also brought in mockingbirds, brown thrashers, and Carolina wrens. She puts the mealworms in a garbage can lid on the grass, where birds can easily see them.

Julie Lundsted and her husband, Jim, have learned to listen carefully to each oriole's song. "Orioles all sing slightly different little ditties," Julie explains. "We have one that has come back for three or four years. He has a very distinctive little tune. We'll hear him in the distance, and it's like, 'Oh my gosh, he's back!'" Jim has learned how to whistle the tune, Julie adds. "That causes the oriole to come in close and whistle right back. It's just a riot!"

A male Baltimore oriole goes for the grape jelly on Nature Products' Oriolefest feeder, which also has a reservoir for nectar and a place for orange halves.

A male Cape May warbler finds grape jelly to its liking in this combination jelly and orange feeder. The Cape May is one of several warblers fond of jelly and nectar.

During nesting season, Shelly says her birds go through 5,000 mealworms every two weeks!

"I never intended to raise mealworms," she explains, "but I just couldn't quit feeding all those babies." Now she farms mealworms in boxes in a spare room of her house.

The summer birds in my central Illinois yard also feed mealworms to their babies. Indigo buntings, song sparrows, bluebirds, robins, catbirds, mockingbirds, brown thrashers, orioles, and Carolina wrens eat them as fast as I put them out.

You can offer mealworms on plastic plates or bowls — any slippery surface that keeps them from squirming away before the birds get them. There are also several varieties of commercially made mealworm feeders, including ones designed to keep out dominating large birds like mockingbirds.

For complete information on raising mealworms and using mealworm feeders, refer to *The Bluebird Monitor's Guide.*

Most BWH experts **feed suet to summer birds.** Some prefer to use no-melt commercial suet cakes in summer, while others offer raw beef suet year-round. Many people I spoke to offered both — and their birds ate it all.

The birds in my yard go through two peanut butter suet cakes every day. Nearly every bird that visits our feeders eats suet and, in summer, brings their young. During migration we've seen yellow-rumped warblers and rose-breasted grosbeaks on the suet. One summer we watched four families of brown thrashers chow down on suet cakes with peanut butter. Other regulars that brought babies to the suet were catbirds, cardinals, indigo buntings, mockingbirds, and Carolina wrens.

Rose-breasted grosbeaks hang out at a seed feeder. Nearly everyone we talked to looks forward to the arrival of their grosbeaks in spring, whether they stay for a few days or for the entire summer.

In Missouri, Sharon Kirkendoll's birds eat one or two suet cakes a day. She likes to experiment with different kinds but says that in summer the favorite is peanut-butter suet cakes. One year she had 10 red-headed woodpeckers from various families that nested in her yard visiting her suet cakes.

Spring migration brings in a few colorful **birds that eat at seed feeders,** including grosbeaks and buntings. It depends upon where you live whether you'll attract rose-breasted, black-headed, or much scarcer blue grosbeaks. Rose-breasted and black-headed grosbeaks love sunflower seeds and will readily eat from any type of feeder.

Buntings eat a variety of seeds. The Sniders, in Texas, told us their indigo and painted buntings prefer chicken scratch on the ground and sunflower seeds from their plants. Shelly DuCharme says her indigo buntings like white millet. My Illinois indigos eat dandelion seeds in the lawn and niger (thistle) seeds with the goldfinches. Michael Wiegand says his lazulis in Idaho go for sunflower seeds.

Grosbeaks and buntings are more likely to nest near a constant food source and will then bring their young to the feeders. "The young rose-breasted grosbeaks are always a treat," says Pricilla Trudell. "They have the mottled look of a bad dye job."

There is enough information about foods and feeders for seedeating birds to fill a book, and since that book has already been written, I'll refer you to *The FeederWatcher's Guide to Bird Feeding,* the first book in this series, for more information about feeding seedeaters. You'll also find an extensive discussion of suet and suet feeders.

A greenish female and brilliant male painted bunting share a meal of mixed seeds on a stump feeder.

A CORNELL BIRD LIBRARY GUIDE

How We Changed Our BACKYARDS for the Birds of Summer

by Susan Day and Jack Griggs

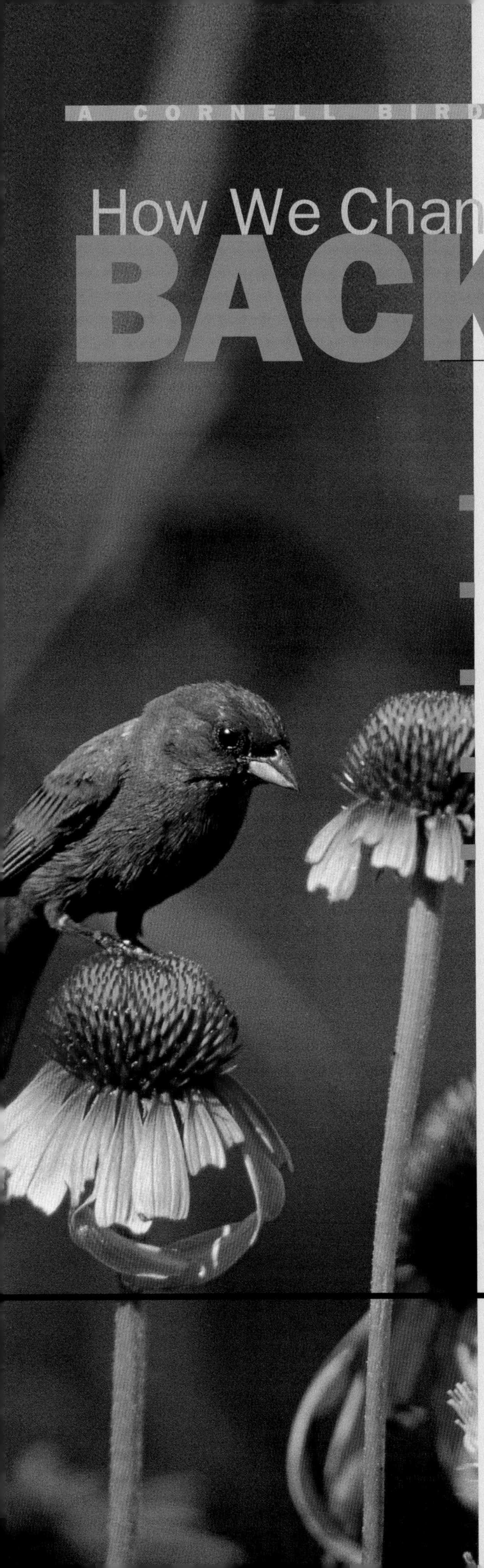

A male indigo bunting perches on a coneflower to feed.

A pair of ruby-throated hummingbird nestlings catch a little shut-eye. This nest was in an oak tree in the yard of co-author Susan Day's neighbor. Yards near extensive woods and water, such as this one, may attract ruby-throats to nest.

This ruby-throat nest is at the top of a porch swing, not in the typical outer branch of a tree. Such odd nesting sites are rare but regular.

Locating a Wildlife Garden — A Bird's-eye View

People who have gone to the trouble of creating backyard habitats for wildlife have a lot of advice and encouragement for others. There is wide agreement among them on how to create habitat to attract hummingbirds and the other birds of summer, but we also encountered unique insights and practices by many gardeners. Eight of the most instructive yards are featured in this chapter. The stories of these yards are filled with advice and tips that will guide you to success in creating your own haven for hummers and summer songbirds.

Several professional landscapers and master gardeners who specialize in gardens for birds and other wildlife were also consulted for this chapter. They and the Backyard Wildlife Habitat experts were unanimous on the most important point: Habitat is the key for attracting the birds of summer.

"I'm amazed at the variety of birds that this small yard attracts because of our habitat changes!" says Julie Lundsted, who lives in a subdivision in Jefferson City, Missouri. "We started landscaping for birds just a few years ago," she adds. "Now I'm sick that the yard is not bigger so that we could do more."

But before you start making changes in your yard, you need to step back and **take a look way outside the box.** What would a bird see if it flew over your area? Picture your garden as a mere patch in the larger neighborhood quiltwork of gardens, wooded parks, overgrown lots, and the like.

"When I first start working with people, they tend to look just at their yard within its boundaries," says Deb Wesselmann, an Illinois landscape designer specializing in wildlife habitat. "I tell them that if the goal is to attract migratory birds, they have to look at their entire area and see what the birds are looking at."

Migrating birds look for continuous areas of natural habitat, watercourses, valleys, and other natural features, and they concentrate within these corridors.

Sandy Vanderbrug, the owner of one of the featured yards (p. 38), observes that the birds don't care about property lines as long as the big picture suits their needs. "We have robins, catbirds, chickadees, rose-breasted grosbeaks, and chipping sparrows that nest in my neighbor's yard, which is a little wilder than mine, and that's fine with me because I get the benefit of it."

The easiest way to improve the big picture is to do what Sandy did, **locate near a large area of good wildlife habitat.** Wildlife gardeners who relocate always make it a priority to move adjacent to the best wildlife habitat they can find, and locating next to water is a big plus. Active birders in many towns know which areas birds find most attractive, so talk to them before relocating.

When Ginny Widrick, longtime Backyard Wildlife Habitat owner, moved a few years ago, she found a new townhouse 40 miles from Chicago that backs up to a forest preserve with a creek running through it. "I picked a wooded corner lot with the biggest backyard I could get," Ginny says. "I had the landscaper plant serviceberries, high bush cranberry, viburnum, currants, wild chokecherry, buckthorn, bayberry, and junipers." It wasn't long before she had orioles nesting in her yard and numerous other summer songbirds visiting it.

If you don't live next to good habitat, if a migrating bird thinks "desert" when it flies over your neighborhood, don't despair. Wildlife gardeners in that situation who created their own small patch of habitat found that some birds will come, and the first time an oriole or a tanager or a hummer shows up, they make sure the neighbors get to see it. You don't really have to promote wildlife gardening to many people; they just need to see the results.

Jim Gallion, of Walkersville, Maryland, says several neighbors have taken note of the wildlife habitat in his yard. "The guy right behind us is adding native plants and reducing turf," says Jim, "and the neighborhood kids are always visiting to look at frogs, butterflies, and birds." As good bird habitat is added to your neighborhood, the birds will add themselves in ever-increasing numbers.

**Constructing a Forest-like Structure —
From Top to Bottom**

Think about where you go to view orioles, warblers, and tanagers. Do these places look anything like your yard or neighborhood? If not, what's different? Most hummers and songbirds from the tropics live and nest in forests or at their edges. To attract these species, you'll need to offer the forest-like structure that most summer songbirds prefer.

"A lot of people think if they just add a few good trees and bushes, they should attract neotrops," says Deb Wesselmann, referring to neotropical migrants, the scientific designation for the summer visitors from Central and South America.

"If people want to create a forest habitat for neotrops," Deb continues, "it helps if they can go out and look at ideal habitat in the wild. If they pay attention to the structure of the canopy and how it shelters smaller understory trees and shrubs, it makes more sense later when we draw up their plans. I try to arrange clusters of trees with shorter understory plants creating a step-down effect along the edges."

By creating multiple levels of vegetation, gardeners mimic the structure found in natural areas and create habitat for all the summer songbirds, no matter which levels they nest and feed in.

Planting a forest-like structure is the typical approach to gardening for summer songbirds, but Miriam Davey has some Zen-like advice on another approach: "Try gardening by not gardening," she says. Miriam is a naturalist and landscape professional from Baton Rouge, Louisiana, and one of the consultants for this book. "Let part of your yard go wild," she says. "By reducing your lawn area, you save time mowing and conserve water resources."

The gardeners whose yards are featured in the next pages all have wild areas, as well as planted or mowed portions of their yards. The proportions vary with the individual.

Providing a canopy level is your first concern, as trees take a long time to grow. Tanagers, vireos, orioles, and many warblers use trees, in some cases the tops of mature trees, for nesting and foraging.

"It takes time to do it, and you have to think about where to plant trees," says Lanny Lincoln, who has spent years improving his Iowa yard. "Ask yourself, 'How big is this going to be? How close together should I plant them? How long will it take to grow? What will they look like at maturity?'"

It is important that there be a diversity of trees in the neighborhood. All the yards featured in this chapter include evergreens, either as trees or shrubs. Evergreens offer year-round cover, often the only shelter available for birds until deciduous trees leaf out in spring. Junipers have particularly dense evergreen tangles and also produce berries for birds.

Several of the gardeners whose yards are featured will explain how the sap and nectar from evergreen and deciduous trees can attract orioles, warblers, and other birds. Of course, insects are what most summer birds eat primarily, and trees serve as hosts to many of the bugs that birds consume.

New suburban developments are often completely cleared of trees before building begins, as they were in Lois Kauffman's neighborhood in Frederick County, Maryland. "The oldest part is 14 years old; the newest is only 4," she says. "A few of the neighbors have planted trees, and I have a fast-growing river birch, some Douglas firs, and a couple of 10-year-old maples. Last year a robin nested in one of the maples for the first time."

For people caught in suburbs with not a large mature tree in sight, Miriam Davey advises, "Plant trees like cottonwoods, sycamores, or whatever grows rapidly in your area." While they grow, says Miriam, "I'd plant the biggest evergreen shrubs I could find, both exotic [non-native] and native. If space is small, I'd run the native and exotic evergreens together, then stand back and let them grow. Many exotics grow quickly. As the natives develop, I'd garden by careful subtraction." Miriam's advice is a possible quick fix, but be careful that the exotics don't become a problem while the natives mature.

You can also plant small trees, such as hollies, hawthorns, or mountain ash. Small trees and shrubs

Trees and shrubs are either evergreen or deciduous. Evergreens are just that — plants that remain green all year. They can have needles, as do pines, spruces, firs, and junipers, or they can be broad-leaved. Holly, live oak, magnolia, box-wood, and pyracantha are examples of broad-leaved evergreens. Deciduous plants, including maples, oaks, hackberry, and dog-woods, shed their leaves each year.

Highway in the Treetops

The treeless Great Plains are the reason we have Baltimore and Bullock's orioles. The two orioles had a common ancestor before the plains divided the North American forest into eastern and western components. The plains separated the birds into two populations and allowed them to evolve independently. In the last century, as people have planted trees in communities on the plains, the two species have followed the treetops to meet again, resulting in mixed pairs and hybrids. Other bird species, including several warblers, have a similar history.

provide **the midlevel structure** of a successful bird garden. They're easy to grow and will mature faster than larger trees. Many produce berries for food, as well as providing cover and nest sites.

In her birdscaping programs, Susan Day (co-author of this chapter) pleads for people to avoid planting a lone small tree or bush in a sea of lawn. Instead, try clustering three of the same-sized trees together. You'll have the best success by grouping shrubs together in masses and layering them by height. Put the tallest species in the back, midsized trees or shrubs in front of them, gradually working down to short bushes or other plants.

Mix evergreens and deciduous species for year-round interest and use by wildlife, and plan your berry-producing plants to ripen in succession.

In Great Falls, Virginia, Elaine Tholen lost much of her understory to browsing deer. "At first I planted things I thought they wouldn't eat," says Elaine. She found that viburnums, serviceberries, and hawthorns were ignored. "But they ate so many plants — even coneflowers — that we had to get a deer fence."

Vines are often forgotten, and they add a valuable element to the structure of a garden. Natives like Virginia creeper *(Parthenocissus cinquefolia)* and muscadine or fox grapes *(Vitus* spp.) have fruit that birds love. Vireos especially seem to like foraging in high-climbing vines.

The vegetation at low levels is particularly important to ground-dwelling birds such as thrushes. In a deciduous forest interior, much of the ground is in shadows and covered with dead leaves. For this reason, many of the gardeners featured in this chapter let leaf litter accumulate in parts of their yards for ground-feeding species. Bill Hilton, Jr., of York, South Carolina, says, "I was the leaf thief of York. I'd pick up bags of leaves from curbside, bring them to my place, and spread them over the ground."

The brown thrasher is a ground-dweller that will readily go up to midlevel in a backyard or forest habitat to enjoy berries such as this serviceberry.

"Leaf litter brings in lots of insects," explains Jim Gallion, who lets his accumulate until late spring when, he says, "We take off the stuff that blows around and compost it." A layer of organic mulch will also act like leaves to create habitat for insects and grubs eaten by ground-feeders.

Sunlight can reach all the way to the forest floor in spring before deciduous trees leaf out. Early blooming flowers absorb the rays. Sunlight also reaches ground level in clearings, bogs, and at forest edges, encouraging the growth of flowers, grasses, ground covers, and briars.

In a garden for wildlife, ground that is open to the light is often utilized for flower beds and lawns. Nearly every wildlife gardener grows beds of nectar flowers for hummers. The gardeners whose yards are featured in this chapter will give you their hummplant choices, and expert Ron Rovansek describes his choices in Chapter 4.

The open areas that we and other wildlife gardeners maintain are dedicated more often to **our needs and uses for a yard** than wildlife's. Yes, you want wildlife, but you can't forget that you live there too. If children use the yard, set aside safe areas for them to play and be careful where you place plants that have thorns. Where you draw the line between your backyard and the wildlife's is a decision that has to fit you. Of course, the line is not a hard one, and much of the yard can be shared.

Connie Toops, a respected songbird habitat specialist had a neighbor on the left side of her property with a traditional lawn and yard. On the right side was a ravine and wild growth. "We wanted to have an open vista look when people drove up to the house, so we planted lawn to meet our neighbor's on that side," says Connie. "We defined planting areas in the lawn with borders and grew native plants in them for the wildlife. On the right side of the house, next to the woods, was where we had our wild meadow and leggier plants."

By defining her wild areas and surrounding them with lawn, Connie made her yard acceptable to her neighbors. Jim Gallion confirms that framing a wild habitat makes it look neat and keeps neighbors happy even when most of the yard is native garden. "I have only about a 2-foot strip of lawn left next to the garden to keep mowed," he says.

Preserving even a small piece of lawn becomes increasingly difficult for many wildlife gardeners. "I have no more lawn left," says Donald Torino, of Moonachie, New Jersey. "I have a patio and deck where I get to sit. I've got to have my spot too."

Miriam Davey recommends a manicured area next to the house. She explains, "On a small lot, the main backyard view from inside the house should look out over a patio or small lawn ringed by hummer nectar gardens and other flower beds backed by shrubs, including evergreens."

Orioles, such as this Baltimore oriole, like the nectar in blossoms almost as much as hummingbirds do.

This common yellowthroat is attracted to a tangle of wild grapes. Tangles and briars are characteristic habitat for a number of warblers and other summer migrants.

And in the remote portions of the yard, Miriam suggests natural growth. Lay out a garden hose or spray-paint where you plan to stop mowing, she says. Make an undulating, natural-looking line, and then, "Let it all grow — the blackberry tangles, trees, shrubs, native and naturalized vegetation. It's fun to see what comes up by itself and to watch the natural succession over several years. The only plants to consider removing are undesirable exotics."

Wherever you draw your line between wild and manicured, Deb Wesselmann says that you need to **make a drawing of your yard** before embarking on any extensive landscaping or cleanup.

"The technique of designing a wildlife garden is similar to that of any other landscape design," she explains. "Start by taking an inventory of what's already in your yard. List all the trees, shrubs, vines, and flowers already growing on your property and nearby, and determine which provide food, shelter, or nesting places for birds.

"Next, on a piece of graph paper, draw your house, patio, driveway, garage, sidewalks, lawn, water sources, and other structures. Include the bird-feeding areas and nest boxes you already have." This drawing doesn't have to be fancy — a rough sketch works fine for most people. The NWF Backyard Wildlife Habitat kit includes graph paper and a landscape stencil for drawing trees, flower beds, and other plantings. If you're good with computers, you may prefer using a landscape design software program.

After mapping the fixed structures, refer to your plant list and add the plant locations to your drawing. This drawing is now the master plan for your bird garden. Make any additions to your garden on the drawing first, then go buy your plants. If something dies, erase it.

The final step in developing your songbird habitat is selecting the plants and planting them. Basic instructions for preparing soil, planting, and maintaining a garden are given in Chapter 3 (p. 99) by Ron Rovansek. His instructions apply to the plants in this chapter as much as they do to hummplants.

For your plant choices, Deb Wesselmann advises, "If your primary goal is to attract neotropical birds, I'd recommend **using native plants**."

Kay Charter, author of *For the Love of Birds*, agrees. Kay and her husband have 47 acres of Backyard Wildlife Habitat in Omena, Michigan, primarily intended for songbirds. "When I put my book out, I didn't realize how important it was to have native plants to attract insects," she says. "Nesting songbirds need insects to support their kids!"

Insects are not generally supported by exotic species as they are by the natives with which they have evolved. "We are plagued with autumn olive, a noxious exotic that the birds themselves spread," continues Kay. "The birds love the berries and drop the seeds everywhere, but it is not a good bird plant because it doesn't host insects." And as autumn olive spreads, it does so at the expense of natives that do attract insects.

Native plants also require less water than most exotics, as Alice Bengel, who lives near Atlanta, Georgia, learned. "We're having a long drought, and a lot of ornamentals in our yard haven't survived," says Alice. "Because outdoor water use is restricted, I came around to landscaping with natives."

There are literally thousands of native species to choose from. Ten of the birds' favorites are described next, and the featured wildlife gardeners will mention some of their best bird plants in the coming pages. There are many more good choices for your locality that you can learn about from local experts.

Exotic (non-native) species lack natural predators and may spread rampantly in their adopted ecosystem, dramatically reducing biological diversity. Learn which plants are considered invasive in your area and avoid planting them.

"Contact a landscape specialist," says Deb Wesselmann. "Join a group," says Miriam Davey. It wouldn't hurt to do both. Local experts can answer questions about your climate and soil conditions, and they'll also know of any city ordinances that might restrict certain plantings.

Backyard Wildlife Habitat stewards from the National Wildlife Federation (see Resources) can assist; so can your local nature center, Native Plant Society, or Audubon Society. Your gardening will be much more productive if you learn what local gardeners already know about plants for your locality.

Planting Natives for Summer Songbirds — Ten Favorite Trees and Shrubs

All of these plants are native to North America and have varieties that grow well in different regions. Because soil conditions and climate differ by region, you should consult a local nursery or plant expert to determine which variety will perform best for you and when its fruit can be expected to ripen.

Cherry, deciduous tree or shrub

TREE FORM
Black cherry (*Prunus serotina*)

SHRUB FORMS
Chokecherry (*P. virginiana*)
Pin cherry (*P. pensylvanica*)

A black cherry tree is a great place to bird-watch when the fruit ripens in summer. Tanagers, grosbeaks, catbirds, orioles, and vireos are just some of the birds that can't resist black cherries. Trees grow quickly and can reach between 50 and 100 feet tall, so if space is a consideration, plant the shrub varieties. There are many other natives within the *Prunus* genus that produce bird-friendly fruits.

Objectionable to some gardeners are the numerous seedlings that sprout wherever birds roost and excrete seeds. Also, black cherry trees can be as messy as mulberries. Plant them away from frequently used areas.

Dogwood, deciduous tree or shrub

TREE FORMS
Flowering dogwood (*Cornus florida*)
Pacific flowering or mountain dogwood (*C. nuttalii*)
Pagoda or alternate-leaf dogwood (*C. alternifolia*)

SHRUB FORMS
Gray dogwood (*C. racemosa*)
Red-osier dogwood (*C. sericea*)
Rough-leaf dogwood (*C. drumondii*)
Silky dogwood (*C. amomum*)

Dogwood trees are small ornamentals that provide excellent nesting and cover sites for birds, as well as clusters of berries. Seventeen species are native to North America. Also included in the *Cornus* genus are shrubs that can be planted in masses or used as screens or hedges for nesting. All produce berries.

Hackberry, deciduous tree

Common hackberry (*Celtis occidentalis*)
Netleaf hackberry (*C. reticulata*)
Sugar hackberry (*C. laevigata*)

Hackberry trees make good shade trees for yards, as well as offering excellent roosts and nest sites for birds. Birds glean insects from leaves (especially warblers during spring migration) and eat the berries in late summer.

Hawthorn, deciduous tree

Cockspur hawthorn (*Crataegus crus-galli*)
Cockspur hawthorn (*C. crus-galli 'Inermis'*, thornless cultivar)
Downy hawthorn (*C. mollis*)
Mayhaw hawthorn (*C. opaca*)
Parsley hawthorn (*C. marshallii*)
Washington hawthorn (*C. phaenopyrum*)
Winter king or green hawthorn (*C. viridis*)

Hawthorns are small trees with pretty spring blossoms followed by thick, bushy leaves that offer excellent nesting cover. Some can be pruned into shrub form for thickets. Most varieties have thorns that keep predators at bay and so aren't appropriate for yards with small children. The small orange/red berries ripen in late summer/early fall.

Holly, broad-leaved tree or shrub

TREE FORMS
American holly (*Ilex opaca*)
Dahoon (*I. cassine*)
Possum haw (*I. decidua*)

SHRUB FORMS
Common winterberry (*I. verticillata*)
Inkberry (*I. glabra*)

Arrowwood viburnum is one of 15 viburnums that are native to North America. The berries of viburnums ripen later than serviceberries and dogwoods, so they work well as late summer food for birds.

Smooth winterberry *(I. laevigata)*
Yaupon holly *(I. vomitoria)*

Many hollies are evergreens; others, such as possum haw and the winterberries, lose their leaves in winter but retain their berries. Dahoon loses its leaves in northern winters but is an evergreen in southern climates. The leaves of most hollies are smooth and leathery. Only the American holly and a few exotics have prickly leaves. Berries ripen late in the year and can persist through winter, to be eaten by early spring migrants. Most hollies bear male and female flowers on separate plants. You'll need one of each to produce fruit.

Juniper, evergreen tree or shrub

TREE FORMS
Eastern red cedar *(Juniperus virginiana)*
Rocky Mountain or western red cedar
   (J. scopulorum)
Western juniper *(J. occidentalis)*

SHRUB FORMS
Common juniper *(J. communis)*
Horizontal juniper *(J. horizontalis)*

Junipers fit well in any type of landscaping and have dense tangles of vegetation that provide outstanding protection. Fifteen species are native to North America. Some non-native varieties are also readily available. Choose a variety that produces fruit.

Mulberry, deciduous tree

Red mulberry *(Morus rubra,* native)
White mulberry *(M. alba,* non-native)

Mulberries are medium-sized trees that we hesitated to include in the 10 favorites because they can be so messy when ripe fruits drop to the ground. But songbird gardeners all rave about the benefits of mulberries in their yards for cover, nest sites, and especially food. Many birds can't resist their juicy, early-ripening fruits. The plants are spread by bird droppings and can be invasive in some areas. White mulberry was introduced in the Southeast and has spread quickly, becoming naturalized in some states. Because they are messy, be sure to plant them away from sidewalks, driveways, or frequently used areas.

Oak, deciduous tree

Burr oak *(Quercus macrocarpa)*
Gambel oak *(Q. gambelii)*
Live oak *(Q. virginiana)*
Northern red oak *(Q. rubra)*
Northern white oak *(Q. alba)*
Willow oak *(Q. phellos)*

Oaks are excellent shade trees for large yards, and they are favorite nest sites for many forest species, including warblers, grosbeaks, and orioles. Migrating birds eat their blossoms and glean insects from their foliage in spring. Acorns provide food for woodpeckers, jays, and other birds, and

The fruit of a mulberry tree attracts this scarlet tanager. It is not unusual to see a half-dozen different birds foraging in a mulberry tree at the same time.

in some areas, hummers feed at the sweet, sticky liquid on the caps of live oak acorns.

Serviceberry, deciduous tree or shrub

TREE FORMS
Allegheny serviceberry *(Amelanchier laevis)*
Canadian or shadblow serviceberry *(A. canadensis)*
Downy or shadbush serviceberry *(A. arborea)*

SHRUB FORMS
Pacific serviceberry *(A. florida)*
Saskatoon or western serviceberry *(A. alnifolia)*

Serviceberries (also known as Juneberries) are one of the earliest berries to ripen in spring. Berries ripen one at a time, and fruit can last for a few weeks. Serviceberries are versatile plants that fit in nearly any size yard. They work well along edges in the understory of woods or as specimens in a landscape. The delicate clusters of white flowers add beauty to spring yards.

Viburnum, deciduous shrub

American cranberry bush or American highbush
   cranberry *(Viburnum trilobum* vars. *'Alfredo
   Compact'* [dwarf form] and *'Wentworth')*
Arrowwood viburnum *(Viburnum dentatum)*
Hobblebush *(V. lantanoides)*
Smooth blackhaw *(V. prunifolium)*
Squashberry or moosewood viburnum *(V. edule)*
Rusty blackhaw *(V. rufidulum)*

Easy to grow and nearly maintenance free, viburnums are great for people who don't want to fuss over their plants. The genus includes 225 species, many of them natives. They range from 4 to 30 feet tall and provide good cover for nesting. Most have showy flowers and colorful fall foliage. Choose varieties that produce berries; some don't.

Pure Fresh Water —
The Center of the Action

Good habitat includes water. Vegetation will attract summer songbirds, but it is water that draws them out of the trees and down to the ground where they can be seen. Without a birdbath, pond, or some other water feature, many birds will pass through the foliage unobserved.

The featured gardeners in this chapter all offer water and feel that it is the center of bird action in a summer garden. Few of us settle for a single water feature, and nearly all of us agree that the gentle dripping and splashing sounds of moving water, such as from small waterfalls, bubblers, and misters, are nothing short of magical in the way they attract birds.

Anything that can hold a shallow puddle of water can be used as a container, and we heard of everything from garbage can lids to satellite dishes being used. Some containers are on the ground; some are on pedestals. None are filled more than 2 inches at the deepest. The summer songbirds have short legs, and none of them swim.

By far, the most popular choice for birdbaths are large terra-cotta flowerpot saucers. Many people keep several under bushes in different parts of their yard. Some add pea gravel or rocks inside the saucer to provide shallow bathing areas.

To create the intoxicating sound of moving water, we heard of contraptions from drippy milk jugs hanging in trees to elaborate in-ground pools. Pam Perry, in Minnesota, just runs a hose to a birdbath. "It's a bowl on a pedestal only a foot off the ground that I filled with a bunch of rocks," describes Pam. "I prop the hose up with a few rocks and let it drip into the bowl. The warblers really love it."

Ginny Widrick, in northern Illinois, made a shallow pond in the ground with a plastic liner and put a pedestal birdbath on top of it. She topped that with a small fountain sprayer. A pump recirculates the water, creating a fine mist at the top, and water trickles down the bath to the ground pool. This multilevel bath attracts all sorts of birds, including hummers, at the mist, says Ginny.

Many elaborate water features are available at your local wild bird supply store. Avian Aquatics, a manufacturer that specializes in water features for birds, offers a complete assortment, including misters, drippers, pumps, waterfalls, pools, and elaborate in-ground baths.

Hummingbirds are particularly fond of misters. Many people we spoke with were quick to share a delightful humm-bathing story. "Hummers love to scoot on their belly along the wet surface of a leaf to bathe," says Bob Sargent, of Alabama. "We cut green leafy branches and put them in the mist to attract hummers to the spray."

Cleanliness of water and water containers is as important as it is with nectar and nectar feeders. If possible, place water where it receives some shade during the day to discourage algae growth. It's also a good idea to keep bird water away from deciduous trees and far enough away from feeders that hulls and droppings don't foul the water.

Plants or dead limbs should be placed near or over water for perches, but avoid planting concealing shrubs next to water to prevent cats from

A covey of bobwhites crosses a rustic wooden fence into Sharon Kirkendoll's front yard to visit a sunflower seed feeder. A male will often stay on a fencepost and stand guard, Sharon says.

The fence line around the Kirkendolls' front yard includes a seasonal variety of flowers, some vines that produce gourds for birdhouses, and a post with a feeding tray used for berries and mealworms.

Sharon Kirkendoll
BWH 30758, Holt, Missouri

"It's a wild yard, and I love it," says Sharon Kirkendoll of the roughly 40-by-70-foot front yard at her home north of Kansas City, Missouri. Sharon and her husband, Mike, live in a small development set in woods and agricultural fields. Lot sizes are large — at least 3 acres — and the Kirkendolls' property includes 17 surrounding acres.

"The habitat is mostly mixed deciduous woods with a farm field behind the house and a constantly flowing creek," says Sharon. The only part that is maintained is the front yard and a strip around the house that is kept mowed to discourage snakes.

"I started gardening here because I wanted birds, and when I got some, I wanted more," Sharon laughs as she explains why her yard is nearly all native plants. She has planted hundreds of bushes, trees, and flowers — many of them recommended by the Missouri Department of Conservation — specifically to attract birds. And she has gotten half the neighborhood ladies involved in bird-watching and gardening for birds too. "They don't want their yards quite as wild as mine," she says, "but they want birds."

"My wildness does have its limits," Sharon says, referring to her yard, of course. "I do pull poison ivy out of my flowers, but if a milkweed or gooseberry comes up on its own somewhere, I just leave it." Each summer her yard looks different, she says, as plants mature and she adds to her landscaping. And as the list of plants in her yard increases, so does her list of birds that are attracted, which now tops 80 species.

Baltimore orioles, rose-breasted grosbeaks, and indigo buntings are migrants that nest regularly on the property. In the summer of 2000, to Sharon's delight, a pair of orchard orioles selected her yard for their nest. Numerous warblers migrate through the yard, although Sharon hasn't tackled trying to identify all the species of the flitty little birds she sees.

Other than nectar for ruby-throated hummers, Sharon doesn't provide any special foods for summer birds. She offers black-oil sunflower seeds, sunflower chips, and niger seed for the seedeaters year-round, along with suet for the woodpeckers. She relies on plants to attract most of the bug- and fruit-eating birds to her yard, and two birdbaths help bring them in close. "I don't spray, so I have lots of bugs for the birds," she says.

"My warblers hang out in the low cotoneasters in front, looking for insects," Sharon continues. "If you have room for just one plant," she advises, "make it a cotoneaster. It's my favorite plant and a real bird magnet." She has planted several varieties, but her favorite is the Peking cotoneaster, which has dark green leaves, no thorns, and grows 6 to 8 feet tall. "The little, bitty spring blossoms aren't showy by human standards," she says, "but the hummingbirds and orioles can't resist them. They sip nectar from the blossoms in spring and then stick around and nest.

"I had a few Baltimore orioles nesting on the property when I first moved here," she continues, "but those numbers have increased, and now the orchard orioles are nesting too." And it's all because of the cotoneaster bushes, she is convinced. "The orioles ignore the nectar feeders until the cotoneasters finish blooming. Then the adults bring their babies to the nectar feeders, which they continue to use until they migrate south in the fall." Sharon says her orioles don't eat oranges. "But they do like to splash in the creek."

Sharon put out a hummer nectar feeder when she moved into her house but had no takers that first year. To draw hummers into the yard where they might find the feeders, she tied pink ribbons to some of her shrubs over winter. "One morning the next spring, I was bird-watching from my bedroom window and noticed a hummingbird flying around those pink ribbons, so I went outside and put out more feeders. Since then I've planted lots of flowers for hummers, including larkspur, hollyhock, sweet William, penstemons, columbines, and purple coneflowers." Now she has several pairs of ruby-throats nesting in her yard each year and using her flowers and feeders — with many more stopping by for a meal during spring and fall migrations.

The trees and bushes in Sharon's woods complement her yard. "The woods are full of raspberries, serviceberries [p. 31], blackberries, and gooseberries," she says, "and the birds eat everything!" There are also plenty of walnuts and acorns in the woods. "Enough to keep most of the squirrels away from my feeders," Sharon says with a grin.

What she really appreciates about the nuts, however, are the woodpeckers that they attract. "I have five different woodpeckers nesting in the woods — downy, hairy, red-bellied, red-headed, and flickers. I make a point to leave seven to ten dead trees per acre for birds. Besides that, I leave any live tree that blows over on the ground." As a result, Sharon gets to watch a lot of woodpeckers come to her suet feeders. "Last fall I counted ten red-headed woodpeckers — parents and babies — at my suet feeders at one time!"

Sharon likes to experiment with suet cakes and says her summer birds prefer the peanut- or peanut-butter-based varieties. "I buy suet cakes by the case for my woodpeckers," she says, and she goes through one or two cakes per day in the summer. Many other birds are regulars at Sharon's suet cakes, including colorful indigo buntings that eat the crumbs that fall to the ground.

For Sharon, attracting birds and gardening go hand in hand. "I figure birds can be my flowers if I ever get too old to mess in my garden," she says.

Mary Lynn and Michael Cervantes
BWH 18412, Fairmont, Minnesota

The Law of Unexpected Consequences has worked in a wondrous way for Mary Lynn Cervantes. Over a span of 20 years, she and her husband, Mike, have gradually improved the habitat of their lot — less than a quarter acre, right in town — hoping to attract birds. The birds came as expected, but for Mary Lynn, they brought with them the unexpected, a change in career.

Inspired by the variety of birds she saw in her yard, Mary Lynn quit her job as a school librarian and is developing a future as a nature photographer and a writer of nature books for young children. "It's wonderful!" she says. "A whole new set of challenges and adventures.

"They say that a nature photographer must travel all over," Mary Lynn continues. "Why? It's a lot easier to see a warbler taking a bath in my backyard than it is to locate one with binoculars off somewhere up in a tree."

The Cervantes' list of summer migrants is up to 40 species, most of them well documented in photographs. Another 30 or so species are summer residents. "We're proudest of the fact that we attract so many migrating warblers — more than a dozen species," Mary Lynn says. Her yard also is a regular stopover for rose-breasted grosbeaks, Baltimore orioles, and every species of thrush that migrates through the region.

So how does a small residential lot with postage-stamp-sized front and back yards become a busy way station on the migrant songbird flyway? Mary Lynn says it helps that there are a lot of mature trees, several lakes, and a slough to attract migrant birds to the area. But she is convinced that the reason so many birds come to her yard is that the feathered travelers cannot pass up the opportunity for a quick bath and a cool, refreshing drink in comfortable surroundings.

"The key to our backyard landscape is our pond," states Mary Lynn. She has added numerous feeders and plants to the yard over the years — more about them later — but, she says, "When we finished our pond and turned on the pumps, it was like the warblers just dropped out of the trees, like they were always there and we didn't know. It was amazing! We drew in birds we never saw before!"

Mary Lynn credits Carrol Henderson of the Minnesota DNR, who wrote *Landscaping for Wildlife*, with giving Michael and her the idea for the pond. "We didn't use a kit — just our own design. It's 18 to 20 inches deep, with two recirculating pumps." One pump feeds a waterfall built of flat rocks that small songbirds flock to. Larger birds such as robins and cardinals often bathe at the other end of the pond, attracted by the sound of splashing water from a small pump-driven fountain.

The pond was built in the shade of a basswood tree rather than out in the open as experts suggest. "There wasn't really any other place for it in my small yard," Mary Lynn says. "But when we dug the hole, we kept chopping into tree roots." They double-lined the pond to help prevent punctures and, Mary Lynn says, "It's worked fine."

Looking like a woodland pond, the Cervantes' backyard water feature attracts numerous birds. Water tumbling over the rocks on the near side forms shallow pools in which small songbirds bathe. Larger birds bathe under the fountain on the far side of the pond, perching on the tree limbs provided for them.

Having the pond in deep shade has proven to be a stroke of luck. To start with, the shade attracts such birds as thrushes, ovenbirds, Kentucky warblers, mourning warblers, and the elusive northern and Louisiana waterthrushes. And because of the shade, Mary Lynn says, "We have very little problems with algae. In early spring, before the leaves come out, we notice some algae, but the minute the leaves appear, the algae disappears."

Nearly all of the Cervantes' yard is in shade, though it wasn't always that way. Mary Lynn explains, "When we first moved here, there were only a few trees. We had such trouble fighting crabgrass in the lawn that we finally decided to plant gardens, trees, and bushes. Mike said it would be OK if he didn't have to mow a lawn."

The yard is landscaped on several levels, offering something for every bird that flies through, says Mary Lynn. "Tanagers and orioles like the trees, the warblers like the bushes, and birds like the towhees and thrushes like the low ground cover." By ground cover, Mary Lynn includes leaf litter. "Most people aren't into stuff like leaf litter," she says. "But the ground-feeding birds love it and keep going through it."

A huge mulberry tree (p. 31) produces the birds' favorite berries. "Anyone else would have cut it down a long time ago." Mary Lynn says. "It makes a mess of our driveway and the street each year, but we have every bird in the neighborhood in that tree."

To discover where Baltimore orioles nest, Mary Lynn and Mike watch them as they take mulberries to their nestlings. They've counted as many as six

The male blackburnian warbler is one of the many spring migrants that has been attracted to the wildlife habitat in Mary Lynn Cervantes' yard.

nesting pairs in their neighborhood. Mary Lynn says the orioles use fibers peeled from dried milkweed stalks to build their nests. "I take the pods off so they don't blow all over the neighborhood, and I save them and put them out the next spring," she says. The orioles use the soft, downy material in the pods to line their nests.

Other popular berry-producing plants in the yard include highbush cranberries, hackberries, dogwoods, and hollies (pp. 30–31). There are so many bushes, shrubs, hedges, and various plants in her yard that Mary Lynn says, "Most people find it difficult to walk through, but the critters love it."

In 1999, Mike planted a mix of native prairie plants in an area next to the road — the only sunny spot in the yard. "Mike was thrilled," Mary Lynn comments. "He got rid of his last patch of grass. Now he can sell the mower and buy more plants!"

The prairie patch proved to be a huge draw for hummers and monarch butterflies, Mary Lynn says. "The plants lasted until almost the first snow." The hummers spend most of their time at the wildflowers in summer, she says, but by fall, "that's when they really go for the sugar-water."

The number of hummingbirds migrating through the Cervantes' yard in fall has increased from a trickle until now, Mary Lynn says, "we have a huge migration. We see hummers upon hummers and can hardly keep the feeders full."

She puts out nectar feeders for both hummers and orioles, but Mary Lynn says her birds can't seem to figure out the difference and regularly visit each other's feeders.

Besides nectar feeders, Mary Lynn sets out oranges in spring for orioles. One year a scarlet tanager came regularly to the orange feeder, Mary Lynn recalls. Scarlet tanagers usually stay out of sight, in the treetops. Having one visit a feeder where it could be seen was a treat. "Everyone in the

A wood thrush lives on the dark, littered forest floor. It is seldom seen in the open but is one of the many forest dwellers that visit the Cervantes' yard.

A female Baltimore oriole gathers milkweed for her nest. Mary Lynn grows the milkweed for monarch butterflies and leaves the stalks to dry over winter for the birds to use in spring.

Arlene Koch
BWH 25986, Easton, Pennsylvania

"I have a 25-acre birdfeeder," says Arlene Koch, describing the property she and her husband, David, own in eastern Pennsylvania near the New Jersey border. "It was originally a barren old pasture," she continues. "We created everything on it from scratch, and it only took 23 long years."

Actually, much of the "birdfeeder" remains as fields. David Koch plows and plants it each year, but the crops are intended for the birds. Koch is a longtime farmer, and he finds it satisfying to plow and plant. "He usually plants in strips," says Arlene, "strips of things like field corn, millet, rape, sorghum, rye, wheat, and of course, sunflowers. He'll plant 50,000 to 60,000 sunflowers of every variety we can find."

Some of the strips are seeded with mixtures, including, of all things, birdseed. "We get large bags of pigeon mix — stuff meant to be fed to pigeons — and plant it," Arlene says. "It grows!" She also gets bags of wildlife mix from the Pennsylvania Game Commission.

Not all strips are plowed every year. "Birds get just as much use out of some strips the second year," Arlene observes, "particularly strips of field corn." And a couple of 2-acre plots are not plowed at all, she says. One is mowed each spring, and the other has been untouched for six years, so now saplings and small trees are starting to develop on it.

The crops attract more than sparrows and the other seedeating birds you might expect. They also attract bugs, and the bugs attract flycatchers,

neighborhood got excited about birds when they saw the scarlet tanager. You could find oranges in nearly every yard." Mary Lynn developed the experience into one of her children's stories.

Rose-breasted grosbeaks stop by for safflower seed. Mary Lynn says that the grosbeaks like safflower as much as they liked the sunflower seeds she used to serve. "We've found that we attract the same kind of birds with safflower that we did with sunflower, and the squirrels don't bother the safflower," she says. The squirrels stay fat on corn from a feeder of their own.

Robins can count on an early spring handout at the Cervantes' yard. "They normally get caught in the cold and snow, so we always put out apples for them," says Mary Lynn. "And we've managed to get a robin nesting in our front evergreen for the last four years because of the apples. I just cut them in slices and put them on the ground."

On a cold, snowy day in spring 2001, Mary Lynn reports that a flock of close to 100 migrating robins descended on her front yard for apples. "I stood in the yard, sliced apples, and tossed them on the ground as fast as I could. I could feel robins flying over my head, and I know if I had held up my hand, they would probably have eaten an apple slice from it. In 24 hours, they must have gone through 10 or 11 five-pound bags of apples, and they ate everything. When they finished, there was nothing left, not a skin, nothing. It was something I'll always remember!" We hope a lot of children will remember it too, for it is soon to be another one of Mary Lynn's stories for children.

Bugleweed is one of the first hummer plants to bloom in Arlene Koch's yard. It is a ground cover with tiny blossoms, but, Arlene says, "when there isn't much else in bloom, the hummers will find it."

Wildflowers, one of many crops that David Koch grows for the birds, extend in a long strip from the Koch's yard. The extensive plantings offer something for every bird.

warblers, and many other migrants. "When you go through the fields, stuff flies up that you aren't supposed to find in fields," Arlene exclaims.

Arlene believes that part of the reason she sees so many different migrants is her location in a farm valley only 2 miles west of the Delaware River and between two ridges running northeast to southwest. It's a natural migration corridor, and as Arlene says, "When the birds migrate, they have to put down somewhere, even if they can't find their first choice of habitat." The Koches offer enough habitat alternatives that their yard list is now an impressive 212 species.

To make the fields more attractive to birds, David has planted eight tall cedar snags, some of them 20 feet high, at different locations throughout the property. All the perching birds use the snags, Arlene says. "I've seen everything from hummers to eagles on them, including a lot of warblers and flycatchers and just about every kind of raptor you'd expect to find in the East."

At the northern edge of the fields is the Koches' house, surrounded by a 3-acre rectangle of yard and flower gardens. A long row of stones that David has removed from the fields over the years marks the border between yard and field. It has gradually grown to 4 feet high in some places and has become an important part of the wildlife habitat. Some birds use the high spots for a lookout; others take shelter inside the pile. Song sparrows and house wrens nest among the rocks.

The yard contains a variety of feeders and foods for birds and several water sources scattered throughout the gardens. When she first started planting in her yard, Arlene says she didn't know

much about gardening for birds. "I knew only that I needed big things, medium-sized things, and little things," she says. Over the years, she has learned a lot. Today trees and shrubs surround the yard and perennials and annuals fill it until "the backyard has very little 'yard' left," she exclaims.

"I grow more perennials than annuals," Arlene says. "But I grow about as many annuals as I can manage just to attract hummers." The salvias are among her favorites, including the widely popular anise sage (p. 58). "It grows as an annual here and gets 6 to 8 feet tall. But it doesn't make much seed, so I have to take cuttings and keep them in the house over winter."

Winter Hummers in the Tropics of Pennsylvania

Each fall after the last ruby-throated hummer has headed south, Arlene removes most of her hummer feeders, but she always keeps two or three up until the beginning of January, hoping to see a winter hummer from the West (p. 47). "Many birders and others who visit our property think I'm crazy to keep hummer feeders up at my place in the snow," she says, but more than 20 western hummers have been recorded in Pennsylvania dating back to November of 1975. "I often get called to identify some of them," she says. "When someone phones between Halloween and Christmas and wants to know how to keep a hummingbird feeder from freezing, I know I'm probably onto yet another western hummer, most likely a rufous."

The hosts of a winter hummer rarely have a hummingbird garden or panoply of feeders. "The people hosting them generally have only one feeder up, and that's only because they forgot to take it down," Arlene observes. With all the inducements she offers hummers, Arlene had faith that eventually a wandering winter hummer would stop by. She was right. On November 9, 2001, a rufous hummingbird found her oasis and stayed for eight days. "Seeing that little rufous and green piece of life catching insects and drinking from the feeders at this time of year almost stopped my heart," Arlene says.

A number of hummplants grow on the north side of the Koch house, including cardinal flowers, tropical sage, crocosmias, anise sage, and fuschias.

Friends in the southeastern U.S. send her seeds of small red morning glory (p. 82), an annual vine that Arlene says is a much better hummingbird plant than two more familiar ones commonly grown in her region, cardinal climber (p. 83) and cypress vine (p. 83). "Although all three of these vines are good for hummers, the small red morning glory blossoms don't close in the afternoon. They stay open all day and seem to have lots of nectar," Arlene says.

The earliest hummer plants to bloom in Arlene's garden are coral bells *(Heuchera* spp.) flowering quince *(Chaenomeles speciosa),* and bugleweed *(Ajuga reptans)* (picture, p. 36). At the other end of the season, when trees are bare and the rest of the world is brown, coral honeysuckle (p. 68) continues to blossom.

"Really great hummer plants that gardeners ignore are cannas," advises Arlene. "I don't think they have much nectar, but hummers constantly feed on the bugs those plants attract." They are worth the trouble of digging up the tubers after the first frost and replanting them in spring, she says.

Arlene has no difficulty identifying the premier hummer plant in her yard — bee balm (p. 55). "It comes in bloom at the end of June just as young hummers are fledging in this part of the country," she says, "and it is their favorite nectar station."

On the subject of nectar stations, Arlene says she puts out her first hummer feeders on the 15th of April. By July, when the hummingbirds are beginning to move around and migrate south, she is seeing 15 to 20 of them at a time and has 15 feeders set up for them. She uses a variety of feeder styles made by various manufacturers.

"The placement of the feeder is more important than the feeder itself," Arlene says. "First, my feeder areas have to be visible from my kitchen and living room windows," she stipulates. "Otherwise,

what's the point?" She notes that her hummers prefer feeders that are open and accessible from at least three directions and are 4 or 5 feet off the ground. Also, she says, "The feeders should be close to cover and in shade for most of the day. Hummers will ignore a feeder in the hot sun in the middle of the day."

Arlene has fun watching hummers at feeders and in her gardens. She enjoys their company and likes searching for and planting new flowers for them. But if you really want to plant a hummer garden, she advises, "plant trees and shrubs first, hang a few feeders, and do the flowers later." It is the cover that provides them safety and allows them to hang around and feel comfortable. "And make sure that the hummers have perches to sit on," she continues. "The perch is more important than the flower. A hummer will claim a flower with a convenient perch above it no matter what flower I place beneath the perch."

Sandy Vanderbrug
BWH 25276, Thornhill, Ontario, Canada
In 1995, when Sandy Vanderbrug and her husband, Jim Petkoglou, moved into Toronto's northern suburbs, their new backyard had a couple of interesting features but not much else. There was a 20-foot-tall cedar hedge along one side, separating it from a neighbor's yard, and a 9-foot-high man-made berm crossing the back of the yard, helping to block the view and noise of a busy railroad track that bordered the rear of the property. The only other landscaping was a few mature trees and several shrubs.

Most birds wouldn't give the yard much notice, Sandy realized, but she could see the potential. She has been feeding birds for years and watching them most of her life. Her father is an avid bird-watcher, and she states, "Birding has kind of been in my blood since I was a little kid."

Sandy noted that the property was adjacent to a greenbelt that included the railroad right-of-way, a golf course, and a city park. There were many large mature trees, and a tributary of the Don River ran through the area. Amid all the city development, the greenbelt was probably a haven for migrating songbirds in spring and fall, Sandy thought. All her yard needed was a little habitat improvement to bring them in.

Sandy and Jim worked on the landscaping together. "I like to think of myself as the architect who designs everything and Jim as my engineer who puts it all together," Sandy says. "Plus, he enjoys climbing trees, working the soil, and digging holes for trees, which really helps."

Sandy and Jim started their yard improvements by adding more trees, including many evergreens for shelter, and a 50-foot stretch of perennials along the side of the yard opposite the cedar hedge.

Next, says Sandy, they transformed the berm into a striking three-tiered stone-terraced garden. The top terrace is about 10 feet deep, the lower ones each about 5 feet deep. The far side of the berm has been left in a more natural state. "I've built myself a secret garden at the top of the berm where no one can see me, and I can bird-watch quietly there," Sandy says. During spring migration, she is up at dawn, "drinking my coffee and watching the warblers. We get beautiful blackburnian, chestnut-sided, magnolia, yellow-rumped, and Wilson's warblers and more," she says.

Besides the spectacular warblers, Sandy is treated to a brilliant array of other migrants — scarlet tanagers, ruby-throated hummingbirds, indigo buntings, wood thrushes, and rose-breasted grosbeaks. Baltimore orioles nest in the area and visit her yard often.

Vireos and flycatchers feed in willows that grow in a gully near the railroad tracks. "It's a buggy area," says Sandy. Wild grape and raspberries grow beside the tracks, and Sandy and Jim have added to the natural vegetation there by planting pines, hawthorn, crab apple, serviceberries, and highbush cranberries (pp. 30–31) for the birds. Fall migrants are attracted to the ripening berries.

Sandy says her garden is in zone 5, "so I need plants that survive cold winters." In addition to hardy perennials, her garden includes rhododendrons, lilacs, a boxwood hedge, and other shrubs.

This is the east side of Sandy's yard during the month of July. Graham Thomas Heritage and Red-Blaze roses, clematis, and pink cranesbill are all in full bloom. The giant delphinium will grow to a height of 12 feet.

Giant delphiniums and more than a dozen varieties of clematis vines are among Sandy's favorites. "We planted everything I could think of for hummingbirds, finches, butterflies, and bugs," she says.

"I try to have flowers for hummers throughout the whole season. The hummers really like coral bells, penstemons, bee balm (p. 55), purple tall garden phlox, columbines (p. 77), sages, and fuchsias (p. 66). I've also planted annuals for big splashes

High berms can be used to screen unwanted views, as Sandy's does. Low berms of gently contoured soil will add visual interest to a flat yard and can be designed to improve drainage.

This spot, on the top of the berm, is where Sandy Vanderbrug likes to sit concealed behind the lilac and bird-watch. A hummingbird feeder with an ant moat hangs from a branch of the willow tree. The obelisk in the background is often used as a perch by birds, especially cardinals, to sing for their mates.

Sandy Vanderbrug

of color, including bright red ivy geranium, million bells, lantana, and a new purple wave petunia that was a big hit."

One of Sandy's treasures is what she describes as "an ugly old Chinese elm tree. It was in terrible condition, having lost branches in winter storms, but I couldn't cut it down because it's a warbler magnet!" Sandy explains that it produces a winged seed in late spring that attracts many different birds. She suspects that there is a gum on the seed husks that the birds like, but she isn't sure. Hummingbirds are also attracted to the tree because it has numerous small branches that they like for perches.

A big sugar maple in Sandy's yard is another great resource for her birds. Sandy taps it and then sets out the sap in a terra-cotta saucer. "Every bird in my yard loves that sap — I don't know any bird that doesn't drink it," says Sandy. Even the squirrels and her dog, Sir Kensington, enjoy the sweet maple sap, she adds.

In February, she explains, "I drill a hole in the tree at an upward angle, hammer in the tap, and hang the bucket on the hook. The sap starts to flow on the first warm spring morning. It's best to place the drill hole on the southeast side of the tree because the sun will warm that side first and the sap will flow more." She cautions that the sap will

keep only a day or two before spoiling. "When you notice that it has turned a little bit yellow, you need to dump it," she advises.

In fall, Sandy puts out McIntosh apples. "I just slice them in half and stick them on a spike on a tree," she says. "Finches and sparrows really chow down on the apples. I purchase the marked-down packs in the bargain bins. Macs are the favorites. The birds just don't like the other varieties of apples as much."

Sandy also has an assortment of feeders in her yard offering something for every bird that might visit. Sunflower, safflower, and niger seeds are provided year-round, as are peanuts and suet. In warm weather, she adds nectar feeders and oranges.

And she doesn't forget water. "I don't have a big fancy pond, although I would really like one," she says. "But I do keep water available all over the place." In addition to two pedestal birdbaths, she has several large shallow dishes scattered about her yard on the ground in summer.

According to Sandy, "Fresh water is essential. All the birds that come to my yard use the water." She has a dripper on one pedestal birdbath that connects to a hose. "It attracts more birds than anything else. In summer, it is a bigger attraction than food."

This is the view up the east side of Sandy Vanderbrug's terraced berm during the month of May. A weeping crab apple is blooming at the right, along with numerous perennials on the berm. Hidden on the ground behind the urn is one of several small water dishes that Sandy places in her garden for the birds to quench their thirst and bathe.

She adds, "I have a little bubbler waterfall from Wild Birds Unlimited on the other pedestal birdbath. It makes a nice sound that draws in the birds. Last year I had two magnolia warblers come into my lilac tree and look at my bubbler like they were trying to figure out what it was. They eventually came in to investigate and took long drinks."

Birds and other wildlife are not the only critters that visit Sandy's garden. Canadian TV producers have taken note of her success at providing habitat for wildlife and featured Sandy's yard on two different gardening shows. "We live in an urban area, and I think that's why our yard is so special," Sandy says. "I tell people that they don't have to live in the country or have a big place to have birds. The birds will be there if people just change the habitat and make it better."

Michael Wiegand
BWH 28151, Pearl, Idaho

In 1999, when Michael Wiegand moved to a rural home near Pearl, Idaho, one of his first goals was to fix up the yard and apply for NWF's Backyard Wildlife Habitat certificate — his fourth! He first began enhancing his property to attract wildlife in 1993 when he lived in San Diego. He was so satisfied with the results that now when he moves, he routinely improves the yard and has it NWF certified. "As a result of all our moves, I've learned that habitat definitely makes a difference," Michael says. When he and his significant other, Stephanie, knew they would be relocating to the Pearl area, he was able to choose their property based, in part, on what they'd learned about attracting birds and wildlife at former yards.

"The first time I visited our Pearl home was in the dead of winter," Michael explains. "A blue ash tree in the yard was covered with goldfinches, so I knew immediately it was a 'birdy' area." He also knew that a stream running through the 4-acre property would be a bird magnet. "It runs about nine months of the year," Michael says. "It goes underground about the Fourth of July, and around Halloween it pops up again, rain or shine." Cottonwoods, willows, Russian olives, and box elder border the creek, making it an oasis in the rolling desert foothills of bitterbrush, sagebrush, and rabbitbrush.

What Michael didn't realize at the time was that the valley that the stream drains — northwest of Boise between the Owyhee Mountains and Boise Mountains — is a natural corridor for migrating birds. Michael now believes that the biggest assets to his yard "are its proximity to a seasonal creek and the migration corridor it lies within." Because of them, Michael tallied more than 60 yard birds in his first year at Pearl — "more than twice as many as I'd seen in my other yards," he exclaims.

Michael Wiegand's house is surrounded by green trees in the upper right of the picture. The food and shelter offered in the yard draw the attention of any birds migrating up the valley.

Western tanagers, lazuli buntings, and yellow warblers are regulars in summer, along with several species that nest in the trees along the creek — black-headed grosbeaks, Bullock's orioles, and yellow-breasted chats that, Michael says, sing as persistently as any mockingbird. The orioles often visit the house to eat orange slices speared to a tree, sip nectar from the hummer feeders, or glean insects from the treetops.

Orioles are also attracted to mugho pines in the yard, Michael says. "We've seen three and four orioles at a time working on the mughos outside the bedroom window." The birds eat from the tips of the branches, but Michael isn't sure whether they are lapping up the plentiful sap or eating the bugs that the sap may attract. "Whatever it is, there's something about those mughos that orioles love," he says.

The mugho pines compliment an abundance of trees — pines and deciduous — and low sprawling juniper bushes that were planted when the house was built in 1980. They provide shade for the house and excellent cover for birds and wildlife. Michael says that a big round blue ash (*Fraxinus quadrangulata*) outside the bedroom window seems to attract the most birds, including migrants. Because of this, he's hung an assortment of feeders from its branches. He's also planted an array of shrubs near the ash that birds dive into for protection from hawks.

Also in place when Michael and Stephanie arrived was a small vineyard. They weren't sure what to do with the six long rows of grapes but soon learned that orioles and robins, among others, love the ripening fruit. In late fall, when the grapes that remain are shriveled-up raisins, pheasants have a feast. The vineyard takes some effort to maintain, but Michael keeps it up for the birds.

Michael Wiegand

Colorful male lazuli buntings visit a seed feeder. For a few weeks in spring and fall, Michael Wiegand has numerous migrating lazuli buntings at his feeders.

To complement the existing trees and attract more birds, Michael added fruiting plants, such as dogwoods, crab apples, flowering quinces, cranberry viburnums, and native hawthorns (pp. 30–31). And he added two large patches of wildflowers especially for birds. "I just tilled up the ground, scattered wildflower seeds, and then watered religiously in spring. I use a mixture that includes native and non-native flowers specifically for the Northwest," he explains.

The wildflower plots are a big hit with the birds, Michael relates. Black-headed grosbeaks nibble on coneflower petals when they're in bloom. Bee balm, penstemons, lupines, and salvias are hummer favorites. Of course, after the flowers go to seed, the sparrows and finches are all over them. Michael delays cleaning up the plots until March, shortly before they germinate again. "I believe that if you're going to tidy up an area, let the birds do their thing first — after all, I did plant it for them!"

Michael also places eight birdbaths and a couple of dozen various seed and suet feeders around the yard to attract birds, and he often has hundreds of feathered visitors in the yard at one time. In summer, some of the seed feeders come down and a dozen or so nectar feeders replace them. "I hang the hummer feeders from hooks off the rain gutter and from trees and shrubs close to the house so I can watch them," he says. He is dedicated to keeping the feeders constantly filled with fresh nectar. "I don't want to lose a single customer with a stale feeder," he remarks.

Black-chinned, calliope, and rufous hummers all arrive at Michael's Pearl home in late April or early May. "We also get an occasional broad-tail if we're lucky," Michael says. Only the black-chins nest in the area. The calliope and rufous hummers tank up and continue on north to nest. They stop back on their way south in late July and August.

"It's interesting to watch their behavior," Michael relates. "In springtime, they won't share feeders, but in fall, they seem to tolerate one another more. It's an amazing show, and sometimes in fall, they'll go through several quart-sized feeders in two days!" He adds, "Calliopes seem to be the tamest, and rufous are the bullies. Female black-chins are the most inquisitive — they peer in the windows to see what I'm doing. Males of all types are feisty and try to dominate multiple feeders. That's why I put out 12 feeders during peak times."

Sometimes the hummers get a little too inquisitive and end up trapped in the house. Michael has developed his own solution for helping them out: "I slowly hold a straw broom up to them, let them land on it, and walk them out the door."

In 2001, Michael and Stephanie opened their yard for hummingbird banders doing research. Michael reports, "In two days we banded 58 hummingbirds. This is one of the first attempts in Idaho to track hummer migration patterns. I'm glad to be part of research on these beauties and will be interested to see if the same birds return again next year. They're my favorite birds, and I can't get enough of them!"

Susan and Richard Day

Michael has a final tip for backyard birders. "It sounds strange, but snags have been about the most popular addition to my property," he exclaims. "All the perching birds use them." He gathers the snags on hikes and plants them in his yard. "I've got quite a collection now," he says. "Big ones, little ones with lots of limbs, some near feeders, and others that I stick in bushes." He also uses one as a fruit station in the main feeding area, where ruby-crowned kinglets snack on apples, and orioles, house finches, and cedar waxwings peck on oranges.

Snags bring in some summer visitors that wouldn't come otherwise — the flycatchers. For three years in a row, western kingbirds that nest nearby have brought their fledglings to the snags in Michael's yard to teach them how to flycatch. "Once we had the whole family — five kingbirds — on this one snag in the backyard. I could tell the parents were teaching them how to hunt for bugs," Michael says with a grin. "Pretty neat stuff."

Susan and Richard Day
BWH #30585, Alma, Illinois

My fascination with gardening for birds, which led me to co-author this book, began with my own yard in 1990. That was when I moved to the home of my new husband, Richard, in rural south-central Illinois. The yard I inherited was 3 acres of lawn interrupted only by a number of trees — hackberry, wild cherry, white pines, pecans, hickory, ash, and oaks. I've always been a plant person and couldn't imagine living in such a barren place, so I soon was talking with Richard about yard improvements.

Richard is a professional nature photographer, and one of his passions is birds. He'd been feeding and photographing them for 15 years when I came on the scene and had recorded a respectable yard list of about 50 species. We knew that with proper habitat, we could attract more, so we decided to create a sanctuary for birds. Now, a dozen years later, the yard list has mushroomed to nearly 170 species, the number of summer birds has at least tripled, and we have more than 40 species nesting in the yard as a result of the landscaping. Our yard is proof that if you plant it, the birds will come.

We started by hiring a landscape designer to help draw a master plan. With such a big yard, we knew it would take several years to complete, so we tackled a new section each year. Since we already had large trees, we focused on shrubs and smaller trees that would grow quickly and offer food and shelter to birds. We also wanted evergreens for shelter and nest sites.

Richard and I studied books and visited local nurseries and public gardens to find the best plants for our area. We live at the northern edge of hardiness zone 6, and I usually try to plant things that will survive zone 5 winters, just to be safe. Most of the plants we grow can be grown in much of the East and Midwest.

We selected native species for the most part, knowing they would grow well in our area, require only minimal maintenance, and be familiar to the birds. Early on, we learned to buy plants from reputable local nurseries rather than discount stores. Cheaper plants raised elsewhere and shipped to our

This is a flower bed in my yard where I spend a lot of time watching birds and butterflies in the summer. Orioles and robins follow me when I pull weeds, snatching insects I disturb in the mulch. Hummingbirds dart in and out of the penstemons, verbenas, salvias, and weigelas that are scattered throughout this bed.

Susan and Richard Day

It is the opening of berry season in our yard, late May. The serviceberries are ripe, and this female Baltimore oriole is an eager customer.

Bright red cranberries mark the close of the berry season, ripening just in time for the last fall migrants.

area sometimes needed to be replaced in a couple of years. Each time we replaced an inferior plant, we not only spent more money, we also lost years of plant growth. It made sense to pay for quality.

Rather than plant a lone bush in an open section of lawn, we clustered groups of them in islands. There are a dozen of these islands scattered about the yard. Each offers a large area for bird feeding and shelter and also creates a border or edge with the lawn. Edges are popular hangouts for wildlife, enough so that the phenomenon is given a name — the edge effect.

We mulch the beds around the berry bushes to keep weeds down and conserve water. Ground-feeding birds like towhees, sparrows, quail, and thrashers scratch for insects in the mulch and leaf litter of the berry beds. Many birds seek shelter from predators beneath the bushes or rest in their shade on hot summer days.

Berries and fruits of most plants are ripe and edible for only a short period. One of our important gardening goals was to have a variety of plants with berries ripening in succession. We wanted a constant supply of berries for the birds.

The first fruits to ripen are serviceberries (p. 31) in late May and early June. My theory is that after a long winter, the birds must be starved for fresh fruit, because serviceberries attract more birds than any other plant in our yard.

We've planted downy and shadblow serviceberries, which mature at different times. The small berries ripen one at a time and are plucked off as soon as they turn rosy-red. We've watched brown thrashers, kingbirds, catbirds, robins, mockingbirds, bluebirds, red-headed and red-bellied woodpeckers, cedar waxwings, and Baltimore and orchard orioles, as well as many resident birds, eat serviceberries.

One pair of Baltimore orioles returns each year to nest in a pecan tree, usually choosing a branch directly above one of the serviceberry bushes. As the female weaves her nest, her mate sings from his perch and stands guard over their food supply.

The small berries of the gray and silky dogwood shrubs ripen after the serviceberries. We've planted 50 or so of them, and they're our bread-and-butter offering for summer visitors. These hardy plants continue to bloom and set an abundance of berries — blue in the silky species, white in the gray — throughout the summer. They begin ripening just in time to feed the first hungry fledglings that the adults bring to our fruit restaurant.

We regularly see robins, mockingbirds, brown thrashers, kingbirds, bluebirds, cedar waxwings, catbirds, and woodpeckers eating at the dogwoods. And with so many bushes in different areas of the yard, we prevent territorial disputes caused by the aggressive kingbirds and mockers. The bullies usually pick their favorite dogwood patch and guard it against intruders while the other birds move to other parts of the yard.

Two viburnums (p. 31) — nannyberry and our native arrowwood — are great places to find birds munching berries in July and August. At the same time, blackberries and mulberries (p. 31) are ripe in brushy, wild areas along a creek that borders part of the yard. Nesting birds busy raising second and third broods make trip after trip to their nests with berries in their beaks. August is also when a huge old wild cherry tree in the front yard starts to rustle with bird activity.

In early fall, just as the first migrating flocks of robins and cedar waxwings appear, the berries on our hawthorn trees (p. 30) begin to ripen. The migrants compete with our summer families of brown thrashers and catbirds for the bright, red-orange berries. They also find wild elderberries in the ditches along our property. Woodpeckers, jays, crows, and squirrels raid the pecans, hickories, and oaks to stock their winter caches. At this time, another viburnum, the American cranberry bush, is just beginning to ripen. Some of its berries aren't ripe until after the migrants move on.

Our resident cardinals, blue jays, bluebirds, and woodpeckers feast on the remaining cranberries. They also eat the fruits from eastern red cedars, junipers, crab apples, and winterberries and other hollies in winter. Crab apples are always the last fruits to be consumed in our yard. Many remain until spring, when early returning robins and cedar waxwings survive on them as they wait for warm weather to arrive and fresh foods to appear.

In addition to the islands of shrubs, we have 16 beds of flowers for birds and butterflies. I'm a flower fanatic, and I wanted to make sure there were blooms to greet the earliest hummingbird and more blooms to last until the last lingering hummer tanked up and departed in fall. I must have done something right because our hummers spend more time in the flowers than at our nectar feeders. Many times when I'm watering the flowers, hummers will bathe in the mist from my wand. No doubt, the birds consider me part of the landscape

Our hummers seem to favor salvias for nectar. There are literally hundreds of species of salvias to choose from. I have a few perennials; however, most salvias are an annual in my zone, so I plant numerous new varieties each year. They and my other hummer plants bloom in succession all season.

The first hummer flowers to bloom in my garden are native and hybrid columbines (p. 77). Next are bleeding hearts, lilac, and weigela bushes, followed by bee balm (p. 55), honeysuckle (p. 68), and penstemons. In midsummer, hummers sip from liatris, garden phlox, cigar plants (p. 73), wisteria, cleomes, million bells, blackberry lilies, and coral bells. Before they leave in fall, they gorge themselves on nectar from agastaches, tithonia, cardinal climber vines (p. 83), cardinal flowers (p. 60), and late-blooming salvias.

Hummers aren't the only birds that visit the flower beds in summer. Orioles nibble on the petals of cup plants, blackberry lilies, and some of my fragrant petunias. Indigo buntings, song sparrows, field sparrows, cardinals, and goldfinches eat the flowers and seeds from coneflowers, hollyhocks, compass plants, cosmos, and others.

Water is another big draw for birds. We knew that, but we had no idea just how many birds we could attract with water. We started with several pedestal birdbaths, but it wasn't until we installed an in-ground Bird Creek kit from Avian Aquatics that the birds started pouring in. The "creek" is only 5 or 6 feet long, and we have lined the bottom with gravel so that the water is just an inch or two deep.

This is part of one of my large island flower beds and includes numerous plants for hummingbirds. Butterfly bushes are in the foreground, blazing star (the upright spiky purple flowers) is at left center, bee balm is at the back, and hollyhocks are to the right of the bee balm. Salvias, phlox, and penstemons are also in the bed.

A rose-breasted grosbeak bathes in a shallow pool near the waterfall in the "creek" in our yard. This commercial kit has attracted all the summer songbirds, including every warbler species, that migrate through the region.

A catbird feeds its nestlings in one of our arrowwood viburnums. Catbirds also frequently nest in the gray and silky dogwoods along the driveway.

The water flows into a reservoir from where it is pumped back up to a little waterfall at the head of the creek.

The shallow, moving water is irresistible to our birds. To make it even more inviting, we've added a few snags for perches next to it and planted some low-growing shrubs nearby. We've counted more than 60 species using this relatively small water source. Of all the backyard improvements we've done, this creek has been the birds' favorite.

In 2001, at least four pairs of brown thrashers nested in the bushes in our yard, some producing three broods. We know of at least five pairs of catbirds that nested that year too. Robin nests appeared in nearly every tree. One day in July, we counted more than 20 active nests in the yard!

Early nesters such as mockingbirds, robins, and brown thrashers select evergreens — hollies, pines, and junipers — for their first broods. Once the deciduous trees and shrubs have leafed out, they often build second nests in them. The hawthorns with their protective thorns are popular nesting spots with brown thrashers, cardinals, mocking-birds, catbirds, robins, and blue jays.

Many birds nest in the clusters of arrowwood viburnums throughout the yard. Even birds that don't eat berries, such as indigo buntings and chipping sparrows, build nests in the viburnums. Eastern wood-peewees, blue-gray gnatcatchers, and yellow-billed cuckoos nest in our trees and hunt insects in the yard. We were thrilled when a pair of warbling vireos wove their nest a few feet away from a Baltimore oriole nest in a cottonwood tree. Across the yard, a pair of orchard orioles raised their brood near a family of eastern king-birds in the top of an old hickory tree.

Bird nests show up in the flower beds too. When I'm weeding the flowers (which I do often, as I have so many of them), I regularly find hidden song and chipping sparrow nests. Pulling weeds loosens the soil and brings insects to the surface. When I'm busy weeding on my hands and knees, I sometimes see orioles and robins just a few feet away hopping through the flowers, capturing bugs in the mulch.

In addition to the 3-acre yard, we co-own an additional 37 adjoining acres. On 5 of those acres adjacent to the yard, we established a native grass and wildflower prairie in 1991. The prairie grasses attract flocks of goldfinches, indigo buntings, and other seedeaters. Orioles come to gather plant fibers for their nests and eat blossoms from cup plants. Hummingbirds dart from plant to plant for nectar, paying special attention to the native penstemons in early spring.

The prairie is also a haven for insects and insect-eating birds. We watch kingbirds, yellow-breasted chats, orioles, peewees, and yellow-rumped warblers catch bugs there. During spring migration, the prairie is filled with warblers that stop for a snack on their long journey north. Many perch on snags we place there for them.

Some birds hide their nests in the cover of the prairie plants. We've found the nests of common yellowthroats, dickcissels, field and song sparrows, woodcocks, meadowlarks, and northern bobwhites in the prairie

In 1996, we developed an 8-acre shallow-water wetland adjacent to the yard and wildflower prairie. It also borders a small woodlot, and a series of trails connects the yard, woods, prairie, and wetlands, so we can stroll through them all and bird-watch.

We designed the wetlands to attract waterfowl, shorebirds, and waders, and it, too, has been a huge success. We've seen nearly every waterbird species possible in this part of the country. Though it may

This female Baltimore oriole is delivering a fat green caterpillar to her nestlings in our hackberry tree. She wove her sock nest almost entirely from white yarn that we put out in a nesting material basket.

My container garden brings hummers onto the deck. This little corner of our deck hums with hummers all summer long. When a plant gets leggy or is finished blooming for the season, I replace it.

not directly attract hummers and summer songbirds, we know it complements what's in our yard and prairie. We planted native grasses, wetland plants, and flowers along the edges, which offer birds food sources. We see many of our yard birds, such as kingbirds and bluebirds, eating insects in the wetland vegetation. Hummingbirds sip nectar from the cardinal flowers (p. 60) we've planted there.

Some of our neighbors are puzzled by what we've done on our property. Since we are fortunate enough to live in the middle of a rich agricultural region, they wonder why we don't grow corn and soybeans. Why would we want a wetland or all those flowers and weeds? But, the way we see it, the fertile soil also produces healthy bushes, trees, grasses, and flowers — an ideal sanctuary for the birds we love. In our opinion, that union of plants and birds makes a perfect marriage!

Carol Foil
BWH 30068, Baton Rouge, Louisiana

"There is not a day that I don't have hummers in my yard," says Carol Foil, who lives on a semi-urban lot in Baton Rouge, Louisiana. Few hummingbird hosts in the East can boast of year-round visitors. Some westerners have resident Anna's or Allen's hummers all year, and a few communities in the Southwest near the Mexican border see an assortment of hummers throughout the year. But east of the Rockies,

there is only the ruby-throated hummingbird, and it leaves in fall — or so the story used to go.

In the winter of 2000–01, more than one thousand hummers were reported east of the Great Plains. And there were nine species in addition to ruby-throats, including such exotics as broad-billed hummingbirds and green-breasted mangos.

Most winter hummers in the East are sighted in the extreme southern band of land kept warm by winds off the Gulf of Mexico. Along the Gulf, the largest concentration is in Louisiana, and within Louisiana, it is the hummgardeners in and around Baton Rouge, including Carol, who record the most winter hummers. "In the winter of 1999–2000, I had five species — rufous, calliope, black-chinned, buff-bellied, and ruby-throated — and at least nine individuals," says Carol.

Carol's lot is deep and narrow, about 100 by 500 feet, with a backyard devoted to wildlife habitat. The original owner was a botanist on the faculty of LSU. "I inherited some wonderful structure," she says, referring primarily to the mature trees and abundant evergreen understory that occupies the back third of her yard. "I have several 80-year-old Buford holly trees and 60- to 70-year-old camellias. They give the birds lots of shelter."

Carol has long enjoyed having birds of all kinds in her yard. She provides a variety of feeders and sources of water for them. When hurricane Andrew

The brilliant red berries on the holly tree (behind the angel's trumpet in the foreground) are the beacons that draw hummers to investigate her yard, Carol Foil believes. "That and the silly-looking red ribbons [right, rear] that Miriam Davey convinced me to tie all around."

***Salvia iodantha* is one of the salvias** that Carol Foil has for winter hummingbirds. "They make a great show in November," she says.

blew through Baton Rouge in 1992 and splintered some of the big pine trees in the yard, she convinced her husband to use the remains to build a large brush pile for birds and other wildlife. But she wasn't inspired to garden for hummers until January of 1997, when a female broad-tailed hummingbird settled into her yard. "I had no idea what it was," Carol says. "Nancy Newfield [nearby hummer expert] came to capture, band, and identify it.

"Until I got the broad-tailed, all I had out for hummers was a few feeders," says Carol. Afterward, she started planting for hummers in a plot near the patio. The plantings have gradually expanded toward the heavily wooded portion at the back of her lot. "My husband likes a bit of lawn, but I'm creeping in on it," she says.

Winter Hummers in Louisiana

Accounts of wintering hummers in southern Louisiana date from February 1934, when an immature male rufous hummingbird flew into the Louisiana State Capitol Senate chamber and was captured by W. E. Anderson. What business the young hummer had before the Senate is not recorded, but considering the feisty nature of rufous hummers and the absence of gardens for them at the time, it can be assumed that he was berating the surprised solons for their lack of hospitality.

Someone must have been sensitive to the bird's complaint, however. By the 1950s, Mrs. W. W. Tennant, of Baton Rouge, was setting out salvias and feeders every winter, and hummers were regularly visiting them. She was the first in Louisiana to record the broad-tailed (1952) and the black-chinned (1955) hummingbird. Over the years, sightings of winter hummers have increased, but so have the pairs of eyes looking for them. Experts debate whether the number of birds is actually increasing or not, and they also speculate about where the birds come from. Do they wander up from Mexico, or do the hummers that nest in the West migrate directly from their nesting territories? There is much interest in banding winter hummers to find answers to these and other questions.

Nearly the entire yard is heavily shaded by trees, so Carol looks for plants that do well without direct sunlight. "*Salvia miniata* [p. 78], *puberla*, and *mexicana* [p. 91] do great in the shade," she says. "*Abutilon pictum*, or flowering maple [p. 88], makes oodles of nectar and is also great for orioles. Some of the other shade-tolerant bloomers that do well in my garden include firespike [p. 92], various pentas, and many justicias, including shrimp plants [p. 89]."

In parts of her yard that get some sun, Carol has numerous salvias. "I plant *Salvia guaranitica* [p. 58], *Salvia* 'Purple Majesty' [p. 58], and lots of *Salvia iodantha*," she says.

"We don't get a freeze every year," says Carol, but she is prepared for freezes that kill the blooming plants in her garden. She keeps lots of late-blooming plants in pots that she can protect in her "greenhouse" of PVC pipe covered with plastic. "It is actually harder to have plants blooming in our hot summer than in winter," she exclaims.

Winter hummers can hang around until the end of March or the beginning of April while they molt into their mating plumage, according to Carol. "My immature calliopes were dull little birds when they came here. When they left, they had beautiful gorgets." Carol says that because of the molts, it is easy to identify individual birds.

By the time the winter hummers leave, the spring migration of ruby-throats is rapidly building. "The first male ruby-throats show up in early March," Carol says, then continues, "I am fortunate to have ruby-throats that actually nest in a swampy area of the yard." Nesting ruby-throats are common farther north, but much less so in southern Louisiana, where Carol lives and where few suburban yards provide the deep cover and nearby water that ruby-throats prefer for nesting habitat.

Fall migration peaks between the second week of September and the second week of October in Carol's yard. "I have huge numbers of ruby-throats," she says. At the height of migration, she puts out about 20 feeders, including 4 of the quart-size Perky-Pet feeders. The feeders are clumped in a large group — so close together that no bird can claim any one of them. A swarm of hummers will slurp peacefully at the big array. "It's cool to see," Carol exclaims. Most of the ruby-throats leave her yard by the end of October, but Carol says a few linger until winter, and she has had some stay throughout winter.

The first winter hummers from the West or Mexico usually arrive in September or October. These early arrivals are generally returnees, birds seemingly in a hurry to get back to the good life on the Gulf. "I had my first returnee show up this fall [2001] on the 24th of September," says Carol. "It was a male rufous hummingbird banded last winter as an immature." People who don't have returnees often don't see winter hummers arrive until November or December.

The current record for returnees is held by a male buff-bellied nicknamed "The Junkyard Dog" by his bander, Nancy L. Newfield, for his extremely aggressive behavior. Nancy banded him as an adult in Susie Nowell's yard in LaPlace, Louisiana, in February of 1993. He reappeared at the yard every year until his last capture in February 2001, when Nancy calculates he was no less than nine years and eight months old. He was so satisfied with his winter residence that he usually arrived in August; one year he showed up in July!

For winter hummers, Carol has a separate feeding strategy. After the fall migration of ruby-throats winds down, she retires the large array of feeders and puts up numerous Perky-Pet Little Beginner feeders. "I distribute them separately to avoid fights. And to make it easy for hummers to find them, I tie red ribbon near them," she says.

Red is the well-known magic color for attracting curious hummers, and gardeners hoping to have their yard graced by a winter hummer make sure they have plenty of it visible. Although Carol is enthusiastic about winter hummers, she claims she has not yet considered doing anything as extreme to attract them as Nancy Newfield has. Nancy painted her entire house red.

Jeanine Falk
BWH 19728, Manhattan Beach, California

Many NWF-certified yards are small — islands of green surrounded by oceans of concrete and buildings. Maintaining these green oases as habitats for birds and other wildlife can be challenging for owners of urban yards, including Jeanine Falk.

Jeanine has lived most of her life in the increasingly urban coastal community of Manhattan Beach, south of Los Angeles. "I've seen a lot of changes," she says. "Years ago, it was rural. We had horses, chickens, and pigs." Farm animals are no longer permitted, but Jeanine says she still manages to keep a pair of ducks without complaint.

The original houses were unpretentious beach cottages on small lots, explains Jeanine. "The closer you got to the beach, the smaller the lots." In 1975, she and her husband, Herm, bought a 50-by-150-foot lot with a small 600-square-foot cottage about a mile from the beach. It was tucked between two other tiny cottages. The cottages occupied only about 10 percent of the area of the lots, so there was plenty of open space, but Jeanine knew that her neighborhood was about to change.

Cottages throughout the community were being torn down and replaced with 4,000-square-foot homes that sprawled over nearly an entire lot. "The yards became very small, and most of the trees disappeared," Jeanine says. "Today it's pretty much back-to-back houses, and it's sad because the complexion of the area has changed."

The Falks loved their little cottage, the 14 trees on the property, and the birds and other wildlife the yard attracted. "But the cottage was a little on the small side," says Jeanine. The Falks wanted larger quarters but were determined to keep the trees, and enough yard for Jeanine to continue to indulge her passion for gardening.

"Every builder we talked to wanted to remove those trees, but we said, 'No way,'" Jeanine emphasizes. One tree in particular, a large ornamental

Jeanine Falk gardens around the pond at the entrance to the Falks' courtyard. Even on Jeanine's small property, there is room for two water features, including this small pond and waterfall.

pittosporum, had been on the property years before the Falks bought it. Its dense, glossy-green, leathery foliage remains on the tree year-round. The Falks first built a patio around the tree and then decided to get their additional living space by constructing a two-story addition to the cottage around the patio.

"We tried our best to maintain the complexion of the property," Jeanine says. "We planned the windows to face our patio because we knew that eventually the only view on either side of us would be two-story stucco walls."

The Falks' plan worked. When Jeanine looks at the trees and plants in her yard, "I forget that I'm next door to huge homes," she says. Because the windows face onto the courtyard, "we don't need any drapes or curtains," Jeanine explains. "It's so pretty seeing the moonlight streaming through a tree into your bedroom."

Hummingbirds — Jeanine gets Anna's and Allen's — are so attracted to the many plants Jeanine provides for them that the Falks have named their property "Hummingbird Hollow."

Jeanine says, "I didn't want to put up a nectar feeder because I wanted to attract hummingbirds with plants if I could." In addition to penstemons, salvias, cigar plants, and other well-known hummer favorites, Jeanine says her pittosporum tree has been wonderful for hummingbirds. Each year the hummers sip nectar from the fragrant little yellow-white blossoms starting around the Fourth of July.

"Right now," Jeanine shares excitedly, "we have two nests of baby Allen's hummers in that patio tree. They were very thoughtful to build one nest we can view from our master bedroom upstairs. The other is visible from the downstairs living area. It's great because we can watch the mothers feeding their babies and the babies exercising their wings only 4 or 5 feet away!"

Scrub jays, hermit thrushes, and orange-crowned warblers are a few of the many other birds that regularly visit the Falks' yard. Most are attracted by the trees and plants. Jeanine does a minimum of bird feeding. For a long time, she only offered one feeder, a wooden hopper filled with a premium seed mixture she gets from her local wild bird supply store.

Recently she has added a tube feeder that she fills with sunflower chips. Nearly all the birds enjoy the easy-to-eat sunflower chips, Jeanine reports. "It's like putting cashews out at a party; everybody wants some." Only the small songbirds can perch on the feeder and eat from it, so Jeanine avoids attracting the many pigeons in the area.

After she discovered the two hummingbird nests, Jeanine added two small, unobtrusive hummer feeders by the patio. "We feel so attached to our baby hummers that we want to make sure they and all the other youngsters leaving their nests have plenty to eat," Jeanine declares.

Pittosporum is a large genus that extends from Australia and New Zealand to the warmer regions of Africa, Asia, and islands in the Pacific.

A pair of nestling Allen's hummingbirds grow up in a nest in a pittosporum tree, just a few feet from Jeanine Falk's window.

To encourage birds to nest nearby, Jeanine makes little bundles of nesting material for them. "I tie string, twine, dryer lint, dental floss, feathers, cat hair, thread or yarn, toothpicks broken in half — anything they can use — in bundles and hang the stuff out in trees where the birds can see them year-round." She was thrilled to see that her hummers used bits of yarn, duck feathers, and dryer lint in their nests and adds, "That's a pretty nice, cushy thing to sit on."

Jeanine also offers two water features for the birds and other wildlife. Near the entrance to the courtyard is a waterfall powered by a recirculating pump. "Hummingbirds especially love the running water," Jeanine exclaims, and so does she. "We can hear the soothing sound of the running water from every room in the house."

The second water feature — a small pond in the backyard — is primarily for Jeanine's pet ducks, but wildlife, including raccoons and opossums, also use it. Once a week, Jeanine cleans the duck pond. She pumps the dirty water out of the pond and uses it like liquid fertilizer. "I spray it on the flowers and the whole backyard area," she says. "I have this great lemon tree, lots of roses, and all kinds of things that are fertilized only with duck pond water."

There is very little that doesn't get recycled at the Falk household. Scraps that the ducks don't eat are composted and used to augment the thin, sandy soil. "We rarely use our garbage disposal," says Jeanine, who teaches community composting classes. "Everything goes into the yard."

To people who think they don't have the space to create a wildlife-friendly habitat, Jeanine offers some good advice: "You don't need to have a big piece of property to create your own little heaven on earth. You can do it on a patio."

Growing PLANTS
for Hummingbirds

by Ron Rovansek

Red-hot poker (Knifophia uvaria) gets its common name from the delicate red to yellow shading of the blossoms on its tall spires.

Many of the hummingbirds that have visited my gardens over the years don't visit the feeders I set out for them. They come for the nectar in the plants I grow. Flowering plants provide a complete hummer diet of nectar plus small insects and spiders. Plants also offer cover, wet leaves for bathing, and places to perch. They will attract far more hummers than feeders will, and beautify your property as well.

This chapter will help you create a hummgarden that fits your climate, your yard (or balcony or porch), the hummers of your region, and the amount of effort you are willing to put into gardening — all of which depends upon choosing the right plants. A hummgarden can be as simple as a few patches of wildflowers that require no more effort than a lawn, or as elaborate as any botanical garden.

I call my most recommended plants the Dozen Dazzlers, and they are the first plants I describe in this chapter. You guessed it, there are 12 of them, and not only are they hummingbird favorites, but they are so easy to grow that anyone who can grow a tomato (even a tough, flavorless one) will succeed with them.

For gardeners eager to try a wider selection of plants than the Dozen Dazzlers or those who are looking for a plant to fill a special niche, I describe about 100 more excellent hummer plants arranged in lists of plants that thrive in similar conditions or geographic areas. The additional plants are typically as attractive to hummers as any of the Dozen Dazzlers. They may require a little more attention to grow than the Dozen Dazzlers, or they may be more specific in their soil, sun, or moisture requirements. The only drawback to some of them is that they are hard to find.

Following all the plant descriptions, you will find basic gardening information (p. 99) that will get you started successfully. Everything you need to know to grow a great hummgarden is in this chapter.

A Dozen Dazzlers — The Hummplant All-Stars

The descriptions of the Dozen Dazzlers that follow are all organized similarly. They start with a summary of the basic information needed by gardeners, stated in common gardening terms. If you are familiar with gardening terms, you can skip directly to the descriptions of the Dozen Dazzlers. If you are new to gardening, read on for the definitions of the terms you'll encounter.

The first information provided is growth habit. Terms like vine, tree, and shrub, which describe growth habits, should need no explanation, but some other terms I use may not be recognized. Herbaceous plants are those without woody stems. The plants typically die back to the ground each winter and sprout again in spring. If herbaceous plants are grown in frost-free areas, the stems may continue to grow, but they do not add annual rings as woody plants do.

Woody plants have stems that add layers of woody growth each year. There are a few plants I describe that blur the line between herbaceous and woody.

It doesn't take a lot of different kinds of plants to create a successful hummgarden. Start with a large patch of just one hummplant, like the bee balm shown above or one of the other Dozen Dazzlers. If you are an inexperienced gardener (or maybe you have the experience to realize you don't have a green thumb), this advice goes double for you.

Perennials are plants that live for many years. Although they may be herbaceous and freeze to the ground each winter, they resprout from their roots the following spring. Annual plants require annual planting; they live for a single growing season, set seed, and die. Many plants commonly grown as annuals are actually tender perennials, meaning that in a frost-free climate they would live for years, but they are too tender — not just the stems but the whole plant, including the roots — to survive winter in most of the U.S. and Canada.

Exposure, the next item in the summary, refers to the amount of sun a plant receives. Some plants need lots of direct sunlight; others thrive in shade. I have categorized the degrees of exposure as sun, partial shade, and shade. Sun means exposure to more than a half day of direct sunlight. Plants that can live in partial shade need only three to six hours of direct sunlight per day, or they can survive on the dappled shade that occurs under trees with a somewhat open crown. Plants that grow with three hours or less of direct sunlight are said to grow in shade. Gardeners in the Deep South and especially the desert Southwest will find that they can grow plants with somewhat less direct sun than I indicate because of the very intense sunlight in their regions.

Hardiness refers to the coldest temperature that a plant can tolerate over winter — and that's all. It has nothing to do with a plant's resistance to disease, humidity, or any other stress. Hardiness is expressed in geographic zones developed by the USDA (map, p. 99). Adventurous gardeners may be able to grow plants a zone or two farther north than the ratings indicate by providing winter protection in the form of thick mulch or plastic enclosures.

I have divided moisture requirements into wet, moist, average, dry, and arid. Wet means the soil is saturated with water or even has shallow standing water. Moist soils are those in which water is always abundant, either because of heavy, frequent watering or because they are in low-lying areas where water naturally accumulates. The line between moist soil and saturated soil is a critical one for plants. While many plants thrive in moist soils, relatively few can survive saturated soils for more than a few days.

Average moisture is found in typical garden soils that will support a lawn or most common garden plants. In dry climates, regular irrigation is required to provide average moisture conditions. In moist climates, occasional watering may be required during dry spells.

Dry soil conditions occur when there is a long time between rains or watering. In the East and Midwest, plants that will live in dry soil do not need any watering. In arid climates of the West, a good watering about once a week is required.

Arid conditions occur in the unirrigated or infrequently irrigated soils of arid western climates.

Blossoms on spikes of tropical sage are arranged in whorls. This recently introduced cultivar, 'Lady in Red', is a compact, red-flowered version that is widely popular as a bedding plant. Other common cultivars include the pink-flowered 'Coral Nymph' and several white-flowered varieties. Hummers eagerly visit them all.

Tropical Sage, Texas Sage, Scarlet Sage
Salvia coccinea

Growth habit: Herbaceous annual or perennial
Exposure: Shade to sun
Hardiness: Zone 9, hardy only to the upper 20s
Moisture: Moist to dry
Height: 3 to 4 feet, occasionally 6 feet
Bloom: Spring until frost, continuous without frost
Propagation: Seed or cuttings

If I could create the perfect hummingbird flower, it would have a long blooming season, adapt to sun or shade, grow quickly from seed in almost any soil, survive even the worst gardeners, and of course, be eagerly visited by hummingbirds. In short, I would invent tropical sage. It is suitable for planting anywhere in North America as an annual, and the fast-growing herbaceous plant produces an endless supply of red tubular flowers held above the foliage on long spikes.

It takes about two months for the seeds of tropical sage to mature into blooming plants, then they flower continuously until interrupted by frost,

Selecting Plants for a Small Yard in Pennsylvania

I began plants for my hummgarden in Easton, Pennsylvania, the winter before I moved there, even before I had selected the property. Since I had no idea what the yard would look like, I opted to start seeds of the most adaptable hummer plant I know, tropical sage. By May, I had about 75 two-inch-tall plants. Our new home turned out to be a suburban property with only about 150 square feet of sunny garden space. The tropical sage plants filled two-thirds of the plot, and after adding a few tomato plants, I had about 25 square feet of sunny ground left for more hummer plants.

I wanted plants that bloomed from July through fall. I didn't expect to see many hummers earlier than that because there was no significant amount of woodlands anywhere near my property for them to nest in. I also wanted perennials rather than annuals that I would have to replant every year. I chose bee balm (p. 55) because it is a favorite hummer perennial that starts to bloom just when I needed it to and because it is native to the area, which means it is perfectly adapted to the region and would need little attention.

Along the north side of the house, there was space among some small shrubs for a few plants. It was a shady, damp location ideal for cardinal flower (p. 60), another superior perennial hummer plant native to the region. The 10 cardinal flowers I planted among the shrubs thrived on about two hours of sunlight per day and bloomed from July through September.

My bedding spaces were filled, but I still had bare fences along two sunny sides of the yard that I knew would be a great place for vines. Coral honeysuckle (p. 68) was a better choice for my small yard than the other great perennial hummer vine for my zone, trumpet creeper (p. 70), which is larger and more aggressive. Coral honeysuckle grows slowly when it is first planted, so to quickly cover the fence, I also planted lots of small red morning glory (p. 82), a fast-growing annual vine. Although small red morning glory dies each year, it is easily grown from seed and produces masses of flowers in time for southbound hummingbirds in fall.

I next added a couple of hanging baskets of 'Gartenmeister Bonstedt' fuchsia (p. 66) on the shady front porch, accompanied by pots of scarlet sage (p. 57). On the sunny back stoop, I placed a large pot that held a plant of anise sage (p. 58) that would become 6 feet tall. The potted plants required far more attention than the plants in the ground, and they added relatively few blossoms to the yard, but they contributed variety to the garden and brought hummingbirds onto the porch for close-up views.

This small collection of plants, anchored mainly by the patches of tropical sage, bee balm, and cardinal flower and aided by a feeder in both the front and back yards, attracted many ruby-throated hummingbirds. As expected, I didn't see any during spring migration or nesting, but from mid-July through early October, I saw as many as 10 at a time battling for ownership of the nectar-rich flowers I had planted.

providing nectar for hummingbirds the entire time. When the pollinated plants begin to produce seed, they attract seedeating birds. In the West, lesser goldfinches are particularly fond of tropical sage seeds, hanging acrobatically on the plants to feed from them.

Tropical sage has a very wide wild range. Its origins are somewhat unclear as a result of its use in, and escape from, gardens throughout the world's subtropical regions dating back to the 18th century. It is common in all of tropical and subtropical Central and South America and may have originated in Mexico.

Tropical sage can occasionally be found growing wild in southern parts of the U.S. It is sometimes considered a native wildflower in Louisiana, Texas, and Florida, although it is probably introduced or escaped rather than a true native. The Latin species name, *coccinea,* is derived from the word for scarlet and refers to the color of the blossoms in wild plants. Some cultivated varieties bear flowers of white or pink.

Gardening with Tropical Sage. Tropical sage is a perennial in frost-free zones. It is hardy only to the upper 20s and is grown as an annual in most of the U.S. It will grow and flower most profusely in full sun and rich, moist soil (as will the majority of flowering plants) but will also endure in poor soil and under trees that deprive it of direct sunlight and normal moisture. It does well interspersed among larger plants or shrubs and makes an easy potted plant. Tropical sage is a great plant for young kids to grow, tolerating even the most neglectful or ill-considered care and sprouting easily from seed.

Insect and disease problems are rare with tropical sage. Only the extremes of moisture conditions — long droughts or saturated soil — are likely to prove fatal. It is drought tolerant by eastern standards, but in dry areas of the West, it will not survive without supplemental water provided at least weekly. Use raised beds if you plant it in very wet spots. It won't survive waterlogged soils.

When different cultivars grow together in a garden, seedlings of mixed parentage will result. Some may have the same color flowers as one of the parents; others may revert to something more like the wild form. The wild plant is taller than most of the popular cultivars, and this seems to prove attractive to hummingbirds. For this reason, I prefer the wild strain, which is not readily available from retail nurseries but is a popular pass-along plant.

Growing Instructions. Seeds of tropical sage are very easily started, needing only to be sprinkled on top of soil and kept moist. Unlike many mint-family

A female ruby-throated hummingbird probes for nectar in a blossom of tropical sage. Because of the abundant bright red blossoms, tropical sage puts on a stunning show when planted en masse. The many blossoms result in an abundance of seeds that usually produce many volunteer seedlings, making it easy for you to share the plant with friends.

plants, tropical sage does not spread vegetatively; it cannot be divided to obtain extra plants, but stem cuttings root readily.

A mulch of gravel, leaves, lawn clippings, or similar organic material will help control weed growth and seems to encourage healthy growth of tropical sage. If you are hoping for volunteer seedlings, however, heavy mulch will reduce their numbers.

In regions with long summers, volunteers can be relied upon to provide a new supply of plants each year, but in colder zones, volunteers won't appear until late spring, and they may not bloom and be of interest to hummers until late summer. In these regions, it makes sense to start plants indoors from seed collected the previous fall.

Plants spaced about a foot apart provide a solid mass of color by midsummer, although tropical sage also adapts well to more crowded situations. Plants respond well to regular water and fertilizer.

Spent flower spikes and calyces — withered, brown, and shabby looking — can be removed. In regions with long summers, the entire plant can be sheared back, creating a more compact growth and prompting a burst of new flowers in about six weeks. It is possible to maintain tropical sage in a very short condition by repeated shearing or even by using a mower set to cut about 4 inches from the ground, but flowers will be few until plants are permitted a little more growth.

Bee Balm, Oswego Tea
Monarda didyma

Growth habit: Herbaceous perennial
Exposure: Sun to shade
Hardiness: Zone 4
Moisture: Moist to average
Height: 4 feet
Bloom: Midsummer
Propagation: Division or cuttings

In the rich woodlands of the eastern U.S., bee balm is one of the most conspicuous wildflowers, lifting its clusters of bright red blooms from stream banks and moist hillsides. It is native from Georgia to New York and Michigan and also occurs in the wild throughout New England, where it is thought to be a garden escape rather than a true native. In the southern part of its range, it grows most often at higher elevations and can be rare in lowlands.

Large stands of bee balm are common along roadsides in the Great Smoky Mountains National Park in eastern Tennessee and western North Carolina, where in July and August the flowers seem to shine under the shade of hardwoods.

The alternate name, Oswego tea, is a reminder that the plant was once used for brewing tea by Native Americans and early European settlers in the Oswego area of New York State.

Gardening with Bee Balm. Ideally suited to growing in perennial borders and woodland gardens, and

Calyces (KAY-le-cees or KAH-le-cees): the cup-like structures from which flowers emerge.

A male ruby-throated hummingbird probes a bee balm blossom. Bee balm begins blooming about the time the first ruby-throated hummers fledge.

naturalizing in shady meadows or roadsides, bee balm is one of the best choices among hummingbird flowers for difficult shady spots. I have seen this plant survive and bloom in deep shade and with intense root competition under trees like maples and ornamental crab apples. However, it grows best in rich, evenly moist garden soils and prefers ample sunlight everywhere except the Deep South.

Bee balm is fully hardy throughout the continental U.S. and southern Canada. It may fail to bloom in zone 8 and warmer, despite vigorous growth. I suspect that this failure to bloom is related to lack of cold during the winter. A few cultivars, notably 'Jacob Cline', are reported to regularly bloom in hot climates. Bee balm is not a drought-tolerant plant compared to most plants from the southern or western U.S. and should be watered at least twice a week in dry climates or when grown in fast-draining soils.

Bee balm is seldom bothered by insects but often afflicted by powdery mildew, which is most prevalent late in summer and appears as a whitish bloom on the leaves. Severe infestations can induce leaf drop and reduce the vigor of the plant, while milder cases only mar the appearance of the leaves and do not seem to affect a plant's health. The best control for powdery mildew is to grow resistant varieties, such as 'Jacob Cline', 'Claire Grace', and 'Marshall's Delight'. Other control options include thinning the number of stems to increase air circulation (dryness restricts the growth of the fungus) and removing dead stems to encourage healthy new growth. Because the fungus overwinters in a plant's dead vegetation, clearing away this matter in fall will help reduce the following year's crop of fungus.

Bee balm plants are widely available in local nurseries and through mail order and come in a vast variety of cultivars. All of the cultivars I have tried attract hummers as readily as the wild strain of bee balm does. The cultivars are available in

A clump of bee balm will spread by stolons (runners) to form an ever larger patch. It can be somewhat invasive in the garden, so it is wise to separate bee balm from less vigorous plants.

several colors ranging from red to purple, many of them being hybrids between bee balm and close relatives such as wild bergamot *(Monarda fistulosa)* or purple bergamot *(Monarda media)*.

Wild bergamot is a pink- to lavender-flowered species similar to bee balm that many gardeners have reported attractive to hummers, although less so than bee balm. Wild bergamot is widely distributed in the eastern states and into the prairies and is more tolerant of drought and heat than bee balm.

Purple bergamot, another widely cultivated eastern native, resembles bee balm but has purple flowers that are attractive to hummingbirds. The white-flowered basil balm *(Monarda clinopodia)* is also similar in structure to bee balm and native to much of eastern North America. For gardeners in the Deep South, where bee balm may not bloom well, a look-alike that is also called bee balm *(Monarda pringlei)* is worth a try.

Growing Instructions. While they can be grown from seed or stem cuttings, new bee balm plants are commonly propagated by dividing clumps or by transplanting rooted pieces of stem that are numerous in any patch. Small plants placed about 18 inches apart should fill a bed within two years.

After several years, a clump may become overcrowded, grow weakly, and bloom sparsely in the center, indicating that the clump should be dug up, divided, the soil reworked with added organic matter and nutrients, and parts of the clump replanted. It can be divided in late August or early September, soon after it has finished blooming — any later and it might not have enough time to establish itself before the first killing frost and survive the winter.

Because new plants are susceptible to being washed out of the ground by winter rains or frost heaving, they should be completely covered after the first frost with organic mulch, such as leaves or pine needles. The mulch should be removed from the tops of the plants in spring, but allowing mulch to remain in between plants will help recreate soil conditions similar to those bee balm experiences in its natural woodland habitat.

Scarlet Sage, Red Hot Sally
Salvia splendens

  Growth habit: Herbaceous perennial, typically grown as annual
  Exposure: Sun to partial shade
  Hardiness: Zone 9 as perennial
  Moisture: Average to moist
  Height: 2 to 4 feet, varies with cultivar
  Bloom: Summer and fall
  Propagation: Seed or cuttings

Some of the best hummingbird plants can be hard to locate commercially, but one top-notch performer is available in almost every retail nursery in North

These spikes of scarlet sage blossoms are the typical bright red, but the countless cultivars range from white to purple and every shade in between.

America, the ubiquitous scarlet sage. It was first brought under cultivation more than a hundred years ago, derived from a Brazilian wildflower.

Aptly named *splendens* in Latin, scarlet sage bears short spikes of brightly colored tubular flowers. It blooms tirelessly through the summer until stopped by frost, which is a major reason for its popularity as a bedding plant.

Gardening with Scarlet Sage. Scarlet sage is a tender perennial that is usually grown as an annual. It can be grown almost anywhere and is a very adaptable plant, doing well in most soils and exposures. It thrives in full sun, provided it receives regular water, and it also blooms nicely in fairly shady locations, especially in regions with a long growing season.

Disease problems are infrequent. The occasional insect problem usually amounts to a few chewed leaves that do little to impair the plant.

Scarlet sage is excellent in mass plantings, and because plants are available, adaptable, and usually very affordable, they are a superb choice for a beginning hummgardener to create a large mass of flowers in one season.

You will likely have many cultivars of scarlet sage to choose from at most nurseries. For attracting hummingbirds, I recommend selecting the tallest red-flowered variety you can find. A few decades ago, the typical plant grew as much as 4 feet tall and had bright scarlet flowers. Now it is more common to find more compact cultivars for sale. Some recent cultivars, particularly the

Cultivar: short for culti-vated variety, a distinctive strain of a plant. Some cultivars are developed by selective breeding or hybridization between plant species; others, called "sports," are the descendants of an atypical seedling that appeared in the wild or in a garden.

shorter ones with flowers other than red, have been reported to be less attractive to hummers than the old-fashioned tall variety.

Growing Instructions. Space plants from 1 to 2 feet apart, depending on the size they will be when mature. The old-fashioned tall varieties can be spaced as much as 3 feet apart and still fill in a bed by midsummer. Ample water and regular fertilizer are required for vigorous growth, and organic mulch is recommended to control weeds and maintain a constant soil environment.

Scarlet sage can be easily grown from seed, and the seeds of old-fashioned cultivars are sometimes offered for sale. Plants grown from seed often exhibit variations. The beautiful Van Houtte sage (p. 78) is generally thought to be a naturally occurring sport, or chance seedling, of scarlet sage. To increase your supply of a favorite cultivar without introducing variations, make cuttings. Scarlet sage cuttings take root easily.

Anise Sage
Salvia guaranitica

> Growth habit: Herbaceous perennial or annual
> Exposure: Sun to partial shade
> Hardiness: Zone 7, annual farther north
> Moisture: Moist to average
> Height: 3 to 4 feet, occasionally 6 feet
> Bloom: Spring through fall
> Propagation: Cuttings, division, or seed

It is often written that hummingbird flowers are tubular, unscented, and red. Anise sage fits only two of these three conditions, but by no means is it only two-thirds of a hummingbird plant. In fact, anise sage, despite the electric blue color of its numerous inch-long tubular flowers, is one of the most favored hummingbird flowers during its peak bloom in mid- to late summer.

Originating in Brazil, Paraguay, and Argentina, this herbaceous perennial gets its Latin species name from the Guaran Indians, with whom it shares its homeland.

Gardening with Anise Sage. Although tropical in origin, anise sage is surprisingly hardy. It survives through zone 7, and with heavy mulch, it can reportedly make it through winters in zone 6. Because it grows rapidly and blooms in its first summer, this perennial also makes an excellent annual plant for zones 5 and 6.

If its attractiveness to hummingbirds doesn't convince you to grow anise sage, think about what its color will add to your yard or garden. On the standard anise sage, striking cobalt blue blossoms emerge from bright green calyces. If you investigate the many cultivars available, you will find other shades of blue, including the light blue flowers of 'Argentina Skies'. The widely available 'Black and Blue' is notable for its dark purple calyces, which give it a distinctly different appearance from the regular plant.

All of the cultivars of anise sage that I know of are great hummingbird plants. Many of them are hard to distinguish from each other. The two strains mentioned resemble the regular plant and are as hardy as it is, although 'Black and Blue' grows a little less vigorously.

A variety called 'Costa Rica Blue' (p. 90) is larger than most others and blooms from fall through spring, making it a popular plant for attracting winter hummingbirds. This variety is

Each brilliant red flower of scarlet sage emerges from an equally brightly colored calyx. A flower may last as little as one day, but the calyces remain bright and colorful for weeks.

A dragonfly explores a blossom of 'Costa Rica Blue' sage. Many insects are attracted to hummingbird flowers if they can reach the nectar.

'Purple Majesty' is a hybrid of anise sage, a cross with *Salvia gesneriflorae* (p. 98). This is a stunning hummplant, although not as hardy as anise sage. In humid heat, it is also prone to fungal stem rot, which can topple stems before they bloom.

thought by some to be a polyploid. Many other varieties of anise sage can be found and all are excellent hummingbird plants.

Anise sage grows rapidly in typical garden soils, provided it gets regular moisture and adequate fertilizer. Insect and disease problems are few. Its main drawback is that it may be hard to find, particularly in more northern areas where it is not perennial. Mail-order nurseries provide a source of plants for northern gardeners.

Growing Information. Most of the varieties of anise sage — all except the large cultivars — spread by short stolons (runners) to form an attractive clump of stems. As clumps grow older, they may begin to grow weakly and produce fewer blooms in the center. The remedy for this is to dig up the clump, divide it, rejuvenate the soil with plenty of organic matter, and replant one of the sections of the clump. With reworked soil and plenty of space, the new transplant will quickly regain its vigor and flower abundantly. The other pieces of the clump can be planted elsewhere or passed along to humm-gardening friends.

Anise sage can also be grown from stem cuttings or seed. Seedlings, which are common in warm-climate gardens, are interesting because they often differ slightly from the parent. Plants spaced about

18 inches apart will produce a solid bed of anise sage within two months. If you are growing them as perennials, you can place these plants farther apart, allowing them more room to spread as they grow.

Regular water, fertilizer, and an organic mulch to control weeds will keep anise sage growing vigorously. You may choose to prune or remove some older stems when they begin to look unkempt.

Standing Cypress, Spanish Larkspur
Ipomopsis rubra

> Growth habit: Herbaceous biennial
> Exposure: Sun to partial shade
> Hardiness: Zone 5
> Moisture: Moist to dry
> Height: 4 to 6 feet
> Bloom: Summer and fall
> Propagation: Seed

Native to much of the southern and eastern U.S., standing cypress is usually found growing wild in sandy soils that support only a sparse growth of trees and shrubs, allowing plenty of sunlight to reach the ground. Pine barrens, dunes, prairies, and disturbed areas such as railroad tracks and road-sides are places to find this drought-tolerant plant.

Existing only as a rosette of feathery leaves near ground level during its first year of growth, stand-ing cypress gives little indication of what is to come

A polyploid is a genetic variation occurring when chromosomes multiply by two, three, or more. Polyploids often result in larger, more robust plants. Many horticultural plants are engineered to polyploidy through the use of chemicals, but it can occur naturally, as is thought to be the case with 'Costa Rica Blue'.

The impressive spires of standing cypress bear hundreds of flowers, usually from June through August, before dying.

in its second summer, when it puts forth striking unbranched stems up to 6 feet tall bearing brilliant red flowers. After blooming, the plant sets seed and dies, completing its biennial life cycle.

Gardening with Standing Cypress. Besides being extremely attractive to hummers, standing cypress is tough and requires little care, characteristics that make it an outstanding hummingbird plant. It is hardy at least to zone 5, free from problems with insects or disease, and drought resistant, surviving without any supplemental water in most of the continent and needing only occasional watering in the driest climates.

The wild strain of standing cypress, which often reaches 6 feet tall, is unparalleled as a hummer plant, but you can also use several cultivated varieties. These are usually closer to 3 feet tall, come in a variety of colors, and often flower in their first year if sown early in the growing season. The closely

related scarlet gilia (p. 76) looks much like standing cypress but is smaller. Standing cypress may occasionally be available as plants but is more frequently sold as seed.

Growing Instructions. As mentioned earlier, standing cypress is strictly a biennial, growing only leaves in its first summer, then flowering and dying its second year. By sowing seeds in two consecutive years, you can quickly establish two generations of the plant, which will then provide a display of flowers each summer if the plants are allowed to reseed.

A single sowing will eventually produce flowers annually because some of the seeds from the first crop will not germinate until two springs later, when they will form the basis of the "off-year" generation. The plants reseed themselves easily in most gardens, but they do not transplant well.

Standing cypress is well suited to naturalized gardens, prairies, meadows, and similar situations where it receives ample sunlight. Supplemental water is necessary only in dry western climates, although occasional water and fertilizer may produce larger, more floriferous plants. Mulch is not required, and thick mulch will tend to discourage self-sowing.

After a flowering stem has finished blooming, it may be removed to encourage the production of more flowers. As the end of the blooming season approaches, however, it is good practice to leave the blooms on and allow the plants to set seeds to produce the next generation. At the end of its second summer, standing cypress will die regardless of any steps the gardener might take.

Cardinal Flower
Lobelia cardinalis

Growth habit: Herbaceous perennial
Exposure: Sun to shade
Hardiness: Zone 3
Moisture: Wet to average
Height: 3 to 4 feet
Bloom: July to September
Propagation: Seed

Growing on sunny stream banks, sandbars, swamps, and moist woods, cardinal flower is native throughout most of the U.S. and southern Canada. Sometimes it can be seen on roadsides or along power line cuts. Spires of cardinal flower erupt with brilliant red, nectar-filled, tubular blossoms just in time to fatten up the hordes of fall hummers on their journey home.

Until ready to send up a blooming spike, cardinal flower exists as a crowded circle of dark green, shiny leaves radiating from a central base, similar to the rosette of leaves on a dandelion. In midsummer, upright stems begin to emerge from the center of the rosette. Leaves grow on the lower part of the stem, and many flowers bloom on the unbranched upper portion. Flowers lowest on the stem bloom first, each one lasting only a day or two. A large plant will produce several spikes that typically bloom from July through September. When blooming is complete, the stems wither and die, but the basal rosette of leaves usually remains green over winter.

Cardinal flower produces abundant tiny seeds that are spread widely by wind and water. Hundreds of tiny seedlings can sometimes be found on a freshly scoured sandbar or stream bank. In the South, these seedlings will often produce blooms in the first year. In northern parts of the U.S. and in Canada, blooming is typically delayed until the second summer.

Gardening with Cardinal Flower. Even though cardinal flowers in the wild prefer moist to wet situations, in the garden they will grow well with only average moisture. Throughout much of the eastern and midwestern U.S. and eastern Canada, cardinal flowers will thrive in either sun or shade in ordinary garden conditions, although they will benefit from supplemental watering during dry spells. In more arid regions, they require regular irrigation at least twice weekly during the growing season, and their soil should be kept moist through the winter as well.

This water-loving plant can also be grown as a pond plant by potting it in a gallon-sized or larger pot and placing the pot in your pond. Cardinal flower will grow and bloom with the pot submerged in water but will do better if the rosette leaves remain above water level.

Slugs or other pests may bother cardinal flowers, and pest damage to unopened flower buds can be a particular problem. Pest problems appear to be more frequent and more severe with garden-grown plants than with plants growing in the wild. Some gardeners report that their planted cardinal flowers are completely consumed by insects while wild cardinal

Cardinal flower, with its brilliant red, tubular blossoms, not only looks like it evolved with hummers, but seems to have a blooming season timed to coincide with the southbound hummer migration.

Hummingbird Gardening in the Great Basin

It was in the month of April that I moved to Reno, Nevada, and I was eager to get started on my hummgarden. I anticipated hummingbirds would begin to arrive in the region late that very month, and I hoped that the southward migration, which starts as early as late June for rufous hummingbirds, would bring a bumper crop of hummers. I wanted my garden to be ready.

As soon as the danger of frost had passed in early May, I planted several patches of anise sage (p. 58), amounting to about 200 square feet of bright blue in my rather large, irrigated suburban yard. These were plants I had started from cuttings the previous fall and kept alive over winter. Although I wasn't sure what type of yard I would have to work with, anise sage is adaptable enough that I was sure I could find a place for this top hummingbird flower.

Beside the driveway was an area of several hundred square feet landscaped with a bed of gravel. There was fabric mesh under the gravel preventing weeds from growing. I wanted to plant hummingbird flowers there, but removing the gravel and fabric would have been too time-consuming. I decided to scatter seeds of tropical sage (p. 53) over the gravel, gambling that this adaptable hummer favorite would take root through the fabric and thrive without pampering.

My gamble paid off better than the local slot machines. With water twice a week, these salvias were 5 feet tall by August and bloomed nonstop for four months starting in mid-June. In the fall, I pulled the frozen plants from the ground, raked the gravel, and the area was back to its initial appearance.

Because I was not familiar at the time with the dry, intermountain climate of Reno, I scouted around town to see what hummingbird plants were doing well. Not surprisingly, I found that sunset hyssop (p. 63) thrived. Another popular local plant was red-hot poker (p. 73). As summer progressed, I discovered plants that I was not familiar with and met many gardeners happy to share cuttings and advice. I usually try only a plant or two of a species that I am unfamiliar with until I understand its requirements and the level of hummer interest in it. I can't resist experimenting with new plants, but I try to take my own advice and dedicate most of my garden space to a few of the best.

Thanks to my large stands of two hummingbird favorites, I enjoyed summer-long hummer-watching in my suburban Reno yard. Black-chinned hummingbirds nest in many western towns and were common from spring through fall in my neighborhood. I also attracted throngs of migrant rufous hummers and the occasional calliope and broad-tailed. Early on, an unexpected Anna's hummingbird decided my garden was a perfect place to take up residence, and it remained after all the others had departed.

A female ruby-throated hummingbird gets its forehead dusted with pollen while it sips nectar from a cardinal flower blossom.

flowers in nearby woodlands bloom abundantly and are free of insect damage. Because of pests, some gardeners find it difficult to maintain cardinal flowers in their gardens and opt for other plants.

Cardinal flower plants are widely sold by local and mail-order nurseries. Many cultivars and hybrids of this plant are available, generally differing from the typical wild plant in the color or size of the flowers and perhaps in hardiness and pest resistance. The cultivars of cardinal flower seem to attract hummingbirds as well as the wild plants.

Growing Instructions. This plant is a perennial, particularly in the northern part of its range, but individual plants tend to survive no more than a few years in the garden. Along the Gulf of Mexico and in Florida, cardinal flower may grow primarily as an annual, with new plants sprouting from seed each spring.

Although a single plant will get larger as it ages, cardinal flowers do not spread into a clump that can be divided to obtain more plants. Cuttings do not readily root, and the usual method to produce plants is from seed. You can readily buy seed or collect it from wild plants.

Seeds should be scattered on the soil surface and kept evenly moist throughout germination and until seedlings are well established. Cardinal flowers reseed themselves abundantly in some gardens and can be found sprouting in flower beds, lawns, and under shrubs. In other gardens, volunteer seedlings almost never occur and seeds must be planted. Apparently, local conditions have a strong influence on cardinal flower survival.

Plants should be located 12 to 18 inches apart to produce a solid show of blooms in late summer. Regular fertilizer is beneficial to the growth of cardinal flowers, but it is not necessary in the rich soil that is typical of their preferred habitat. Pruning is usually not necessary, as basal leaves are the only vegetation cardinal flowers produce until they are ready to put forth their flower spikes. Any flower spikes that are removed may not be replaced by the plant.

Cardinal flowers may rot if mulched during the winter and so should be left unmulched, particularly in milder regions. In regions with cold winters, a mulch of leaves may help protect the basal rosette from desiccation by cold winds, but the mulch should be removed from the plants when the snow melts in spring.

Trick or Treat?

Some sources state that cardinal flower attracts hummingbirds only by virtue of its bright red blossoms, tricking hummers into pollinating it without providing any nourishment in return. Like the story of hummers hitching a ride south on the backs of geese, it is a myth. Cardinal flowers produce nectar in good quantities. The myth may have started because cardinal flowers, like any hummingbird plant, may not contain noticeable volumes of nectar at all times. Even when a plant is producing good quantities of nectar, the blossoms will be temporarily empty after a hummingbird visit. Hummingbirds quickly learn which plants offer a treat of nectar. They are not likely to be tricked into pollinating any plant for long unless it offers up the expected sweets.

Sunset Hyssop, Licorice Mint
Agastache rupestris

Growth habit: Herbaceous perennial
Exposure: Sun
Hardiness: Zone 4
Moisture: Arid to average
Height: 4 feet
Bloom: June to August
Propagation: Seed or cuttings

Sunset hyssop (HIGH-sup) is a distinctive plant with an odd combination of orange flowers, mauve calyces, silvery green foliage, and a scent that combines licorice, mint, and root beer. It seems to have been pieced together by an imaginative child.

The plant is, of course, a product of nature and is native to the dry mountains of southern Arizona and Mexico at elevations between 5,000 and 7,000 feet. In the wild, this herbaceous perennial occurs only in scattered locations amid ponderosa pines or in piñon-juniper woodlands, often on rocky slopes, as indicated by the species name (*rupestris* means "occurs near rocks"). The abundant flowers appear during July and August in the wild and are arranged at the tips of the stems in spikes.

Gardening with Sunset Hyssop. Sunset hyssop is a perennial, hardy through winter at least through zone 4. It is well suited to difficult situations such as rocky soils on southern exposures. In its native western mountain habitat, it easily tolerates dry soils that are low in organic matter. In richer, moister soils, it will grow more luxuriantly and may bloom longer than wild plants usually do, but it is not well suited to the ample, regular watering typical of many gardens, nor does it grow well in hot and humid parts of the Southeast.

In the garden, sunset hyssop is a charmer. Not only is it a treat for the eye, but the plants fill a garden with their unusual and delightful fragrance when they are brushed by a passerby. No common disease or insect problems are reported, and like many mints, sunset hyssop is said to be avoided by browsing deer.

Because it is relatively new to horticulture, sunset hyssop is usually available only from native plant specialty nurseries or through mail order. There are several close relatives and agastache hybrids that are equally sought out by hummingbirds, including Texas hummingbird mint (p. 72). *Agastache aurantica* and *A. mexicana* are also worth a try, although these western natives are most at home in dry climates.

Several hybrids of the hummingbird-friendly agastaches are available, some of them reportedly more tolerant of the regular water and rich soils of most gardens than the species are. Hybrids to try include 'Firebird' and 'Tutti-Frutti'.

The beautiful spires of sunset hyssop bloom in their first year when grown from seed.

Growing Instructions. Sunset hyssop grows easily in much of the West, but in many other parts of the country, the planting location must be chosen with care. Eastern and midwestern gardeners should choose the driest location in their yards, such as a south-facing wall with an overhanging roof or a south-facing sunny slope. The soil under sunset hyssop should dry out between waterings, so in the East and Midwest, a well-drained soil or sunny slope is the ideal location.

One way to minimize the problems associated with living in the wrong climate is to place sunset hyssop in a large planter or raised bed, which will help the soil around the roots to drain quickly.

Gravel makes a good mulch for this and other dry-climate plants, especially in moist climates. It holds the soil in place without encouraging excessive moisture, and it creates a slightly hotter, drier microclimate near the soil surface than organic mulches or bare soil. Organic mulches should be used sparingly near the base of this plant, especially in winter, when too much mulch can encourage rot.

Unlike many other plants in the mint family, sunset hyssop does not spread vegetatively. It remains as a single plant, which makes it safe to grow among less vigorous plants. It can be grown easily from seed — sprinkle seeds onto prepared soil and keep moist — or cuttings can be rooted.

Like many perennials, transplants survive winter better if they are replanted early enough in the growing season to allow a couple of months of growth before frost.

The upright, spiral-shaped flowers of Turk's cap remind many observers of hibiscus flowers that have not yet opened fully or have finished blooming and curled up again.

Turk's Cap, Wax Mallow, Sultan's Turban
Malvaviscus arboreus var. *drummondii*

Growth habit: Lax to upright or climbing woody shrub

Exposure: Sun to shade

Hardiness: Zone 7

Moisture: Dry to moist

Height: 4 feet, 8 feet if supported

Bloom: May to November

Propagation: Cuttings or seed

The brilliant red flowers of Turk's cap typically contain 20 to 30 percent sugar and are very popular with hummingbirds. The blossoms are followed by small red fruits that are eagerly eaten by many birds and mammals.

Turk's cap grows as a sprawling, woody shrub native to woodlands and forest openings from Central America to southern Texas, where it blooms throughout much of the year. It also thrives in gardens farther north and has been naturalized in much of the southeastern U.S., where cold winters limit its blooming season to summer and fall.

Although they are woody, the aboveground portions of Turk's cap will not survive hard freezes, and in zone 7 and sometimes 8, plants sprout from the roots each spring, reaching 4 feet or taller by autumn.

Gardening with Turk's Cap. In the garden, Turk's cap is a versatile plant that can fill many roles.

Giant Turk's cap (p. 90) is a larger shrub than Turk's cap, bearing similar but larger flowers that hang down from their stems. It is often called *campanitas* (little bells), its common Spanish name.

It is tolerant of drought and also thrives in moist conditions. It grows easily in almost any soil and will perform well in full sun or shade. It blooms longer and more profusely in sunny locations but will have larger, lusher leaves if kept shaded.

It can be grown as a tall ground cover, especially in shady situations. It will grow as an upright shrub if grown against a foundation or wall in full or nearly full sun. With some encouragement, it can be made to climb a trellis, fence, or larger shrub.

Turk's cap is one of the larval host plants of the abundant gray hairstreak butterfly, and the small green caterpillars that appear on the plant consume not only leaves but also flower buds, sometimes halting the production of mature flowers. The caterpillars are reportedly eaten by hummingbirds and a wide variety of other birds, which is a good reason to leave the caterpillars on the plant. But if spraying is necessary, use BT, a pesticide derived from the bacterium *Bacillus thuringiensis,* which is toxic only to moth and butterfly larvae.

Throughout the South, Turk's cap is occasionally available from local nurseries, especially those that specialize in native plants. Many mail-order nurseries also supply it, but be aware that this plant is called by a wide variety of names, as listed above. It is easier to identify by its Latin name, although even that is confusing. The currently accepted Latin name is *Malvaviscus arboreus* var. *drummondii,* but *Malvaviscus drummondii* is also regularly used.

Giant Turk's cap (p. 90) was formerly considered the same species as Turk's cap. It is much larger than Turk's cap, forming an upright shrub as tall as 10 feet. Giant Turk's cap accepts the same wide variety of growing conditions as its smaller cousin.

Growing Instructions. Although it can be grown from seed, Turk's cap is more often grown from cuttings about 6 inches long, taken from pieces of semiwoody stem the diameter of a pencil.

Cuttings set out in spring should grow into plants 2 or 3 feet tall and about as wide by their first summer, and they may bloom. The plants will spread by rooting of the lower branches to form a clump within a few years. Occasional applications of fertilizer and supplemental water in dry climates will encourage faster growth and abundant flowers.

A mulch of leaves, shredded bark, or pine needles will help control weeds and protect the roots over winter. Occasional pruning to control the size or shape of the plant can be done at any time.

Mexican Honeysuckle
Justicia spicigera

> *Growth habit: Herbaceous perennial, semiwoody shrub*
> *Exposure: Sun, shade in the desert Southwest*
> *Hardiness: Zone 8*
> *Moisture: Average to dry*
> *Height: 4 feet*
> *Bloom: Year-round*
> *Propagation: Seed or cuttings*

Despite their extreme temperatures and lack of rainfall, the deserts of the Southwest are home to many hummingbirds. The inhospitable conditions push many flowering plants past their limits, but a few hardy hummingbird plants thrive in the desert. One of the best of them is Mexican honeysuckle.

Mexican honeysuckle is native from Mexico into South America and is widely grown in warmer parts of the U.S. The leafy, evergreen shrub produces spikes of orange tubular flowers almost non-stop throughout the year.

Gardening with Mexican Honeysuckle. Not only is Mexican honeysuckle a great plant for desert gardens, but it grows well throughout the U.S. in zones 8 and warmer. Gardeners fortunate enough to live in these balmy climates will find that the versatile Mexican honeysuckle can fill many niches in their gardens. It grows as a tall ground cover, a low hedge, or among other plants in a desert landscape. It also grows well in containers.

In the desert, Mexican honeysuckle requires irrigation but only a modest amount; deep waterings every week or two are usually just right. In moister climates, it requires good drainage and can typically thrive on rainfall alone. It can tolerate the hottest reflected sun, yet will grow in full shade in the desert. In more humid climates, however, gardeners find that it blooms better with at least a few hours of direct sun.

This plant is usually free of problems, but occasional white fly infestations may occur. Keeping plants vigorously growing can reduce white fly problems, and to this end, occasional fertilization is helpful. Spraying the plants with soapy water helps control the infestations.

Mexican honeysuckle is readily available in retail nurseries in the Southwest and can be found in better-stocked retail outlets throughout the warmer regions of the U.S. It is also available through mail-order catalogs. I am not aware of any named cultivars of this plant. It may be confused with the similar *Justicia leonardii,* but this error should cause little worry; these two look-alikes are both great for hummers and equally versatile in the garden.

Growing Instructions. Plants should be placed about 2 feet apart to provide a solid mass of color within the first year. If your plants begin to look ragged or if frost damages them, pruning them back to within a few inches of the ground in spring will encourage fresh new growth.

Mexican honeysuckle, which blooms year-round, makes an excellent foundation for a desert hummgarden, filling gaps in the blooming times of other plants.

Mulching the soil will help control weeds and maintain soil moisture, but plants grown without a mulch don't seem to suffer. Mexican honeysuckle can be propagated readily either by seed or cuttings.

Honeysuckle Fuchsia, 'Gartenmeister Bonstedt' Fuchsia
Fuchsia triphylla

Growth habit: Tender perennial herb or semiwoody shrub

Exposure: Full sun to shade

Hardiness: Zone 8, grown as annual in colder zones

Moisture: Average to moist

Height: 3 feet as an annual

Bloom: Constant in warm weather

Propagation: Cuttings or division

Fuchsias are native mainly to Central and South America, with a few species occurring in the Caribbean. A couple of far-flung members of the genus are found in New Zealand and islands of the tropical Pacific.

Models of diversity, fuchsias vary from prostrate ground covers to trees. A number of species have edible fruits, including the beautiful *Fuchsia boliviana,* which is cultivated for its berries in South America, and *Fuchsia excorticata,* the fruits of which are eaten in its native New Zealand.

Fuchsia diversity reaches its peak in the cool, high elevations of the tropical Andes Mountains of South America, an area that also supports a very high diversity of hummingbird species; hardly a coincidence, I think. All fuchsia plants, whatever their growing habit, can be recognized by their distinctive flowers, which generally hang as pendants below arching branches.

Only a few of the hundreds of species of fuchsia are widely used as ornamentals outside their native range, but thousands of cultivars and hybrids have been developed, and new varieties are introduced regularly. Unfortunately, most of them, including many of the newer and most common hybrids, are, at best, marginal hummingbird attractors. For hummingbirds, look for a fuchsia with single — not frilly — flowers. The typical hybrid fuchsias with large, frilly flowers offer little nectar, and what little is produced lies behind the frills, inaccessible to hummingbirds.

The notable exceptions to the hummer-unfriendly hybrids are the triphylla or honeysuckle fuchsias. With their long, open tubes; abundant nectar production; and year-round blooms, the triphylla fuchsias are hummingbird favorites. Triphylla fuchsias are a group — cultivars and hybrids — that clearly have *Fuchsia triphylla* as a parent because of their distinctive appearance. Native to Hispaniola in the Caribbean, *F. triphylla* was the first fuchsia discovered by science, gathered in 1703 in the Dominican Republic by Father Charles Plumier.

A male ruby-throated hummingbird is attracted to a hanging basket of 'Gartenmeister Bonstedt' fuchsia, which has long been the most popular of the triphylla fuchsias.

Gardening with Honeysuckle Fuchsia.

One of the most widely available of all the honeysuckle (triphylla) fuchsia cultivars is 'Gartenmeister Bonstedt'. It produces clusters of orange-red flowers throughout the warm months of the year.

Like many other fuchsias, 'Gartenmeister Bonstedt' can be grown in the ground, where it will form a small semiwoody shrub. It makes a good hummer plant as a shrub, but the reason it is one of the Dozen Dazzlers is because it is an outstanding plant for a pot or hanging basket.

A hummer plant in a pot or hanging basket is like a feeder that you don't have to fill or scrub. You can bring hummers right to a window or onto a porch or deck by using potted plants to attract them. And when the hummers aren't feeding, you still have the beauty of the plants to brighten the surroundings.

'Gartenmeister Bonstedt' is a reliable performer. It seldom has a problem with disease, but it can become infested with aphids or white flies. These can usually be treated by spraying the plants with soapy water.

Fortunately, 'Gartenmeister Bonstedt' is resistant to the fuchsia mites that have devastated so many other fuchsias in parts of the country. These mites are prevalent in central and southern California, where they burrow into stems and disfigure or kill fuchsias. The insecticides required to protect fuchsias from fuchsia mites are quite toxic and should be kept out of a hummgarden.

There are a number of other triphylla fuchsia cultivars, and they all are similar in appearance and hummer appeal to 'Gartenmeister Bonstedt'. Some of the more common are 'Mary', 'Thalia', 'Borneman's Best', and 'Insulinde'. Some cultivars are sold simply as honeysuckle fuchsia. The cultivar names aren't important as long as the plant is one of the triphylla fuchsias.

Growing Instructions. 'Gartenmeister Bonstedt' is widely sold as an annual, often already planted in a hanging basket. Avoid dark-colored pots, which will absorb solar energy and overheat the roots. Many growers emphasize the need for a loose potting soil, and the soil should be kept consistently moist. Give the plant regular water and fertilizer.

You can place a pot where it gets a considerable amount of direct sunlight, or you can place it in shade. It will grow well in either case. A few hours of direct sunlight or a full day of the filtered shade under tall trees is probably the ideal exposure.

Although honeysuckle fuchsias are featured as potted plants, gardeners shouldn't neglect them as bedding plants. Placed about 2 feet apart in a sunny or partly sunny bed, they will grow to fill the

The frilly blossoms on this hybrid fuchsia are very different from the single flowers of a triphylla fuchsia (left). This fuchsia is undoubtedly a poor plant for hummingbirds.

Year-Round Hummgardening in Southern California

It was in the month of November that I moved to Huntington Beach in sunny southern California. In most of the rest of the U.S., gardens were through blooming and hummers were long gone by this date, but in Huntington Beach, the resident Anna's and Allen's hummers would soon be nesting. As always, I was eager to interact with them. Unfortunately, my garden space was nothing more than a small lawn surrounded by concrete walls — but it was sunny.

I relied on two hummplant stalwarts, anise sage (p. 58) and tropical sage (p. 53), for my largest plantings. The anise sage I started as small plants, and they began blooming in March. Tropical sage, which is a year-round bloomer in frost-free Huntington Beach, was started as seeds scattered on a prepared bed. I also added several plants of Mexican bush sage (p. 74), an outstanding perennial for warm climates, to my garden.

Because there were no trees in my yard, I wanted to add some plants that would grow to provide cover as well as blossoms for hummers. At a nursery, I found an inexpensive Cape honeysuckle (p. 98) that was already good-sized and blooming. I knew it would require regular pruning to keep it in bounds in my small yard, but it would also provide some of the needed cover. Then I was fortunate enough to rescue two 5-foot tree tobacco plants (p. 95) from a construction site. These plants quickly grew into small trees and provide nectar-filled flowers year-round.

After I established the plants that would be the backbone of my hummgarden, I began to experiment with some of the many other hummingbird flowers that thrive in California's pleasant Mediterranean climate, including aloe vera (p. 93–94), pitcher sage (p. 87), and giant cuphea (p. 89). In order to utilize the vertical space of the garden walls, I added Chilean glory vine (p. 82), providing it with strings to climb. Hummingbirds began to visit my yard as soon as the flowers started blooming.

bed by midsummer, blooming all the time. Beds are displayed to good advantage on a slope or atop a wall, where their pendant flowers can be easily reached by hummingbirds.

'Gartenmeister Bonstedt' fuchsia is occasionally trained as a "standard" in frost-free areas. A standard is a plant with a bare central stem topped by branches and leaves. Fuchsia standards are generally about 4 feet tall, including 3 feet of bare stem. They can grow as high as 5 feet.

Potted fuchsias can be kept alive through the winter. Remove all of the green stems and leaves in fall, trimming the plants back to about two-thirds of their original size. Store them in a dark and very cold, but not freezing, location. The soil should be moderately dry. In the spring, move the plants to a warm, bright location and water them. They should

A coral honeysuckle vine twines over a large shrub, studding it with trumpet-shaped blossoms.

begin to put out green growth again. It is possible to keep fuchsias alive for many years this way.

New fuchsia plants can be started from cuttings, and occasionally honeysuckle fuchsias can be divided. Look for shoots that emerge several inches from the parent plant. After they have grown for a while, carefully cut the shoots, with an intact piece of soil and roots, from the parent with a sharp knife.

Coral Honeysuckle, Trumpet Honeysuckle
Lonicera sempervirens

> Growth habit: Woody vine, evergreen to deciduous
> Exposure: Sun to partial shade
> Hardiness: Zone 4
> Moisture: Moist to average
> Height: Up to 15 feet
> Bloom: Spring through fall, sometimes winter in
>   Zone 8 and warmer
> Propagation: Cuttings or seed

This twining vine (sidebar, p. 83) with thick, rich-green leaves bears many clusters of distinctive 2-inch tubular flowers — red on the outside, yellow inside. It is a widespread but generally uncommon native of most of the East, where it occurs naturally in woodlands, on stream banks, and in sunny woodland openings.

Coral honeysuckle is a very bird-friendly plant. It utilizes hummingbirds as its major pollinator, and its seeds are spread by a variety of birds that relish the juicy red fruit that follows the flowers.

In zones 7 and warmer, coral honeysuckle often lives up to its Latin species name, *sempervirens,*

Gardenless in Louisiana

Baton Rouge, Louisiana, offers great opportunities for a hummgardener, but when I was there, I lived in an apartment that presented few possibilites (sidebar, p. 101). So to keep my thumb green and learn about hummgardening in Louisiana, I joined a community garden. The garden was located in a suburban part of town. It offered ample space, sunshine, and plenty of good gardeners from whom I could learn the tricks of gardening in the Deep South, but it was in an open field more than 100 feet from trees or any other cover, and I worried that hummingbirds would be hesitant to visit such an exposed location.

I began by visiting a few local nurseries to see what plants were offered for sale, and I had the immediate good fortune to run into Miriam Davey, one of the most enthusiastic and knowledgeable hummingbird gardeners anywhere. She introduced me to the plants that thrive in the heat and humidity of Louisiana, and the hummgardeners that grow them in Baton Rouge. Following advice that I would learn was excellent, I began by planting large stands, at least 25 square feet, of hummingbird favorites. The first seeds I planted in spring were tropical sage (p. 53). If you've been reading carefully, you'll note that tropical sage has been the backbone of each of my four gardens described in this and other sidebars. It has thrived everywhere I planted it.

Having lots of space to work with, I planted large stands of many other hummingbird plants, including southern favorites such as cigar plant (p. 73), cypress vine (p. 83), Turk's cap (p. 64), pineapple sage (p. 90), and giant cuphea (picture, p. 73). When I learned about the regular sightings of western hummingbirds in south Louisiana each winter, I began to try winter-blooming flowers, such as Mexican sage (p. 91), forsythia sage (p. 90), orange abutilon (p. 88), and winter shrimp plant (p. 89). I eventually tried dozens of plants, some that thrived and others that failed, but through trial and error I learned to rely on large stands of a few hummplants that thrived in the area — and the concept of the Dozen Dazzlers was born.

The community garden site, far from natural woodlands, lacked a local breeding population of ruby-throats, so my garden was essentially hummerless each spring and early summer. However, starting in July, a half-dozen or more ruby-throats would be in the garden at any one time. Before the last ruby-throats departed in November, they would be joined by western hummingbirds, including calliope, broad-tailed, black-chinned, and particularly rufous hummingbirds. These wanderers arrived in small numbers, usually one or two at a time, but provided great excitement for me and the many other Louisiana birders who awaited their arrival each winter.

which means evergreen, but farther north it usually sheds its leaves in winter.

Gardening with Coral Honeysuckle. Coral honeysuckle is an outstanding hummingbird vine. It has a neat appearance, a long blooming season, and doesn't grow so fast that it threatens to swallow an entire garden the way some larger vines do. It is hardy as far north as zone 4, reportedly even zone 3, and is equally at home south to central Florida. Unlike many hummingbird-pollinated vines, such as the ipomoea species (pp. 82–83), coral honeysuckle is a perennial.

Because of its restrained growth, coral honeysuckle is perfect for a medium-sized trellis, a fence, or a porch railing. Like most vines, it requires at least a half day of sunlight to bloom well. It prefers rich soil and regular moisture, although in the wild it can sometimes be found in dry, sandy soils.

Insect and disease problems are rare, and the only maintenance coral honeysuckle seems to require is occasional winter pruning if you want to limit its size. Occasionally gardeners find that a plant has mysteriously died in the garden. The cause may be related to the overuse of fertilizers, which should be applied sparingly.

There are several cultivars available in addition to the species (wild strain), and all are easily found in retail nurseries or through mail order. Commonly sold cultivars include 'Alabama Crimson', which has redder flowers than the species, and a yellow-flowered variety called 'Sulphurea'. All the cultivars seem to be just as attractive to hummingbirds as the species.

A related plant is Hall's or Japanese honeysuckle *(Lonicera japonica)*, which is similar in appearance to coral honeysuckle but bears yellow or white flowers that are less tubular and more flared at the mouth. This widely available plant is visited by hummingbirds, but it is so rampant a grower that it has become an invasive weed in many areas and is usually avoided by gardeners.

A few hybrids between *L. sempervirens* and *L. japonica* are available. While less rampant than *L. japonica,* they are also a little less attractive to hummingbirds than *L. sempervirens.* Named hybrids include *Lonicera x Heckrottii,* often called 'Goldflame' honeysuckle or 'Pink Lemonade' honeysuckle.

Growing Instructions. A twining vine, coral honeysuckle requires a strong, permanent support that allows it to become larger and more floriferous each year. The supporting poles or rails should be no bigger than about 3 inches in diameter.

One interesting way to grow this vine is to plant it next to a large shrub and allow it to twine through its neighbor. The best shrubs for this are those that do not require shearing, which would damage

A young ruby-throated hummingbird probes the flowers of a coral honeysuckle. Hummingbird flowers typically have long tubes with both male and female sexual organs sticking out beyond the end of the tubes. Pollen from the male stamens may be deposited on a hummer, or pollen that was deposited on the hummer by another flower may be transferred to the female pistil, pollinating it.

Trumpet creeper is a large, vigorous vine with gaudy, large flowers. The flowers are usually orange-red, but occasionally sports of different hues are seen.These wild sports, which include red- and yellow-flowered varieties, seem to be just as attractive to hummingbirds as the more typical version of the plant.

roots reluctantly and sometimes only after several months. You can also remove seeds from the red berries and try planting them, or you can transplant one of the occasional volunteer seedlings that may appear near shrubs where fruit-eating birds perch.

Trumpet Creeper
Campsis radicans

Growth habit: Woody, deciduous vine
Exposure: Full to part sun
Hardiness: Zone 5, zone 4 as a perennial
Moisture: Average to moist
Bloom: June to September or later
Height: Up to 60 feet or more
Propagation: Seed

Looking like a prop from a Tarzan movie, trumpet creeper is an impressively large woody vine that seems to belong in a rain forest, not here in the eastern U.S. draped in oaks, pines, and other trees along woodland edges and fencerows. However, hummingbirds battling over ownership of the abundant clusters of large orange-red flowers plainly feel the plant grows exactly where it belongs.

The hummingbirds, of course, are right; trumpet creeper is among the northernmost representatives of Bignonacea, a large family of tropical plants. It is native throughout the eastern and central U.S., from New Jersey to Florida and Texas to Indiana, where it occurs most conspicuously along woodland edges and fencerows. It also grows along forested stream banks and within moist woodlands, where it can climb 50 feet or more to reach the direct sunlight it requires for abundant flowering.

Vines such as trumpet creeper are an important component of bottomland hardwood forests throughout the Southeast. By covering tree trunks with vegetation and creating tangles of cover high off the ground, they add an extra dimension to the landscape, a very important one to the many birds that utilize the cover, nectar, and berries that various vine species provide.

Trumpet creeper climbs by aerial rootlets that grow wherever the vine touches a solid surface, allowing it to scale large trees or flat walls. It may appear to be smothering the trees that support it, but trumpet creeper generally does no more harm than leaving rootlet marks on buildings or trees after the vines are removed.

Gardening with Trumpet Creeper. Although native only to the East, trumpet creeper grows well throughout most of the U.S. and southern Canada, provided it receives regular water and sunlight. It is hardy as a woody vine to zone 5. Through zone 4, it may be frozen back to the ground each winter but will grow several feet in summer and bloom if given a location in full sun. In the Deep South, it may bloom from May into October.

the honeysuckle and greatly reduce its flower production. Unlike Japanese honeysuckle, coral honeysuckle will not completely cover a shrub or tree but will exist as an interesting addition to the larger plant, providing flowers and fruit for birds.

Occasional pruning, best done during the winter, will help keep this vine in check along a fence or trellis where its size may be a concern. A single vine can cover 20 feet or more of fence after several years, so a spacing of 10 to 20 feet between plants is sensible. Regular water throughout the year will result in vigorous plants with steady growth. Plants can live for years in a favored location. An organic mulch will help control weeds between plants.

Coral honeysuckle is normally purchased as a plant. It can be started from cuttings but will strike

Trumpet creeper makes an invaluable addition to any hummgarden that can accommodate its large size and tendency to spread. Its exuberant growth adds a character that is generally lacking from the manicured suburban environment. Given regular moisture and occasional fertilizer, it is a reliable performer, growing rapidly and producing abundant flowers. Pest and disease problems are rare.

Trumpet creeper is readily available in nurseries and by mail order. A number of select varieties with flowers that are larger or of a different hue than the wild form are available in the horticulture trade, and occasionally a plant with flowers of an unusual color appears in the wild.

The flowers of such hybrids as 'Madem Galen', horticulturally known as *Campsis x tagliabuana,* are larger than the flowers on wild plants, and although ruby-throats will feed from them, the flowers verge on being too large for the birds to easily utilize.

Growing Instructions. This plant has a reputation for being invasive because many gardeners treat it like a small vine. Trumpet creeper is a large plant, and left to itself, it will sprawl from tree to tree and to any other object it can reach. Unless you are willing to keep an eye and a pair of garden shears trained on it, the plant should be separated by at least 5 feet from those trees, shrubs, and buildings that you don't want covered with a vine.

If you grow trumpet creeper on a sturdy support, isolated from other objects in your garden, you can create a stunning specimen in a small space. Grown on a treated 8-foot-long 4-by-4 post, trumpet creeper will weave its woody branches out several feet around the post, creating the appearance of a shrub or small tree. Make sure the support you use is sturdy; trumpet creeper is not a reasonable choice for a small trellis.

Isolating a trumpet creeper also makes it easy to control the suckers the plant sends out. In addition to simply sprawling, the plant spreads by producing new shoots, called suckers, from its extensive root system. If the plant is surrounded by several feet of lawn, the lawn mower controls the growth by clipping the suckers.

Trumpet creeper can be grown from seed or stem cuttings, or a plant can be started by digging a small root sucker, with a section of roots, from a wild plant. Although fast growing once established, this vine can be rather slow growing at first. Newly planted vines may take several years to flower, particularly in northern areas or shady locations.

Trumpet creeper has the longest tubes of any native hummingbird-pollinated plant in the U.S., and this female broad-tailed hummingbird has to thrust half her head into the 3-inch long, thick-walled flower to reach her nectar reward.

The Supporting Cast —
Plants for Specific Conditions

Are you ready to explore beyond the Dozen Dazzlers? Here are more proven hummer favorites organized by climate and other categories. Most of the best hummingbird flowers under cultivation in the U.S. and Canada are on one or more of my lists, but there are many plants that aren't, and some of them can be very good. There is no such thing as a complete list of hummplants. Hummers tirelessly investigate new plants and so do hummgardeners. There is an endless supply of plants to try, and new ones are constantly being brought under cultivation.

The first four lists are of plants suitable for specific combinations of sun and moisture. Gardeners throughout the continent should consult these lists for plants that suit their growing conditions. Each of these four lists is complete. In the list of plants for sunny, moist places, for instance, you will find all the plants that I recommend for growing in a garden exposed to full sun and receiving regular water. Each plant is described, or a reference is given to a page where it is described.

Plants are organized alphabetically by their Latin names so that plants in the same genus are mentioned consecutively. The order is not based on merit.

Following the first four lists are a number of specialized lists. Most of them are a complete listing of recommended plants for a particular niche. Some specialized lists are not inclusive but are lists of additional plants that excel in a particular region — the humid Southeast, the desert Southwest, Texas, or zones 9 and 10. Gardeners in these regions will want to use these lists to supplement the plants they choose from other lists and from the Dozen Dazzlers.

Many hummgardeners hate being told that a plant they want can't be grown in their yard. They take pride in being able to cater to a specific plant's requirements and growing it where it isn't supposed to grow. So even if you don't live in the desert Southwest, if you have a genuine green thumb, you'll want to read the list for the desert Southwest and all the other lists.

Although growing a wide variety of plants is by no means necessary to attract hummers, trying new plants, learning from failures, and discovering which flowers are most popular with the hummers in your yard is part of the fun of hummgardening.

To speed up the learning process, supplement the information in these pages with that from local gardening sources. Connect with other gardeners, or join gardening groups and seek out the wildlife gardeners in them. Not only will you find out what plants others in your area have had luck with, but you'll uncover a source for the plants themselves. Horticultural collecting and swapping is a bug that seems to infect most hummgardeners.

A Selection of Hummplants for —
Sunny, Moist Places

The plants on this list do well in — and in some cases require — a half day or more of full sun. They also require moisture throughout the summer. If you can grow normal lawn grasses without watering them, then you can typically keep these plants happy without supplying additional water. In dry regions, or during a dry spell anywhere, you will need to water these plants to keep them growing vigorously.

Texas Hummingbird Mint, Mosquito Plant, Double Bubble Mint *(Agastache cana)*
Growth habit: Herbaceous perennial
Exposure: Sun
Hardiness: Zone 5
Moisture: Average to dry
Height: 4 feet
Bloom: Summer to frost
Propagation: Seed or cuttings

This native of west Texas and New Mexico is one of the more adaptable species of agastache. It will grow in dry western climates with only occasional supplemental irrigation and will also tolerate moister climates or more frequent irrigation as long as the soil is well drained.

For moist soils, several hybrids are available that offer a wider range of colors and a longer blooming season. *Agastache* 'Firebird' does well in average soil and bears dark red flowers most of the summer and fall, and *Agastache* 'Tutti Frutti' bears spikes of pink flowers continuously from midsummer to frost. *Agastache* 'Desert Sunrise' is an aromatic hybrid between *A. cana* and *A. rupestris* (p. 63).

A wildlife garden receives a periodic watering. Most flowering plants do their best with regular watering and full exposure to the sun.

Cigar plant *(Cuphea x 'David Verity'),* shown above, is often misidentified as *Cuphea ignea.* 'David Verity' is hardier, grows taller, has larger flowers, and is a better hummplant than *C. ignea.*

Indian Shot *(Canna indica)* (p. 80)

Cigar Plant, Mexican Cigar *(Cuphea x* 'David Verity')

> *Growth habit: Herbaceous perennial, semiwoody*
> *shrub in frost-free areas, annual in colder regions*
> *Exposure: Sun or partial shade*
> *Hardiness: Zone 7*
> *Moisture: Average to moist*
> *Height: 4 feet, 6 feet or more in frost-free areas*
> *Bloom: Summer to frost*
> *Propagation: Cuttings*

This hybrid is probably the most widely grown orange-flowered cuphea. In sun, it is a dense, compact shrub covered with inch-long orange flowers. It is surprisingly hardy, returning from the roots in zone 7 if protected with a thick, airy mulch of pine straw or dry leaves soon after the first killing frost.

Hardy Fuchsia *(Fuchsia magellanica)* (p. 78)

Honeysuckle Fuchsia *(Fuchsia triphylla)* (p. 66)

Red-Hot Poker, Torch Lily *(Knifophia uvaria)*

> *Growth habit: Herbaceous clumping perennial*
> *Exposure: Sun*
> *Hardiness: Zone 5*
> *Moisture: Moist to dry, good drainage*
> *Height: Leaves to 3 feet, flowers to 5 feet*
> *Bloom: Color and bloom time vary*
> *Propagation: Division or seed*

Giant cuphea *(Cuphea micropetala),* shown above, is probably one of the hybrid parents of 'David Verity', together with *C. ignea.*

There are numerous species of knifophia, all originating in Africa, and many hybrids as well. The old standard red-hot poker, bearing spikes of red, orange, and yellow flowers, has been hybridized to produce a wide range of colors and bloom times. Some of the smaller hybrids with flowers reaching less than about 2 feet high don't seem to get as much attention from hummingbirds as the larger varieties. (picture, p. 51)

Standing Cypress *(Ipomopsis rubra)* (p. 59)

Copper Iris *(Iris fulva)* (p. 81)

Cardinal Flower *(Lobelia cardinalis)* (p. 60)

Turk's Cap *(Malvaviscus arboreus* var. *drummondii)* (p. 64)

Scarlet Monkeyflower *(Mimulus cardinalis)* (p. 82)

Bee Balm *(Monarda didyma)* (p. 55)

Cape Fuchsia *(Phygelius x rectus)*

> *Growth habit: Shrubby perennial or annual*
> *Exposure: Sun*
> *Hardiness: Zone 7, possibly farther north*
> *Moisture: Average to dry*
> *Height: 5 feet*
> *Bloom: Summer to fall*
> *Propagation: Cuttings*

Mexican bush sage bears lots of interesting purple and white flowers and has attractive silvery foliage. The blooms appear in waves. As one wave ends, the next set of new stems appears at the base of the plant, indicating that the old ones can be removed to make ready for the show to start over.

The many varieties of *Phygelius x rectus* are hybrids of several species, reportedly including *P. capensis* and *P. aequalis,* native to the mountains of South Africa, where their nectar-rich blossoms are pollinated by sunbirds. Several varieties with different color flowers are available, and all are attractive to hummingbirds. These tall plants with their pendulant, tubular flowers make a striking addition to a sunny garden and can be grown as annuals.

Tropical Sage (*Salvia coccinea*) (p. 53)

Autumn Sage (*Salvia greggii*) (p. 80)

Anise Sage (*Salvia guaranitica*) (p. 58)

Mexican Bush Sage (*Salvia leucantha*)
  Growth habit: Herbaceous perennial or annual
  Exposure: Sun
  Hardiness: Zone 7
  Moisture: Average
  Height: 4 to 5 feet
  Bloom: Summer through fall as perennial
  Propagation: Cuttings or division

Because it is attractive and easy to grow, Mexican bush sage is widely planted, especially in the southern tier of states. It blooms for much of the year in frost-free areas. With some winter protection, it is hardy into zone 7. Farther north, it can be grown as an annual but will not flower until September or later. Consequently, it isn't recommended where the first frosts occur before late October.

Belize sage (*Salvia miniata*) (p. 78)

Scarlet Sage (*Salvia splendens*) (p. 57)

Van Houtte Sage (*Salvia vanhoutte*) (p. 78)

Scarlet Betony, Scarlet Hedgenettle
(*Stachys coccinea*)
  Growth habit: Herbaceous perennial
  Exposure: Sun
  Hardiness: Zone 6
  Moisture: Moist to average
  Height: 2 feet
  Bloom: March to October
  Propagation: Seed or cuttings

This outstanding red-flowered Texas native is generally a low-maintenance plant in the garden. It grows wild in moist areas and will grow well in typical garden conditions with weekly watering during dry periods of the summer.

**A Selection of Hummplants for —
Sunny, Dry Places**

Gardeners in much of the West are faced with a difficult set of conditions, including cold winters; hot, dry summers; and low humidity. These factors combine to make it difficult or impossible to grow many of the garden plants that thrive elsewhere in North America. Fortunately for westerners, there are many species of native plants that are ideally suited to the climates and soils of dry western regions, and the best of the hummplants are listed here.

Gardeners in other parts of the country who face problems caused by rocky or sandy soils that dry out rapidly after a rain will also find useful plants in this list. Many of these plants will grow in the humid climates of the Midwest and Northeast, but they are not likely to survive the hot, humid summers of the Southeast.

Texas Hummingbird Mint (*Agastache cana*) (p. 72)

Sunset Hyssop (*Agastache rupestris*) (p. 63)

Indian Paintbrush (*Castilleja* spp.)
   Growth habit: Herbaceous perennials
   Exposure: Sun
   Hardiness: Varies with species, some to zone 3
   Moisture: Dry to wet, varies with species
   Height: Most species to about 3 feet
   Bloom: Summer
   Propagation: Seed or division
These striking North American natives with red or orange tips to their paintbrush-shaped flowers are hummer staples in western meadows. Indian paint-brushes are partial parasites, obtaining some of their sustenance from the roots of nearby plants, especially grasses. In the garden, they are often slow to become established. In spite of this, many gardeners feel they are worth the effort they require.

Red Yucca (*Hesperaloe parviflora*)
   Growth habit: Clump-forming, semisucculent
      perennial
   Exposure: Sun to partial shade
   Hardiness: Zone 5
   Moisture: Dry to average
   Height: Leaves to 3 feet, flowers to 6 feet
   Bloom: Summer and fall
   Propagation: Seed or division
Red yucca is a native of Texas and New Mexico but survives winters much farther north. This highly

Scarlet betony sends up an abundance of spikes with red flowers that bloom over much of the year.

drought-tolerant perennial tolerates a wide range of soils and, because of its drought and heat toler-ance, makes an excellent choice for a large planter in a sunny location where regular watering will not be convenient.

A male ruby-throated hummer sips nectar from a Texas paintbrush (*Castilleja indivisa*). The many species of Indian paintbrush are characteristic plants of western mountain meadows and are hummingbird staples.

A male broad-tailed hummingbird feeds at the bright blue blossoms of Rocky Mountain penstemon, one of the showiest wildflowers of the southern Rockies.

Scarlet Gilia (*Ipomopsis aggregata*)
  Growth habit: Herbaceous perennial
  Exposure: Full sun to partial shade
  Hardiness: Zone 4
  Moisture: Average to dry
  Height: 2 feet
  Bloom: Summer
  Propagation: Seed

The bright red flowers of this widespread western wildflower (picture, p. 114) are seen in deserts, mountain meadows, and many habitats in between. It adapts well to dry western climates but is less vigorous in humid eastern climates, where its larger relative, standing cypress (p. 59), is better adapted.

Standing Cypress (*Ipomopsis rubra*) (p. 59)

Mexican Honeysuckle (*Justicia spicigera*) (p. 65)

Turk's Cap (*Malvaviscus arboreus* var. *drummondii*) (p. 64)

Eaton's Firecracker, Scarlet Bugler (*Penstemon eatonii*)
  Growth habit: Herbaceous perennial
  Exposure: Sun
  Hardiness: Zone 4
  Moisture: Average to dry
  Height: Leaves to 1 foot, flowers to 3 feet
  Bloom: Spring and early summer
  Propagation: Seed

This Arizona native thrives in the arid West, tolerating dry summers and cold winters, but does not grow well in humid eastern climates. The bright red tubular flowers inspired the "firecracker" name.

Eaton's firecracker is reported to live longer when given limited water during the summer.

Pineleaf Penstemon (*Penstemon pinifolius*)
  Growth habit: Shrubby perennial
  Exposure: Full sun to partial shade
  Hardiness: Zone 4
  Moisture: Average to dry
  Height: 2 feet
  Bloom: Summer
  Propagation: Seed or cuttings

Because of its small size, pineleaf penstemon is one of the best of the native penstemons for smaller gardens and adapts well to rock gardens or sunny, arid hillsides. It should be placed in the front of borders, not intermixed with taller plants.

Rocky Mountain Penstemon (*Penstemon strictus*)
  Growth habit: Herbaceous clumping perennial
  Exposure: Sun to partial shade
  Hardiness: Zone 3 in the West
  Moisture: Dry to average
  Height: 2 to 3 feet
  Bloom: May through July
  Propagation: Seed or division

This is one of the easiest to grow of the many species of penstemon native to the western U.S. It spreads to form clumps and is useful as a ground cover for hillsides, road embankments, and similar areas. Rocky Mountain penstemon is highly drought tolerant once established, but in wet regions, it may not survive.

Pineleaf penstemon is a small plant with red tubular flowers. Older specimens resemble a low-growing shrubby pine.

There are a number of other native penstemons worth trying in dry soils, including *P. cardinalis, P. barbatus,* and *P. pseudospectabilis.*

Tropical Sage *(Salvia coccinea)* (p. 53)

Autumn Sage *(Salvia greggii)* (p. 80)

California Fuchsia, Hummingbird Trumpet
(Zauschneria spp.)
  Growth habit: Herbaceous perennial
  Exposure: Sun
  Hardiness: Varies with species, some to zone 5
  Moisture: Dry to average
  Height: Varies from 1 foot to 3 feet
  Bloom: Summer and fall
  Propagation: Seed or cuttings
Many species of zauschneria are native to the western U.S., including *Z. californica, Z. arizonica,* and *Z. latifolia.* All are excellent hummingbird plants, and one variety or another will grow well almost anywhere in the West. Sprawling plants with abundant orange-red blossoms, California fuchsias are well suited for a dry hillside or rock garden. These relatives of fireweeds are sometimes included in the genus *Epilobium.*

A Selection of Hummplants for —
Shady, Moist Places

These plants do well in the diffuse or dappled light beneath tall trees or in places where they get less than a half-day's direct sunlight, providing they receive adequate moisture. Many do better with increased sunlight but are sufficiently shade tolerant that they may continue to bloom with as little as an hour or two's direct sunlight a day or with no full sun at all if the shade is diffuse and not deep.

Soil moisture and the presence of tree roots, which compete for moisture and nutrients, influence the usefulness of shady spots for hummingbird plants. One indication that growing conditions may be difficult in a shady spot is a lack of grass. This often results as much from dense tree roots as from shade. Many trees are so thirsty for moisture during the summer that the soil beneath them becomes dry very soon after a rain, and some trees produce chemicals that restrict the growth of other plants beneath them.

Few hummingbird flowers will grow well with both intense root competition and shade. Where these two factors are both severe, it may be better to opt for plants such as woodland wildflowers, ferns, or ground covers, and leave the hummplants for better locations. One way to grow flowering plants under trees with extensive shallow roots is to use pots or planters. Try plants on this list or check the list of houseplants for hummingbirds (p. 85), moving them outside for summer and indoors for winter.

On shady hillsides in dry regions of the West, hummingbird plants must tolerate both shade and a lack of water. These plants are adapted to dry soils for much of the summer, but many western plants can adapt to moist eastern climates if planted on well-drained soils that resemble those of their western homeland.

Eastern Columbine *(Aquilegia canadensis)*
  Growth habit: Herbaceous perennial
  Exposure: Shade to partial sun
  Hardiness: Zone 4
  Moisture: Average to moist
  Height: 3 feet
  Bloom: Spring
  Propagation: Seed
Eastern columbine is a favorite spring nectar source for hummingbirds. This wildflower self-seeds to produce a slowly spreading group of plants. It is particularly at home on hillsides where fallen leaves don't build up excessively. It is native throughout much of eastern North America.

Eastern columbine raises its red and yellow bell-shaped flowers over rocky outcroppings throughout the eastern U.S.

Honeysuckle Fuchsia *(Fuchsia triphylla)* (p. 66)

Hardy Fuchsia *(Fuchsia magellanica)*
  *Growth habit: Herbaceous perennial, shrub in
    frost-free climates*
  Exposure: Sun to shade
  Hardiness: Zone 5
  Moisture: Moist to average
  Height: 4 feet, to 6 feet in frost-free regions
  Bloom: Summer to fall, year-round where frost-free
  Propagation: Cuttings

This adaptable perennial will produce its abundant purple and red pendant flowers with only a few hours of sunlight or in dappled shade, although in more northern areas, it will appreciate more sunlight. A native of cool temperate climates in Chile, it will not tolerate the hot summers of the Deep South and Florida but thrives farther north and in much of the West.

Spotted Jewelweed *(Impatiens capensis)* (p. 81)

Belize sage bears bright red fuzzy flowers even in very shady conditions.

Cardinal Flower *(Lobelia cardinalis)* (p. 60)

Turk's Cap *(Malvaviscus arboreus* var.
drummondii) (p. 64)

Bee Balm *(Monarda didyma)* (p. 55)

Red-Flowered Currant *(Ribes sanguinium)*
  Growth habit: Shrub
  Exposure: Sun to shade
  Hardiness: Zone 5
  Moisture: Moist to average
  Height: To 10 feet
  Bloom: Spring
  Propagation: Cuttings or seed

The clusters of small red flowers on this native of the Pacific Northwest are a major source of food for rufous hummers as they arrive on their nesting grounds early each spring. It is a must-have plant for gardeners in this region and will grow well in many other parts of the country. Several cultivars are available from mail-order nurseries.

Tropical Sage *(Salvia coccinea)* (p. 53)

Autumn Sage *(Salvia greggii)* (p. 80)

Belize sage *(Salvia miniata)*
  Growth habit: Herbaceous perennial
  Exposure: Sun to shade
  Hardiness: Zone 9, grown as annual farther north
  Moisture: Average
  Height: 3 feet
  Bloom: Summer and fall
  Propagation: Cuttings or seed

Belize sage is one of the best salvias for shade. It is reliably hardy only in zone 9, but grows fast enough to be a valuable annual. It is available from many retail nurseries in the South but usually must be ordered by mail farther north.

Scarlet Sage *(Salvia splendens)* (p. 57)

Van Houtte Sage *(Salvia splendens* 'Van Houttei'
or *S. vanhouttei)*
  Growth habit: Herbaceous perennial
  Exposure: Shade to sun
  Hardiness: Zone 9, grown as annual farther north
  Moisture: Moist to average
  Height: 5 feet
  Bloom: Late summer and fall
  Propagation: Cuttings

This South American beauty (pronounced "van HOOT sage") will reach 4 feet or more in a single growing season if given a few hours of sunlight or dappled shade. It produces a spectacular show of maroon flowers emerging from calyces of the same color. Cuttings must be taken in fall, before a killing

Indian pink spreads to form a small colony of plants with an abundance of red and yellow (not pink) trumpet-like blossoms. As it continues to spread, it can be divided to start new plantings.

frost, to provide plants for the next season. The cuttings root easily and should be kept in a sunroom or near a window that gets good light. Van Houtte sage is well worth the effort for gardeners who can expect frost-free weather into October. It is usually sold only by mail-order nurseries.

Indian Pink (*Spigelia marilandica*)
 Growth habit: Herbaceous perennial
 Exposure: Shade to partial sun
 Hardiness: Zone 5
 Moisture: Average
 Height: 2 feet
 Bloom: Spring
 Propagation: Division

Indian pink is native to the deciduous forests of the southeastern U.S. Like many woodland wildflowers, it blooms in spring before deciduous trees fully develop their leaves and block the sun from reaching the woodland floor. Indian pink thrives in a humus-rich soil, benefits from a mulch of fallen leaves, and is hardy through zone 5 with some extra winter mulch.

**A Selection of Hummplants for —
Shady, Dry Places**

Few hummingbird plants can succeed in dry soil and shade. The deeper the shade, the fewer the plants that can meet the challenge. The plants on this list do well in dry soils and can tolerate partial shade. Fortunately, most dry-climate trees are open and don't cast deep shade, so plants on this list can grow beneath them. Gardeners willing to water regularly will find additional choices in the list for

shady, moist places, but before deciding to water heavily under a tree, you should make sure that the extra water won't adversely impact the tree.

Soap Aloe (*Aloe saponaria*)
 Growth habit: Succulent perennial
 Exposure: Sun to partial shade
 Hardiness: Zone 8
 Moisture: Arid to average
 Height: Leaves to 1 foot, flowers to 3 feet
 Bloom: Fall through spring, mainly
 Propagation: Division

This African succulent is the most cold hardy of the aloes, surviving the occasional hard freezes of zone 8. Soap aloe makes a rugged, drought-tolerant potted plant or can be grown in the ground. It produces a 3-foot-tall panicle of pink tubular flowers.

Western Columbine (*Aquilegia formosa*)
 Growth habit: Herbaceous perennial
 Exposure: Sun to shade
 Hardiness: Zone 4
 Moisture: Dry to average
 Height: 3 feet
 Bloom: Spring and summer
 Propagation: Seed

The nodding red and yellow flowers of this species closely resemble those of eastern columbine (p. 77), but this species is native to the dry climates of the West. The Arizona columbine, *A. desertorum,* produces many orange and yellow flowers and is a better choice for gardeners in hot low-elevation sites.

Mexican Honeysuckle (*Justicia spicigera*) (p. 65)

Autumn sage blooms throughout the warm months to feed hungry hummers such as this male ruby-throated. A variety of blossom colors is available.

Turk's Cap *(Malvaviscus arboreus* var. *drummondii)* (p. 64)

Gooseberries and Currants *(Ribes* spp.)
   Growth habit: Shrub
   Exposure: Sun to shade
   Hardiness: Varies, with several species hardy
      throughout the West
   Moisture: Dry to average
   Height: To 5 feet
   Bloom: Spring and summer
   Propagation: Cuttings or seed
There are many species of gooseberries and currants, all of them placed in the genus *Ribes.* Many of them, particularly western species, are valuable nectar sources for hummingbirds in spring and early summer. Among the many possibilities to try are fuchsia-flowered currant (p. 87), mountain gooseberry *(R. montigenum),* golden currant *(R. aureum),* and gummy gooseberry *(R. lobbii).* Most native currants and gooseberries are not widely available in the horticultural trade. The best way to identify good local species may be to spend time watching hummingbirds in the wild.

Tropical Sage *(Salvia coccinea)* (p. 53)

Autumn Sage *(Salvia greggii)*
   Growth habit: Woody perennial or shrub
   Exposure: Sun to partial shade
   Hardiness: Varies with cultivars, some to zone 6
   Moisture: Dry to average
   Height: 3 to 4 feet, larger in frost-free areas
   Bloom: Spring through fall
   Propagation: Cuttings or seed
Autumn sage adapts to a wide variety of growing conditions. It will generally grow as a shrub in zone 8, and some cultivars can reach 6 feet in height. Farther north, this Texas native grows as a perennial, freezing to the ground each winter and returning to a height of about 3 feet. There are many hybrids with *Salvia microphylla* (p. 91), a close relative and look-alike, and they are also great for hummingbirds, including the many-color varieties of *Salvia x jamensis.*

A Selection of Hummplants for —
Wet Places and Ponds

These plants can be grown in soils that are consistently saturated — too wet for most hummplants to grow well. Such places include springs, seeps along hillsides, areas near ponds or flowing water, or a low spot where runoff creates a mud hole. Saturated soil conditions are more common in regions with abundant rain but can occur in arid regions at natural wetlands or as a result of irrigation runoff.

   All the plants listed here are suitable as pond plants, except *Impatiens capensis,* which may not tolerate constant inundation and whose seed will not sprout in water. The others can all be grown in pots placed in a pond so that the soil surface is an inch or two under the water surface. If you start these plants in pots outside your pond, introduce them slowly to the water, lowering the pots an inch or so each week or two. This will enable the plants to adapt to their surroundings.

Indian Shot *(Canna indica)*
   Growth habit: Clump-forming herbaceous perennial
   Exposure: Full sun to partial shade
   Hardiness: Zone 7; in colder zones, roots can be
      dug and stored in cool place over winter
   Moisture: Wet to average
   Height: 4 to 6 feet
   Bloom: Summer to fall, year-round where frost-free
   Propagation: Seed or division
Indian shot is a wild form of canna with small red flowers. Other small-flowered varieties also attract hummers, but the large-flowered hybrids commonly sold as *Canna x generalis* or *C. x orchiodes* hold little appeal for hummingbirds. The common name comes from reports that the hard seeds were once used as pellets in shotguns on their native Caribbean islands. Watch for damage from caterpillars.

This is the wild form of canna. Its small red flowers are hummingbird favorites.

This canna, *Canna x generalis* **'Pretoria',** is typical of the large-flowered hybrids that hummers ignore.

Spotted Jewelweed (Impatiens capensis)

Growth habit: Annual
Exposure: Shade
Hardiness: Reseeds to zone 4
Moisture: Moist to wet
Height: 4 to 6 feet
Bloom: July through September
Propagation: Volunteers from seed

This eastern native is an abundant hummplant in the Appalachians, yet I have seldom seen plants or seeds for sale. It is best established by transplanting a few young plants from the wild in spring. Collecting wild plants is not normally acceptable, but spotted jewelweed always produces far more seedlings than can mature in the available space, so removing some will not affect the wild population.

Once established, spotted jewelweed will reseed itself and can be thinned for strongest growth. Seeds of wild plants can be planted, but they must be cold-conditioned (p. 101), and the ripe pods fling seeds several feet, making seed collection a challenge.

Copper Iris (Iris fulva)

Growth habit: Perennial in much of the country
Exposure: Full sun
Hardiness: Zone 4
Moisture: Moist to wet
Height: 2 feet
Bloom: Spring
Propagation: Division

This copper-colored cousin of the widespread blue flag iris is a native of the Southeast. Unlike many irises, which are pollinated by bees, this one is pollinated by hummingbirds. It may be affected by iris root borers, but removing the fall foliage, which contains eggs of the borers, will help contain damage.

Cardinal Flower (Lobelia cardinalis) (p. 60)

Spotted jewelweed has distinctive sac-shaped yellow blossoms with dense orange-red spots on parts of the inner surfaces.

This scarlet monkeyflower is growing streamside at Madera Canyon in Arizona. The plant produces many seeds (and seedlings) each year.

Scarlet Monkeyflower *(Mimulus cardinalis)*
Growth habit: Perennial in much of the country
Exposure: Full sun to shade
Hardiness: Zone 5
Moisture: Wet to average
Height: 3 feet
Bloom: Spring to fall
Propagation: Seed or volunteer

This native of California and the Far West grows naturally on stream banks. It produces scarlet flowers throughout the summer. Stems may begin to look ragged by midsummer, but they can be trimmed to keep the plant in shape. Like many other western natives, scarlet monkeyflower may not survive the hot, humid summers in Florida and along the Gulf of Mexico.

**A Selection of Vines —
The Hummers' Choices**

Vines add a unique element to a garden, covering a fence or wall with flowers or adding interest to a

Cypress vine has bright red flowers and a lacy green foliage that make it a garden favorite.

shrub or tree used to support them. Fortunately for lovers of vines and hummingbirds, there are a number of excellent vine choices for a hummingbird garden. Unfortunately, flowering vines do not do well in shade. They like plenty of sunshine, rich soil, moisture, occasional fertilization, and a suitable support (sidebar, p. 83).

Trumpet Creeper *(Campsis radicans)* (p. 70)

Chilean Glory Vine *(Eccromocarpus scaber)*
Growth habit: Perennial twining vine
Exposure: Sun
Hardiness: Zone 8, annual elsewhere
Moisture: Moist to average
Height: 10 feet as an annual
Bloom: Summer and fall
Propagation: Seed

Chilean glory vine grows fast enough that it can be used as an annual. It climbs by tendrils and twining. Although the typical flower color is red, varieties with orange or yellow flowers are also available.

Small Red Morning Glory *(Ipomoea coccinea)*
Growth habit: Annual twining vine
Exposure: Sun
Hardiness: Grows well to zone 5
Moisture: Moist to average
Height: 10 feet
Bloom: Summer and fall
Propagation: Seed

This widespread Central American vine is considered a native in much of the southern U.S. It is a problematic weed in farm fields of the South, but

Cardinal climber is the best of the annual vines for regions with a short season.

it is not a problem in gardens, where it is easily grown and reseeds abundantly.

Cypress Vine (Ipomoea quamoclit)

Growth habit: Annual twining vine
Exposure: Sun
Hardiness: Grows well to zone 5
Moisture: Moist to average
Height: 6 feet
Bloom: Summer and fall
Propagation: Seed

This is a popular pass-along plant in the Southeast because of its self-seeding ability and its attractive flowers and foliage. In cool mountain climates, however, this native of the South American tropics may not grow well.

Cardinal Climber (Ipomoea x multifida)

Growth habit: Annual twining vine
Exposure: Sun
Hardiness: Grows well to zone 5
Moisture: Moist to average
Height: 10 feet
Bloom: Summer and fall
Propagation: Seed

This hybrid between cypress vine and small red morning glory blooms earlier in the summer than either parent and so is a better choice for areas with shorter summers. Like both of its parents, this vine sets lots of seeds, but the seeds usually do not survive winter outdoors and should be collected and stored inside for spring planting.

Coral Honeysuckle (Lonicera sempervirens) (p. 68)

Firecracker Vine (Manettia cordifolia)

Growth habit: Perennial twining vine
Exposure: Sun
Hardiness: Zone 7
Moisture: Average to moist
Height: 6 feet
Bloom: Summer and fall
Propagation: Division

Some vines can grow so fast that they threaten to take over a garden. The not-too-vigorous growth and abundant red flowers of firecracker vine make it a very desirable garden plant. It will spread slowly to form a clump of roots that can be divided to obtain extra plants.

Flag of Spain (Mina lobata, sometimes Ipomoea lobata)

Growth habit: Annual twining vine
Exposure: Sun
Hardiness: Grows well to zone 5
Moisture: Moist to average
Height: 10 feet
Bloom: Summer and fall
Propagation: Seed

The flowers of this plant fade from red to orange, then white, as they age. The presence of all three colors on the vine gives the plant its common name. This tropical member of the morning glory family, like the ipomoeas described previously, is easily grown but may not thrive in cool mountain climates.

Support for Climbing Vines

The support a vine requires depends on the kind of climber it is. Some vines, including pole beans and those in the morning glory family (ipomeas and others), climb by twining. They wrap their stem around a support in an upward spiral that in the northern hemisphere always goes clockwise when viewed from the ground facing upward. Twining vines require a support no larger than about 3 inches in diameter, around which they can wrap themselves; they cannot climb larger supports or walls.

Some climbing vines use tendrils — small, string-like, twisting appendages — to wrap around a support. Tendril climbing vines, including peas and the Chilean glory vine, typically do not wrap their main stem around their support. They need wire, string, other plants, or branches no larger than about one-half inch in diameter on which to climb.

Another way vines can climb is by aerial rootlets that grow from their stems and attach themselves to a surface. English ivy, trumpet creeper, and Cape honeysuckle climb this way, which enables them to climb walls, large tree trunks, or almost any other surface. These vines are typically long-lived, large, woody vines that require a permanent sturdy support.

Other vines climb with twining leaf stalks — which work a lot like tendrils — or by scrambling, a method used by some vine-like plants that lean on, lie on top of, or otherwise use nearby plants for support without really being a vine. No leaf-stalk climbers are listed in this book, but many of our plants, notably shrimp plant (p. 98), island bush snapdragon (p. 86), climbing penstemon (p. 86), and rosebud sage (p. 93), can behave as scrambling vines when they are grown among other, larger plants.

A Selection of Trees —
The Hummers' Choices

For most of the U.S. and Canada, there are few trees that are very attractive to hummingbirds. For gardeners in zones 9 and warmer, however, there are several excellent choices included in the list of additional plants for zones 9 and 10.

Red Buckeye (Aesculus pavia)
Growth habit: Small tree or tall shrub
Exposure: Sun to partial shade
Hardiness: Zone 6
Moisture: Moist to average
Height: 15 feet
Bloom: Spring
Propagation: Seed

This native shrub or small tree occurs in the wild in moist, rich forests of the Southeast. The spikes of tubular red flowers appear with the northward migration of ruby-throated hummingbirds in spring.

Mimosa, Silk Tree (Albizzia julibrissen)
Growth habit: Small tree
Exposure: Sun
Hardiness: Zone 6
Moisture: Moist to dry
Height: To 30 feet
Bloom: Summer
Propagation: Seed

This Asian tree grows wild throughout much of the eastern half of the country. It is considered an invasive weed in many places and, for that reason, is not recommended. However, in regions where silk tree is firmly established as a naturalized plant, there is little additional harm to be done by someone who plants it in a garden. The pink powder-puff-shaped flowers do attract numerous hummingbirds and butterflies. It is drought tolerant enough to survive in the driest soils in the eastern U.S.

Desert Willow, Desert Catalpa (Chilopsis linearis)
Growth habit: Tree or large shrub
Exposure: Sun
Hardiness: Zone 5, but untested in wet winters of the East and Midwest
Moisture: Arid to average
Height: To 30 feet
Bloom: Summer
Propagation: Seed

Desert willow is not a willow but is related to the catalpas. It is native throughout the desert Southwest from southern Utah and Nevada south into Mexico but will survive farther north. It bears spectacular flowers in shades of pink or white in the summer. Desert willow is extremely drought tolerant once established and will tolerate the hottest locations in the desert Southwest.

A Selection of Hummplants —
for Hanging Baskets and Small Pots

These plants thrive in the demanding conditions of a fairly small container. They tend to drape over the edges, making them ideal for hanging baskets.

Fountain plant (Russelia equisetiformis) is widely planted in gardens in the tropics and frost-free areas of the U.S. It blooms almost year-round if not touched by frost.

Hardy Fuchsia *(Fuchsia magellanica)* (p. 78)

Honeysuckle Fuchsia *(Fuchsia triphylla)* (p. 66)

Fountain Plant, Coral Plant *(Russelia equisetiformis)*

    Growth habit: Herbaceous perennial or annual
    Exposure: Sun
    Hardiness: Zone 9 as perennial
    Moisture: Average to dry
    Height: 4 feet
    Bloom: Summer and fall
    Propagation: Layering

This unique Central American plant thrives in hot, sunny spots and will grow well in a pot with watering only once or twice per week, although it will grow faster with more frequent water. The arching, leafless stems bear small red tubular flowers. Fountain plant is propagated by layering (p. 102).

Fountain Plant *(Russelia sarmentosa)*

    Growth habit: Herbaceous perennial
    Exposure: Sun to partial shade
    Hardiness: Zone 9; protect from frosts elsewhere
    Moisture: Average
    Height: To 2 feet tall; branches may extend
        horizontally or drape up to 4 feet
    Bloom: Most of the year
    Propagation: Cuttings or layering

This Mexican native is much like *R. equisetiformis* (above), with which it shares identical common names and similar arching stems with small red flowers. *R. sarmentosa* is smaller and thus a better choice for a small pot. New plants can be obtained from cuttings or by layering.

A Selection of Houseplants — The Hummers' Choices

The plants on this list are usually grown indoors as houseplants. All of them will bloom if they are given enough light, and their flowers, which can appear at any time of the year, are attractive to hummingbirds. One way to grow impressive houseplants is to move them outside to a shaded location each summer. In this way, the plants on this list can enhance a very shady area under a tree or on a covered porch that otherwise would not support hummingbird flowers.

    Outdoors, these plants need shade, but indoors, they appreciate the brightest conditions available, as in a south-facing window. Plants are easily stressed when they are moved into or out of a yard. An indoor plant will lose leaves or even be killed if it is placed where it gets much direct sunlight. Conversely, plants that have become used to some direct sun while outdoors will often turn yellow and drop leaves if they are abruptly moved indoors away from the sun in fall.

Aphelandra squarrosa, **with its white-lined leaves,** is one of several plants known as zebra plant.

Zebra plant *(Aphelandra squarrosa)*

    Growth habit: Herbaceous perennial
    Exposure: Shade
    Hardiness: Zone 10; grown as a houseplant
    Moisture: Average
    Height: To 3 feet
    Bloom: Erratic
    Propagation: Cuttings

This neotropical shrub is widely available as a houseplant. It bears spikes of tubular yellow flowers.

Columneas *(Columnea spp.)*

    Growth habit: Trailing perennial
    Exposure: Shade
    Hardiness: Zone 10; grown as a houseplant
    Moisture: Let dry slightly between waterings
    Height: 1 foot or less; may hang several feet
    Bloom: Erratic
    Propagation: Cuttings

The many species and numerous hybrids of columnea are popular houseplants among collectors. These plants from the Neotropics bear tubular flowers in many colors and are pollinated by hummingbirds in their native habitats. *Aeschynanthus* is a similar genus from the Old World that produces good hummingbird flowers.

Christmas Cactus, Thanksgiving Cactus *(Schlumbergera spp. and hybrids)*

    Growth habit: Herbaceous perennial
    Exposure: Shade
    Hardiness: Zone 10; grown as a houseplant
    Moisture: Average to dry
    Height: 3 feet
    Bloom: Typically fall and winter, sometimes spring
    Propagation: Cuttings

An Anna's hummingbird pierces the base of a Christmas cactus blossom to get at the nectar instead of probing the opening of the blossom.

There are many cultivars of Christmas cactus derived from several neotropical species. They typically flower in fall and winter, and to set flowers, they require either cool temperatures, with nights in the 40s, or a regular progression of decreasing daylight. Keep them in a shady spot outdoors, and when fall comes, the cool nights will cause flower bud formation. Once a plant begins to set buds, it can be moved indoors if you wish and will still produce flowers. Colors range from red to white to purple.

A Selection of California Native Plants — The Hummers' Choices

Distinguished from the rest of North America by its warm Mediterranean climate and isolated by mountain ranges and deserts, California has developed a diverse and unique flora. Dozens of native species have evolved for pollination by California's abundant hummingbirds. Adapted to winter rains and dry summers, many California native plants do not grow well in gardens with abundant summer moisture and should be watered only occasionally in summer.

California native plants have their own devoted gardeners, and ample horticultural advice is available in books and on the Internet. This list includes some of the more widely grown California natives that are excellent hummingbird plants.

Western Columbine (*Aquilegia formosa*) (p. 79)

Indian Paintbrush (*Castilleja* spp.) (p. 75)

Desert Willow (*Chilopsis linearis*) (p. 84)

Ocotillo (*Fouquieria splendens*) (p. 94)

Island Bush Snapdragon (*Galvezia speciosa*)
  Growth habit: Herbaceous perennial or scrambling, shrubby climber
  Exposure: Sun to shade
  Hardiness: Zone 8
  Moisture: Dry to average
  Height: 10 feet or more with support
  Bloom: Spring through fall
  Propagation: Cuttings or seed

This adaptable plant from the Channel Islands, off the coast of southern California, bears its tubular red flowers through most of the year. Island bush snapdragon can grow as a hillside ground cover, climb a bush or trellis, or stand alone, in which case it will form a mound about 4 feet high and many feet across. It tolerates some summer water.

Scarlet Gilia (*Ipomopsis aggregata*) (p. 76)

Chuparosa (*Justicia californica*) (p. 94)

Climbing Penstemon (*Keckiella cordifolius* or *Penstemon cordifolia*)
  Growth habit: Semiwoody shrub or climber
  Exposure: Sun to shade
  Hardiness: Zone 8
  Moisture: Dry
  Height: 10 feet with support
  Bloom: Summer
  Propagation: Cuttings or seed

This red-flowered hummplant is one of several keckiellas that are excellent hummingbird plants for native gardens. Until recently they were included in the genus *Penstemon* and known as climbing or shrub penstemons. They will tolerate occasional summer water.

Tree Mallow (*Lavatera assurgentifolia*)
  Growth habit: Small tree or large shrub
  Exposure: Sun
  Hardiness: Zone 9
  Moisture: Dry
  Height: 10 feet
  Bloom: Most of the year
  Propagation: Seed

A fast-growing native of the Channel Islands, tree mallow is related to hibiscus, which is evident from the pink flowers. It tolerates some summer water.

Cardinal Flower (*Lobelia cardinalis*) (p. 60)

Scarlet Monkeyflower (*Mimulus cardinalis*) (p. 82)

Scarlet Bugler (*Penstemon centranthifolius*)
  Growth habit: Herbaceous perennial
  Exposure: Sun
  Hardiness: Zone 8
  Moisture: Arid to dry
  Height: 4 feet
  Bloom: Spring
  Propagation: Seed

The brilliant red flowers of this southern California native are similar to those of several southwestern penstemons. It will tolerate occasional summer water.

Red-Flowered Currant (Ribes sanguinium) (p. 78)

Fuchsia-Flowered Currant (Ribes speciosum)
Growth habit: Thorny deciduous shrub
Exposure: Sun to light shade
Hardiness: Zone 8
Moisture: Dry
Height: To 6 feet
Bloom: Winter and spring
Propagation: Seed

Inconspicuous for much of the year, this thorny shrub bursts into bloom in winter, bearing hundreds of fuchsia-like red flowers that hang from its branches. It should be given only occasional water in summer or none at all.

Cleveland Sage (Salvia clevelandii)
Growth habit: Herbaceous perennial or semiwoody
        shrub
Exposure: Sun
Hardiness: Zone 8
Moisture: Dry
Height: 5 feet
Bloom: Summer
Propagation: Seed, division, or cuttings

This blue-flowered sage blooms later in the summer than many other California natives and thus is

valuable in a natives-only garden. Several hybrids are available that tolerate more than the occasional summer wetting that this species accepts.

Pitcher Sage (Salvia spacathea)
Growth habit: Herbaceous perennial
Exposure: Sun to shade
Hardiness: Zone 8
Moisture: Dry
Height: To 5 feet
Bloom: Spring and summer
Propagation: Division, cuttings, or seed

Pitcher sage grows among the scattered oaks and chaparral of southern and central California. It adapts well to gardens if the soil is allowed to dry out slightly between waterings.

Woolly Blue Curls (Tricostema lanatum)
Growth habit: Shrub
Exposure: Sun
Hardiness: Zone 8
Moisture: Dry
Height: 4 feet
Bloom: Spring and summer
Propagation: Seed

Woolly blue curls grows wild in the mountains of southern California. The fuzzy blue flowers are held for a long period. Wooly blue curls should not be watered once established.

California Fuchsia (Zauschneria californica) (p. 77)

Pitcher sage has dramatic spires of red blossoms. It forms a clump that can be divided.

Woolly blue curls is a handsome shrub with a charmingly descriptive name.

This broad-billed hummer is stealing nectar from an orange abutilon. Blossoms whose petals overlap at the base are usually good nectar sources.

The petals on this orange abutilon hybrid do not overlap (note the sliver of green visible between the petals). It is probably a poor nectar source.

A Selection of Plants — for Winter in the East

The growing interest in attracting western-breeding hummingbirds to eastern gardens in late fall and winter (p. 47) is the reason for this list. As the number of western hummers reported as far north as New England and the upper Midwest continues to increase, gardeners well north of the Gulf of Mexico are investigating late-blooming, cold-tolerant plants.

One way to evaluate the nectar production of an abutilon is to tap a flower against the palm of your hand. A good nectar producer will often leave a drop or two of sugary nectar on it. A poor nectar source will have little or no nectar, and even a good source may be dry on a windy day, after a hummer visits, or at other times.

Winter hummingbird gardeners look first for plants that bloom in winter. The next thing they want to know is a plant's cold tolerance. Cold tolerance is not the same as hardiness. Cold tolerance is the ability of a plant to hold its flowers and continue blooming despite subfreezing temperatures. Hardiness is a plant's ability to merely survive cold weather, often underground, so that it can resprout in spring. The two characteristics are often curiously unrelated. Some plants are cold tolerant but not very hardy, and vice versa.

In this list, the extra characteristic, "Cold tolerance," is provided. Poor cold tolerance means a plant will typically lose its flowers with the first kiss of frost, when temperatures reach a degree or two below freezing. Moderately cold-tolerant plants will usually hold their flowers in a heavy frost, with temperatures at or just below 30 degrees. Good cold tolerance means a plant can retain its flowers when temperatures drop to the upper 20s, and plants with excellent cold tolerance will still bloom when temperatures fall to the mid- or lower 20s.

For best results, place plants in a protected location. The coldest area in your yard will be in the open, away from trees and buildings. The last part of your yard to freeze is likely under an overhang along the side of the house or below a large window or glass door. Trees, especially evergreens, also offer protection from frost.

Covering plants on cold nights is another trick to extend their blooming season. Your source of heat is the ground, so cover your plants all the way to the ground. Place the covers on a support other than the plant if possible. Plant parts touching the covers will often freeze.

Bare ground will yield more heat than mulched soil, so you may want to delay the application of fall mulch until your plants have finally been nipped by a frost. A light bulb placed under the covers will also generate heat, but be sure to use outdoor-rated lights.

Orange Abutilon, Flowering Maple, Chinese Lantern *(Abutilon pictum)*

Growth habit: Small tree or shrub
Exposure: Sun to shade
Hardiness: Zone 8, maybe colder
Cold tolerance: Good
Moisture: Moist to average
Height: To 15 feet
Bloom: Nearly year-round, heaviest in fall and spring
Propagation: Cuttings

This rather weak-stemmed small tree is a favorite of winter hummingbird gardeners because of its good cold tolerance and its large size, which provides both cover and numerous orange bell-shaped flowers for hummers. A plant of uncertain origin, it is reportedly hardy far north of zone 8 if its roots are given a heavy winter mulch, but it dies to the ground with a

hard freeze. There are many hybrid abutilons, and winter hummers will readily visit those that produce ample nectar. Hybrids can be grown in the same manner as orange abutilon, but hardiness varies.

Giant Cuphea, Mexican Cigar (*Cuphea micropetala*)

Growth habit: Herbaceous perennial
Exposure: Sun
Hardiness: Zone 8, zone 7 with protection
Cold tolerance: Poor
Moisture: Moist to average
Height: 5 feet
Bloom: Fall and winter
Propagation: Cuttings or seed

Giant cuphea, a shrubby Mexican wildflower, puts on a spectacular show of flowers, each one red at the base, orange in the middle, and yellow at the tip, like old-fashioned candy corn. (picture, p. 73)

Winter Shrimp Plant (*Justicia brandegeana* in part)

Growth habit: Sprawling or climbing herbaceous
perennial
Exposure: Sun to partial shade
Hardiness: Zone 7
Cold tolerance: Good
Moisture: Dry to moist
Height: 4 feet; can climb higher with support
Bloom: Winter
Propagation: Cuttings

This is one of the best winter hummingbird plants, holding its blossoms through moderate freezes and

producing abundant nectar throughout the winter months. Except when in bloom, it can be difficult to distinguish winter shrimp plant from the summer-blooming shrimp plants commonly sold in retail nurseries. There are several species in this neotropical genus that can be confusingly similar to the two forms of *J. brandegeana*. One, *J. fulvicoma,* may be distinguished by its orange flowers and bracts.

Nurseries may occasionally sell winter shrimp plant, but cuttings from other hummgardeners are your most likely source.

Winter Honeysuckle (*Lonicera fragrantissima*)

Growth habit: Shrub
Exposure: Sun to shade
Hardiness: Zone 5
Cold tolerance: Excellent
Moisture: Moist to average
Height: 8 feet
Bloom: Winter to spring
Propagation: Cuttings

Of all the hummplants, winter honeysuckle will bloom in the coldest weather, its flowers surviving nights in the teens. When the weather turns warm, the plant produces a delightful aroma. It blooms from November through March in zone 9, and the farther north it grows, the later it blooms. Blossoms don't appear until March in New Jersey, too late for nearly all winter hummingbirds. This Asian shrub blooms on two-year-old wood and shouldn't be sheared or flowering will be greatly reduced.

Coral Honeysuckle (*Lonicera sempervirens*) (p. 68)

Winter shrimp plant has flowers with a pinkish blush. The "shrimp" are made up of colored bracts (modified leaves) and are usually less curved in winter shrimp plant than in summer-blooming shrimp plants.

Summer-blooming shrimp plants (p. 98) bear white flowers. Both winter- and summer-blooming plants have brown or purple spots inside the flower. The "shrimp" can be a variety of colors.

Giant Turk's Cap (*Malvaviscus penduliflorus* or *M. arboreus* var. *mexicana*)

Growth habit: Shrub
Exposure: Sun to shade
Hardiness: Zone 8, where it freezes to ground
Cold tolerance: Poor
Moisture: Moist to average
Height: 10 feet, less if frozen by winter weather
Bloom: Winter
Propagation: Cuttings

This spectacular neotropical relative of Turk's cap (picture, p. 64) is useful as a hedge, specimen plant, or in masses. It usually doesn't produce its red flowers until November, and the bloom is often spoiled by early frosts in northern parts of zone 8.

Costa Rica Blue Sage (*Salvia* 'Costa Rica Blue')

Growth habit: Herbaceous perennial
Exposure: Sun to shade
Hardiness: Zone 8, zone 7 with protection
Cold tolerance: Good
Moisture: Moist to average
Height: 6 feet
Bloom: Fall through spring
Propagation: Cuttings

This blue-flowered sage may be a polyploid of anise sage (p. 58). The good cold tolerance and winter hardiness make it an easy plant to maintain for gardeners in zone 8. If killed by winter freezes it will regrow in spring, begin to bloom in late summer, and continue blooming abundantly through winter unless again interrupted by freezing weather. Costa Rica blue sage tends to sprawl and makes a good mass planting under trees.

Pineapple Sage (*Salvia elegans*)

Growth habit: Herbaceous perennial or annual
Exposure: Sun to partial shade
Hardiness: Zone 8 as perennial
Cold tolerance: Moderate
Moisture: Moist to average
Height: 4 feet
Bloom: Fall and winter
Propagation: Cuttings

Pineapple sage, native to Central America, is one of the more widely available winter hummingbird flowers. It is a staple of more northerly winter hummingbird gardeners, who grow it as an annual. It is frequently in the herb section of a nursery because of its occasional use in cooking.

Forsythia Sage (*Salvia madrensis*)

Growth habit: Herbaceous perennial
Exposure: Sun to partial shade
Hardiness: Zone 8, zone 7 with protection
Cold tolerance: Poor

Pineapple sage get its common name from its fragrance, and its Latin species name *(elegans)* from its elegant appearance.

Mexican sage grows vigorously and sets numerous purple flowers. For the best bloom set, limit any nighttime lighting.

Moisture: Moist to average
Height: 6 feet
Bloom: Fall and winter
Propagation: Cuttings or division

This easily grown sage from Mexico makes an intriguing addition to any hummgarden. Hummers eagerly visit its yellow flowers, and its unusual square stems make it visually interesting even when not in bloom. Although it is fully hardy at least through zone 8, it is not cold tolerant and is killed to the ground by a light freeze. It is sometimes eaten by caterpillars.

Mexican Sage *(Salvia mexicana)*
    Growth habit: Herbaceous perennial or annual
    Exposure: Sun to partial shade
    Hardiness: Zone 8 as perennial
    Cold tolerance: Moderate
    Moisture: Moist to slightly dry
    Height: 6 feet
    Bloom: Fall and winter
    Propagation: Cuttings

Mexican sage bursts into a show of striking purple flowers in October. Although it is not always hardy, even in zone 8, it is easily grown from cuttings and in a good location can reach 6 feet tall as an annual. Frequent pruning of the stem tips in spring and summer will create a bushier plant with more flowers in fall. Another fall-blooming, half-hardy, Mexican salvia worth a try is *S. iodantha.*

Little-Leaf Sage *(Salvia microphylla)*
    Growth habit: Shrubby perennial or annual
    Exposure: Sun to partial shade
    Hardiness: Zone 7 as perennial
    Cold tolerance: Good
    Moisture: Dry to moist
    Height: 4 feet
    Bloom: Almost year-round
    Propagation: Cuttings or seed

Little-leaf sage sometimes blooms through nights in the upper 20s, and for this reason, it is a valuable addition to a winter hummingbird garden. This red-flowered, long-blooming sage is native to west Texas and Mexico. It is used to dry conditions but also thrives with regular water.

**A Selection of Additional Hummplants —
for the Humid Southeast**

Gardeners in humid areas of the Southeast have special opportunities and challenges. Their plants enjoy a long growing season with plenty of rainfall but must cope with heat, humidity, abundant insects in summer, and occasional frosts in winter. The steamy summers overwhelm some plants that originate in temperate North America, and winter freezes kill a lot of the tropical plants that thrive in the hot summers.

Little-leaf sage is similar in appearance and closely related to autumn sage (p. 80).

Most of the Dozen Dazzlers thrive in summer in the Southeast, and so do many of the plants recommended for the various combinations of sun, shade, moist, and dry conditions. Plants on the additional list for Texas will also do well in the Southeast. And if those aren't enough choices, here are some more that excel in the humid Southeast. For plants that bloom throughout the winter, consult the list of winter plants for the East.

Gardeners living a bit farther north may also want to try some of these beauties but should be prepared to provide winter protection, such as heavy mulch and a southern exposure. Gardeners in the warmest parts of the Southeast can grow many of the additional plants for zones 9 and 10 (p. 97).

Javanese Glory Bower, Pagoda Plant
(Clerodendrum speciosissimum)
    *Growth habit: Woody shrub, woody perennial in
        areas with frost*
    Exposure: Sun to partial shade
    Hardiness: Zone 8
    Moisture: Moist to average
    Height: To 12 feet
    Bloom: Summer and fall
    Propagation: Division

This is a large plant that has escaped cultivation to grow wild in southeastern Florida. Its 3-foot panicles of bright red flowers, held atop a 6-foot stem bearing large, glossy leaves, make it a spectacular addition to gardens throughout the humid Southeast, but it is not suited for small gardens. New pagoda plants may appear several feet from the parent and can be dug up and transplanted.

Coral Bean, Cardinal Bean, Cherokee Bean
(*Erythrina herbacea*)
> Growth habit: Woody perennial or small shrub
> Exposure: Sun to partial shade
> Hardiness: Zone 8
> Moisture: Dry to wet
> Height: To 6 feet
> Bloom: Spring
> Propagation: Seed

This southeastern native occurs naturally on sandy soils and will tolerate most any garden soil. It has sharp thorns and so should not be planted in high-traffic areas. Coral bean's spikes of 2-inch tubular red flowers are most abundant in full sun. This plant may take several years to reach flowering age if started from seed.

Firebush, Scarlet Bush (*Hamelia patens*)
> Growth habit: Shrub
> Exposure: Sun
> Hardiness: Zone 8; dies to ground in hard freeze
> Moisture: Average to moist
> Height: 5 feet in zone 8, higher where frost-free
> Bloom: Summer and fall, longer if not frozen
> Propagation: Usually by cuttings

Firebush is native to the Caribbean islands, Central and South America, and central and south Florida. In addition to hummingbirds, the orange flowers attract butterflies that are large enough to reach the nectar at the base of the tubular flowers. Fruit-eating birds enjoy the berries firebush produces. Propagation can be done by division if suckers appear, and cuttings can be taken from soft wood.

Red Ginger (*Hedychium coccineum*)
> Growth habit: Clump-forming herbaceous perennial
> Exposure: Sun to partial shade
> Hardiness: Zone 8, zone 7 with protection
> Moisture: Wet to average
> Height: 6 feet
> Bloom: Summer
> Propagation: Division

This moisture-loving Himalayan native is easy to grow and will form an impressive clump in a few years. The 6-foot-tall leafy stems and foot-long spikes of orchid-shaped orange flowers make it an exotic addition to a southern garden. Apparently because of differences among cultivars, some gardeners find that this is a hummer favorite, while others note only occasional hummer visits. Many other species of hedychium gingers are grown in the South but receive only scant attention from hummers.

Firespike (*Odontonema strictum*)
> Growth habit: Herbaceous perennial
> Exposure: Shade to partial sun
> Hardiness: Zone 8, zone 7 with protection
> Moisture: Moist to average
> Height: 5 feet
> Bloom: Late summer and fall
> Propagation: Cuttings

In spite of its tropical appearance, this plant is surprisingly hardy and one of the best shade-tolerant choices for the Deep South. Cuttings root easily, making it a popular pass-along plant. Its one drawback is susceptibility to a disease that distorts the leaves and flower spikes.

A coral bean plant attracts the attention of a female black-chinned hummingbird. If the blossom is fertilized by the feeding hummer, the resulting seed will be a shiny red bean.

Firebush is a fast-growing shrub that makes an excellent hedge but may require some pruning.

A young male ruby-throated hummingbird hovers at a cluster of firebush blossoms. Except for the green leaves, all the visible parts of firebush are red or orange.

Darcy Sage (Salvia darcyi)

    Growth habit: Herbaceous perennial

    Exposure: Sun to partial shade

    Hardiness: Zone 7

    Moisture: Average to dry

    Height: 3 feet

    Bloom: Summer

    Propagation: Division, cuttings, or seed

This sage is new to horticulture in the U.S., being introduced from Mexico in the 1980s. It has proven to be an adaptable, easily grown perennial in warmer climates, and hummingbirds eagerly visit its bright red blooms. Darcy sage is fairly drought tolerant once established, but will need weekly watering in arid western climates.

Rosebud Sage (Salvia involucrata)

    Growth habit: Herbaceous perennial

    Exposure: Sun to shade

    Hardiness: Zone 8, zone 7 with protection

    Moisture: Average

    Height: 6 feet

    Bloom: Late summer and fall

    Propagation: Cuttings

Rosebud sage makes a spectacular show with dozens of spikes of bright pink tubular flowers. It is an adaptable plant that will bloom in almost continuous shade or will thrive in full sun. The similar and closely related *S. puberula* is also a good plant for hummingbird gardens and may be difficult to distinguish from *S. involucrata*. Both are native to Mexico.

**A Selection of Additional Hummplants —
for the Desert Southwest**

The desert Southwest is home to lots of hummingbirds, and the plants in this list are some of their favorites. They thrive in the hot, dry, and nearly frost-free climate of larger cities, such as Phoenix and Tucson, Arizona; El Paso, Texas; and Palm Springs, California. Gardeners in southwestern cities with cooler winters may find that some of these plants will not survive the winter.

Most of the plants in the list for sunny, dry places (p. 74) will also grow in the desert, and with regular watering, most plants on the sunny, moist places list (p. 72) can be grown there as well. Mexican honeysuckle (p. 65), one of the Dozen Dazzlers, should be on every desert gardener's must-have list.

Aloe Vera, Barbados Aloe, Burn Plant (Aloe barbadensis)

    Growth habit: Succulent perennial

    Exposure: Sun to partial shade

    Hardiness: Zone 9

    Moisture: Arid to average

    Height: 3 feet

    Bloom: Winter and spring

    Propagation: Division

The succulent, lance-shaped, spiny-edged leaves of aloe vera are familiar throughout the world, thanks to its popularity as a houseplant and burn remedy. Much less familiar to most people are the 4-foot spikes of flowers the plant produces when

Spikes of orange tubular flowers tower over this aloe vera. Some plants produce yellower flowers.

grown outdoors. It blooms in winter and spring and often at other times of the year as well.

This drought-hardy African plant makes an interesting low-maintenance ground cover in a desert garden, with a single plant gradually spreading to as much as 10 feet wide. New plants can be obtained by separating a small plant, or pup, from the parent plant. Although aloe vera is quite drought tolerant, watering every week or two will keep the leaves more succulent and better for use in case of burns. There are many other species of aloe that are suitable for southwestern gardens in zone 9 and warmer, including soap aloe (p. 79). Many of the other aloe species have compounds in the leaves that make them a skin irritant, so make sure you have aloe vera *(aloe vera* means "true aloe") before you apply aloe to your skin.

Desert Honeysuckle *(Anisacanthus thurberi)*
 Growth habit: Shrub
 Exposure: Sun
 Hardiness: Zone 8
 Moisture: Arid to average
 Height: 4 feet
 Bloom: Most of the year
 Propagation: Cuttings
This plant is similar to flame acanthus *(A. wrightii)* (p. 96) and bears many orange-red flowers off and on throughout the year. It is native from Arizona and New Mexico south.

Baja Fairy Duster *(Calliandra californica)*
 Growth habit: Evergreen shrub
 Exposure: Sun to partial shade
 Hardiness: Zone 8
 Moisture: Arid to average
 Height: 6 feet
 Bloom: Spring through fall
 Propagation: Seed
The Baja fairy duster is native to southern California and the Baja Peninsula, where it brightens desert washes with its numerous red flowers resembling small powderpuffs. It can survive without watering once established but will bloom much longer if watered. It is generally evergreen but may become partly deciduous if stressed by drought or cold.

Ocotillo, Candlewood, Slimwood, Coachwhip, Vine Cactus *(Fouquieria splendens)*
 Growth habit: Tall shrub
 Exposure: Sun
 Hardiness: Zone 8
 Moisture: Arid to dry
 Height: 15 feet
 Bloom: Spring
 Propagation: Cuttings
Ocotillo is one of the characteristic plants of the Sonoran and Chihuahuan Deserts. Throughout much of the year, it exists as an upright cluster of leafless, thorny, wooden stems, but for several months in spring, it is topped by brilliant clusters of orange-red flowers that provide abundant nectar for the hummingbirds of the desert. The leaves appear following a rain and are dropped when moisture disappears.

This plant is recommended only for desert climates. In humid parts of zones 8 and 9, it may grow but will not flower because its bloom period is partially controlled by the changes in desert humidity. This fiercely spiny plant is grown by inserting large (3 feet or longer) cuttings directly into the soil where a plant is wanted.

Chuparosa *(Justicia californica)*
 Growth habit: Semiwoody shrub
 Exposure: Sun
 Hardiness: Zone 8
 Moisture: Arid
 Height: 3 feet
 Bloom: Spring
 Propagation: Cuttings
Chuparosa is native to the Sonoran Desert from Texas to California and south into Mexico. It occurs naturally only in nearly frost-free parts of the desert.

Red Justicia *(Justicia candicans)*
 Growth habit: Herbaceous perennial or semiwoody shrub
 Exposure: Sun to partial shade
 Hardiness: Zone 8

Moisture: Arid to average
Height: 4 feet
Bloom: Year-round
Propagation: Cuttings

This Mexican native, sometimes mistakenly called *Justicia ovata,* bears tubular red flowers held in spikes above the plant.

Tree Tobacco *(Nicotiana glauca)*
Growth habit: Small tree or large shrub
Exposure: Sun
Hardiness: Zone 9
Moisture: Arid to average
Height: To 20 feet
Bloom: Much of the year, especially spring
Propagation: Seed

Introduced from South America, tree tobacco grows abundantly along farm ditches, roadsides, and near water in much of California, southern Arizona, and south Texas and throughout most of Latin America. A fast-grower, tree tobacco is easily started from the abundant tiny seeds it produces. Occasional pruning will help control its rather weedy growth habit.

Parry's Penstemon *(Penstemon parryi)*
Growth habit: Herbaceous perennial
Exposure: Sun, partial shade in the desert
Hardiness: Zone 6
Moisture: Arid to dry
Height: 3 feet
Bloom: Spring
Propagation: Seed

This southwestern native grows readily from seed and thrives in deserts. It will also grow farther north

A male Anna's approaches the bright yellow blossoms of tree tobacco. The plant is a spring staple for migrating hummingbirds, as well as such residents as Anna's.

where summers are dry, but it will not tolerate much water. Other penstemons that do well in the Southwest and attract hummers include Eaton's firecracker (p. 76), desert penstemon *(P. pseudospectabilis),* and superb penstemon *(P. superbus).*

**A Selection of Additional Hummplants —
for Texas**

Much of Texas has a climate that combines wilting heat with occasional heavy rain and humidity, creating a unique set of conditions for gardening. Many of the Dozen Dazzlers will grow well in Texas. Turk's cap (p. 64), standing cypress (p. 59), autumn sage (p. 80), and scarlet betony (p. 74), all Texas natives, are regional favorites. But gardeners in Texas have some good choices in addition to the

A male Allen's hummingbird visits a chuparosa plant. The red flowers of chuparosa (meaning "hummingbird" in Spanish) brighten the harsh desert washes that the plant favors.

The large red flowers of mountain sage are favorite nectaring stops for migrating hummers in fall.

Flame acanthus would be a small nondescript shrub if not for the many tubular red flowers it produces.

Dozen Dazzlers and plants found in the lists for sunny, shady, dry, and moist areas.

This is a list of a few additional plants that seem to thrive in the soils and climate of Texas. Texas is a big state, and this list is skewed toward plants that thrive in the more populated parts, such as Houston, Dallas–Fort Worth, Austin, and San Antonio.

Gardeners in far west Texas should also examine the list of plants for the desert Southwest (p. 93), and those in east Texas should consider the plants listed for the humid Southeast (p. 91). Gardeners in the warmest parts of south Texas can grow many of the plants on the list of additional plants for zones 9 and 10 (p. 97).

Flame Acanthus (*Anisacanthus wrightii*)
 Growth habit: Shrub
 Exposure: Sun
 Hardiness: Zone 7; may freeze to ground in winter
 Moisture: Arid to average
 Height: 4 feet
 Bloom: Summer
 Propagation: Cuttings or seed

Flame acanthus blooms all summer in hot, dry, sun-baked spots where other plants would turn to dust. It can grow without watering throughout most of its native Texas but also does well with watering and in the humid Southeast. In zones 8 and warmer, it may become large but can be pruned anytime to control its size and shape. Flame acanthus is well suited to a large container.

Big Red Sage (*Salvia penstemonoides*)
 Growth habit: Herbaceous perennial
 Exposure: Sun to partial shade
 Hardiness: Zone 7
 Moisture: Average to arid
 Height: 6 feet
 Bloom: Summer
 Propagation: Seed or division

This showy Texas native, which bears 5-foot spikes of magenta flowers, was considered extinct until several wild colonies were discovered in central Texas. Since then it has become popular with hummingbird gardeners and native plant enthusiasts in Texas and elsewhere. It prefers an alkaline soil, and grows well when mulched with limestone gravel. Once established, it will grow without watering in most of central Texas but will need additional water in arid portions of west Texas

Mountain Sage (*Salvia regla*)
 Growth habit: Deciduous shrub or woody perennial
 Exposure: Sun to shade
 Hardiness: Zone 8 as shrub, zone 7 as perennial
 Moisture: Dry to average
 Height: 6 feet as shrub, usually shorter as perennial
 Bloom: Fall
 Propagation: Seed or cuttings

This native of the Big Bend region in southwest Texas bears its large red flowers in the fall. It is hardy through most of the state and prefers some protection from midday sun.

**A Selection of Additional Hummplants —
for Zones 9 and 10**

The northern edge of zone 9 marks the approximate southern limit of regular subfreezing weather, an important factor determining which plants can be grown. Gardeners living south of this line can grow a wide variety of plants unsuited for gardens farther north. Some of the best hummplants for frost-free gardens are listed here.

Much of California, including the main population centers as far north as the Bay area, is frost free. So are parts of the Southwest, Texas, and the Southeast, and gardeners from one of those areas should be sure to consult the list of additional hummingbird plants for their region as well.

Tree Aloe (*Aloe arborescens*)
Growth habit: Succulent shrub
Exposure: Sun to partial shade
Hardiness: Zone 9
Moisture: Dry to average
Height: 8 feet
Bloom: Winter
Propagation: Cuttings or division

Tree aloe grows into a shrub and each winter bursts into flower with many 2- to 3-foot spikes of brilliant orange flowers. Landscapers in southern California often use this slow-growing plant, one of many aloes that can be successfully grown in the state. Native throughout Africa, aloes range in stature from ground covers to trees up to 30 feet tall, and all bear spikes of tubular flowers that attract hummingbirds. To view the many species of aloe, visit a botanical garden that has a large collection.

Most species grow best in full sun and require only occasional watering or none at all once established.

Bottlebrush (*Callistemon citrinus*)
Growth habit: Tree
Exposure: Sun
Hardiness: Zone 9
Moisture: Dry to average
Height: To 25 feet
Bloom: All year
Propagation: Cuttings

Bottlebrushes have long been a standard landscaping tree in warmer parts of California and Arizona, south Texas, and Florida. This Australian import is one of the easiest and best hummingbird plants for zones where it is hardy. Its abundant bright red flowers, held high above the ground, are irresistible to hummers. A similar plant, weeping bottlebrush (*C. viminalis*), grows well in most of California but is a bit less tolerant of heat and cold than *C. citrinus*.

Eucalyptus (*Eucalyptus* spp.)
Growth habit: Tree
Exposure: Sun to partial shade
Hardiness: Zone 9
Moisture: Dry to average
Height: Some as tall as 90 feet
Bloom: Mostly winter but varies
Propagation: Cuttings or seed

Australia is home to the many species of eucalyptus in cultivation in California, Arizona, and frost-free portions of Texas and Florida. Among the best for hummers is *Eucalyptus sideroxylon*, which bears abundant clumps of red flowers during the winter

An immature male Anna's hummingbird investigates the brilliant blossoms of a eucalyptus tree. These flowers attract not only hummingbirds but also warblers, orioles, and finches, which may be as interested in the insects drawn to the flowers as they are in the flowers themselves.

months in California. Blue gum *(E. globulus)* and Red River gum or red gum *(E. camaldulensis)* eucalyptus are invasive species that should not be grown.

Grevilleas *(Grevillea* spp.)
Growth habit: Shrub
Exposure: Sun to partial shade
Hardiness: Zone 9
Moisture: Dry
Height: Varies
Bloom: Varies with species
Propagation: Seed

There are many species of Australian grevilleas in cultivation and a number of hybrids are available as well. Among the shrub species grown in California, some spread along the ground and grow only 2 feet tall. Others can be large shrubs, and one, the silk oak *(Grevillea robusta),* becomes a large tree that produces masses of long yellow blooms in spring. All grevilleas are evergreens and grow best with restricted water during the summer.

Shrimp Plant *(Justicia brandegeana)*
Growth habit: Semiwoody shrub, herbaceous
perennial
Exposure: Sun to shade
Hardiness: Zone 9
Moisture: Moist to dry
Height: Up to 5 feet
Bloom: All year
Propagation: Cuttings or seed

This neotropical plant gets its common name from the shape of the clusters of bracts that produce the tubular white flowers. It is an adaptable, easily grown, semiwoody shrub or perennial, and blooms throughout the year in frost-free climates. Many varieties are cultivated. Most differ from each other in the color of the "shrimp" (pictures, p. 89).

This striking red flower is one of many beautiful grevilleas originating in Australia. Many, if not most, of them are good hummplants.

Pineapple Sage *(Salvia elegans)* (p. 90)

Salvia gesneriflorae
Growth habit: Shrub or herbaceous perennial
Exposure: Sun to partial shade
Hardiness: Zone 9
Moisture: Average
Height: To 10 feet as shrub, 6 feet as perennial
Bloom: Winter through spring
Propagation: Cuttings or seed

This large salvia, which has no common name, bears impressive spikes of big red flowers throughout the winter. Because of its size, it makes an ideal focal point for a winter hummingbird garden, along with several other Mexican sages, such as *S. mexicana* (p. 91) and *S. iodantha.*

Cape Honeysuckle *(Tecomaria capensis)*
Growth habit: Woody vine or shrub
Exposure: Sun to partial shade
Hardiness: Zone 9
Moisture: Dry to average
Height: 6 feet as shrub; can climb 20 feet or more
Bloom: Most of the year
Propagation: Cuttings

Cape honeysuckle is another adaptable plant that is a landscaping stalwart throughout the warmer parts of the U.S. This African import is a large plant that can cover a wall or be grown as a ground cover for large areas, producing spikes of attractive orange tubular flowers throughout the year.

Cape honeysuckle, with its large orange flowers, is named for Cape Province in its native South Africa.

Making Them Grow —
The Basics of Gardening

You don't have to be an experienced gardener to successfully grow a patch of hummingbird flowers. Starting a hummgarden can be as simple as choosing a spot, breaking up the ground, and setting young plants in the soil. If you have ever grown flowers or vegetables, you know how it's done. Most of the plants I recommend, including all of the Dozen Dazzlers, will thrive under the same conditions that produce healthy tomatoes or marigolds.

If you haven't gardened before, my first bit of advice is to ask family, friends, or neighbors who garden for their advice. Before you think I am passing the buck, let me assure you that the next few pages include lots of gardening advice. However, they won't answer all the questions you might have, such as how early in spring is it safe to start planting in your area? All gardeners have learned much of what they know from other gardeners.

What follows is a **review of the basics** that will get you started growing beautiful plants and attracting glittering hummingbirds.

Plants may be grown from seed or cuttings, by layering, or by dividing clumps (pp. 101–102), but the easiest way to start a plant, and the way I would recommend for any beginner, is to buy young plants that a nursery has already started. Look for compact, sturdy plants that are a healthy green, and don't focus on buying plants that already have flowers. A healthy plant will always outperform a weaker one in the long run, regardless of which one starts blooming earlier.

Choose a sunny location for your plants if one is available. Some of the Dozen Dazzlers will do very well in shade, but nearly all plants do better with a half day or more of sun. A plot should be at least 25 square feet if possible, and 50 square feet of a single flower is even better. Hummingbirds are generally more comfortable near cover, so keep your garden within 50 feet or so of trees or shrubs if you can.

Once you've selected your garden spot, you need to prepare the soil. Gardeners sometimes do extensive preparation of bedding soil so that many different kinds of plants will flourish, but if you select your plants carefully to match the soil and moisture conditions in your garden, all you really need to do is loosen the soil and get rid of any grass or weeds. If not removed, grass and weeds will compete with your plants for moisture and nutrients, weakening them and possibly causing them to die. Later I'll discuss techniques to get rid of grass and weeds (p. 102) and to improve your garden soil (p. 103).

Soil preparation can be done with a plow or rototiller, but on a small plot, it is typically done with a spade-type shovel. Although hoeing or scraping the soil may at first seem an easier way to prepare a garden than spading it, I find that using a shovel does a better job and is actually much easier.

The upper foot or so of soil is turned over, burying any grass and loosening the soil so that air and water can filter through. Spading should be done when the moisture in the soil allows it to crumble easily. If a clay soil is too moist or too dry, it will be hard to work and will not break up. After turning the soil, roughly level the surface with a rake.

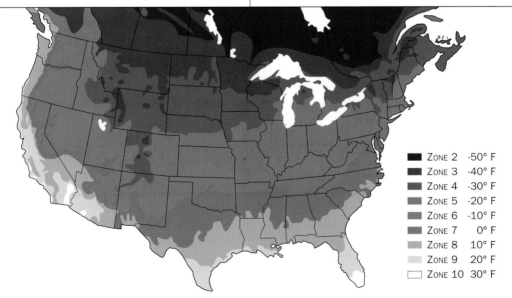

	Zone 2	-50° F
	Zone 3	-40° F
	Zone 4	-30° F
	Zone 5	-20° F
	Zone 6	-10° F
	Zone 7	0° F
	Zone 8	10° F
	Zone 9	20° F
	Zone 10	30° F

This is the USDA Plant Hardiness Zone map of the United States and southern Canada. Plants are classified by zone according to the coldest temperature they will tolerate. Each zone denotes a 10-degree (F) difference in the average annual minimum temperature. To use the map, locate your community, note the color of the zone surrounding it, and match that color to the key at the right.

A single hummplant, even a favorite such as this autumn sage, doesn't provide enough food to keep a hummer's attention for long.

A large patch of flowers will be recognized by passing hummers as a resource worth staying around for.

Rocks, large weeds, and clumps of roots can be removed. This is the time to add granular fertilizer (p. 105) if you intend to fertilize. Scatter handfuls evenly over the soil.

If turning the soil is not possible, simply remove any grass or weeds before digging holes for plants. Whether your ground is tilled or not, the planting hole should be a little larger and slightly deeper than the pot the plant is growing in.

To get the plant out of the pot, place one hand over the soil surface, with a finger on either side of the stem. Turn the pot over with your other hand, loosen the pot from the soil, and carefully remove it. If you have trouble getting the pot off, check to see that roots haven't grown out through a hole in the bottom. If they have, simply cut them off.

As you remove the pot from the plant, be careful not to disturb the ball of soil around the roots. Good contact with the soil is essential for the survival of the roots. If you see a lot of roots pressed along the edge of the potting soil, you can loosen them or cut them to encourage new root growth.

When you place the plant in the hole, backfill the hole so that the potting soil surface is about even with the garden soil surface. Carefully fill the hole around the plant, making sure to create good

contact between the garden soil and the potting soil and leaving no large air pockets. Soil should be tamped to help consolidate air pockets that may remain after you backfill. I use my hands to firm the soil when working with smaller plants, and my feet when planting large perennials, shrubs, or trees.

After planting, thoroughly water the garden and keep watering every second day or so for the first couple of weeks. As they send roots into the soil, plants rely less on frequent irrigation and more on moisture in the soil, but you will need to be attentive with water during the entire first growing season. Even very drought-tolerant plants take a season to become well established in a garden.

Once established, plants need little maintenance during the growing season. To control weeds, I mulch (p. 104) the soil around my flowers, but occasional hand weeding or hoeing works too.

Established plants usually benefit from a monthly application of water-soluble fertilizer (p. 105) if a time-release granular fertilizer was not used when the soil was prepared. Simply follow the package directions. Avoid fertilizing in fall unless you live in a frost-free climate. You don't want to induce fresh growth that will be damaged by cold weather.

You can make many plants grow fuller and produce more blossoms by pinching the stem tips. When the tip of a growing stem is removed, many plants respond by producing two new stem shoots on opposite sides of the main stem and at the spots where the last pair of leaves join the main stem. For plants that bloom from the stem tips, more stem tips means more flowers. You should stop pinching the stem tips of most plants about two months before flowers are expected. Continued pinching will remove the newly forming flower buds.

Making Spade Work Easy

I start spading in a corner of my garden plot, digging a hole about as deep as the blade of the shovel is long and maybe a foot in diameter. Once the hole is dug, I cut a slice of soil from the edge of the hole by placing the shovel tip on the ground and driving the blade in with my foot. Then I pick up the slice and turn it over on the far side of the hole. In this manner, I work my way across the garden, turning the soil as I go. I can make the work match my strength by varying the thickness (and thus the weight) of the slices of soil.

Removing dead stalks and stems will improve the appearance of a garden, and some perennials will produce another round of flowers if they are cut back after they bloom. You may want to cut a plant back close to the ground or remove only a small part of the stem, depending on the type of plant and your personal preferences.

Perennials that are fully hardy in your region will require even less maintenance in winter than they do during the growing season. Once the stems are frozen, they can be pruned back to about 6 inches tall, but I let mine stand until spring to provide winter food and cover for birds.

Half-hardy perennials survive winter more easily if they have thick mulch covering them. Fallen leaves are great for this purpose, and I prefer oak leaves because they don't get as soggy as other leaves, but any leaves will do. Other excellent mulches include pine needles, straw, or even hay, although hay may contain lots of weed seeds.

After half-hardy perennials have frozen, trim them back to about 1 foot tall and completely cover the bed, plants and all, with a foot or more of mulch. In spring, after danger of frost has passed, remove the mulch, being careful not to break any new stems that may be sprouting. The dead foot-tall stems help identify the locations of the plants.

Some dry-climate perennials are prone to rot during winter when they are mulched because the mulch prevents soggy soil from drying out. Use only a light mulch of pine straw or gravel over the soil to prevent this problem.

Growing plants from seed is easy, and it's free if you collect the seed yourself. Many garden plants regularly set seed. The seeds appear near the base of flowers that were pollinated and are typically inside a fruit or protective structure of some kind.

Ripe seeds are typically brown or black and have a more or less hard shell. The part of the plant that contains them may turn brown or straw-colored and die when the seeds are ripe. Fruit usually turns a bright color when ripe. Unlike fruit, seeds do not overripen, but they do tend to fall off the plant when ripe, so don't wait too long to pick them. Ripe seeds can be removed without harming the plants.

After collecting seeds, leave them uncovered until they are fully dry and hard. You can then put them in a covered jar and store them in the refrigerator until spring. Seeds from cold-climate plants are conditioned not to sprout until they have experienced cold weather, so it is necessary to store them in a cold place for at least four to six weeks to simulate winter. This adaptation ensures that the seeds don't sprout in fall, when the seedlings would be killed by winter, but lie dormant until spring.

The seeds of some plants may require dampness as well as cold to be able to sprout. These seeds can be prepared by layering them with wet paper towels or damp soil and storing for four to six weeks in the fridge. Many tropical plants produce seeds that are ready to grow as soon as they ripen, but they can be stored over winter in a refrigerator without harm.

Seeds can be sown in spring as soon as the danger of frost has passed. Most seeds should not be sown after midsummer if the plants that grow from them are expected to survive winter. They need time to grow and establish themselves. Exceptions are the many temperate-zone wildflowers. Their seeds can be sown in late fall. The cold and moisture of winter will prepare them to sprout the following spring.

To plant seeds, cover them with a layer of soil about equal to the diameter of the seed. Small seeds can simply be sprinkled over the top of the soil. Keep the soil evenly moist from the time you sow the seeds until the seedlings are several inches tall.

Many perennials spread vegetatively (not by seed) to form a clump. For these plants, it is easy to **divide clumps to get new plants.** But before you try to divide a plant, do a little exploratory digging around the base to be certain that there really are at least two parts that can be separated, with each having its own stems, crown, and roots. Some plants may appear to have spread into a clump but will really consist of a single crown with many stems. These plants cannot be easily divided.

A plant can be divided in the ground by carefully slicing part of the clump away from the main clump. Use a shovel with a sharp blade for this, and make vertical cuts around the division at least a foot deep to sever all connecting roots. The stems near the cuts may die, so don't try to divide too small a piece.

If You Can't (or Just Don't Want to) Dig

It can be very difficult to prepare a garden under large trees. The limbs cast shade. The roots compete for moisture and nutrients and make tilling impossible. Nevertheless, some hummplants are at home under trees. Outside my Baton Rouge, Louisiana, apartment, the only garden spot was under magnificent live oaks with extensive shallow roots. To make things worse, there was a sparse lawn of Bermuda and St. Augustine grasses, two aggressive and difficult pests to eradicate from a flowerbed. But these difficulties didn't stop me from having a hummgarden, and similar circumstances shouldn't prevent you, either.

I piled autumn leaves 3 feet deep on the area I wanted to become a flower bed, and around the edges, I dug a shallow trench to separate the garden from the surrounding grass. The leaves quickly compacted to less than a foot deep, and over the first winter, worms, fire ants, armadillos, squirrels, at least one helpful turtle, and countless other creatures helped break them down further and mix them with the soil underneath. By the next summer, what had been hard clay began to resemble loam, and the grass was completely gone. Without any tilling, I planted flowers in the new bed. They flourished, and the soil continued to develop over the years, helped by generous additions of fallen leaves each autumn.

In areas with cold winters, the decomposition process may take a year or even longer, as little decomposition or mixing of soil and leaves occurs when it is cold. This method of flower bed preparation may be used in open locations also. In all cases, be careful to keep any grass or weeds out of the decomposing leaves.

Carefully move the new division with a ball of soil around its roots and transplant it. The new plant will have lost much of its roots, so trim the aboveground portion of the plant back by at least 50 percent to help balance leaves with roots. Refill the hole next to the parent plant with soil to protect the plant's roots.

Another way to divide some perennials is to dig up the entire clump in one or more large pieces and then divide using a sharp-bladed shovel. Some tough-rooted perennials, such as red-hot poker, may require considerable violence to divide them, so don't be timid. Alternatively, you can try to tease apart the intertwined roots and stems, which will save more of the plant but will take much extra effort.

Perennials that tend to form a clump of plants also tend to become less vigorous in the center of the clump after years of growing in the same location. The remedy for this is to dig up the clump, divide it into several pieces, and replant them in less crowded conditions. The soil can also be turned over and enriched with organic matter during replanting.

Starting plants from cuttings is the preferred method of propagation for many species. Some plants do not set seed reliably in a garden, and others grow faster from cuttings than they do from seed. Cuttings also produce a plant identical to the parent, which allows for the reproduction of hybrids and cultivars.

Getting cuttings to take root is a game of percentages. For some plants, maybe 90 percent of the cuttings I have tried have rooted. With other plants, the percentage is much lower, and some plants will not typically grow from cuttings at all. There are rooting hormones that are said to increase the chances that a cutting will take root, but many plants will root without them. Scratching the surface of a cutting may stimulate root formation by exposing inner tissue layers to the soil.

Some plants can be propagated by layering. **Reproducing a plant by layering** is accomplished by covering a portion of a lower branch with soil, causing it to take root. The branch is not cut from the plant, and the leaves at the end of the branch should not be covered, so that the branch can continue to grow. Eventually roots will form, and the branch can then be cut from the parent plant and transplanted. Many hummingbird flowers will self-layer — lower branches will spontaneously strike roots when they touch the soil. Other plants can be very slow to root by layering. An American holly I layered took nearly three years to strike roots.

A frequent problem in soil preparation is **getting rid of grass and weeds,** especially when converting a patch of lawn to a garden. Tilling seldom actually kills grass; most lawn grasses resprout quickly. Some grasses can be controlled by pulling, hoeing, or mulching. Others, particularly Bermuda

To make a cutting, sever a piece of a stem just below a leaf node. A cutting is typically 4 to 6 inches long and must include at least two pairs of leaf nodes.

but also St. Augustine, centipede, and Kentucky bluegrass, can be difficult garden weeds. Any small piece that is not removed from a garden will form a plant and quickly spread.

If you are unsure what variety of grass you have, examine the edges of your lawn. A problem grass has probably spread, or is aggressively trying to spread, into shrubs and out onto sidewalks or driveways.

If you have an aggressive lawn grass on your prospective garden plot, you should get rid of it before tilling. There are three ways this can be done. You can smother the grass, kill it with an herbicide, or remove the top couple of inches of sod. Removing sod is heavy work, and you must be very careful not to leave behind any piece of the grass to resprout.

Smothering grass is usually effective but can take several months. Use a thick light-blocking layer of leaves, wood chips, cardboard, plywood, or black plastic sheets. If the plastic sheets are thin, it may take several layers to keep light out. Grass covered in this way may die in a few weeks in hot weather, or it may survive for months in cool weather. The grass will quickly turn from green to yellow or white, but it won't be dead until it is completely dull brown.

Because of the time and trouble required to completely smother healthy grass (particularly Bermuda), some gardeners prefer to kill it with the herbicide

Remove all except the top leaves and push the cutting halfway into damp sand, soil, potting soil, or sometimes plain water. Be sure a leaf node is buried, because roots generally form near leaf nodes.

Roots have sprouted on this cutting. They may take several weeks to appear and are signaled by new growth aboveground. Keep the cuttings moist and in a bright-spot out of direct sunlight until they are growing strongly and ready to be transplanted.

glyphosate (Roundup or several other brands). This herbicide decomposes when it touches the soil, becoming harmless, and planting can be done one month after treatment.

A thick lawn will probably not be completely killed by a single application of herbicide, so allow a couple of weeks for new growth to appear and re-apply herbicide if necessary. If you are planning to herbicide a lawn, keep it watered and mowed prior to spraying; actively growing grass is more readily killed because it absorbs herbicide better.

Be very cautious using glyphosate herbicides to kill grass in a flower bed, as they are not selective and will kill any vegetation they touch. If you find that you have aggressive lawn grasses growing in your flower beds, you will have to pull them by hand, and sometimes pulling them doesn't stop their spread. I have had several flower beds that became so thoroughly infested with Bermuda grass that I had to dig up all the plants, remove the grass, and replant the garden.

Your plants will probably grow better, and you will be able to grow a wider variety, by **improving your garden soil.** Although there are good humm-plants for almost any soil, the best growing conditions are a nutrient-rich soil that is neither too sandy nor too full of clay. Soil with lots of clay does an excellent job of retaining water and nutrients for plants, but in low areas, the soil can stay permanently waterlogged. On higher ground or when there is a long time between rains, clay soil can bake nearly as hard as pottery and become impossible to work.

The easiest way to deal with waterlogged clay soil is to grow cardinal flower or a few other plants that thrive in it (p. 80). In order to grow a wider variety of plants, create raised beds to encourage water to run off. Make the soil for your raised beds from your own clay soil enriched with organic matter. The organic matter you add to the clay not only will provide nutrients but will encourage good drainage.

Don't import a sandy soil mix for a raised bed, as is often recommended. The sandy mix will drain rapidly and require frequent watering. Soon the water will saturate the clay soil underneath it.

The Real Dirt on Soil

Soil is made up of mineral particles, organic matter, and voids (open spaces) filled with water and air. Mineral particles — the broken-down remains of rock — range in size from gravel (the largest particles), to sand, silt, and finally clay, the smallest particles. A loam soil is a mixture of sand, silt, and clay, and the best loams have plenty of organic matter in them as well. In typical soils, organic matter is the component that gives the soil a dark brown or black color, which is why dark color is associated with rich soil. In general, most plants grow best in an organic-rich, loamy soil. Fortunately for gardeners, even the poorest soils can be enriched by adding organic matter.

A protective mulch around the plants helps keep this garden attractive, healthy, and easy to maintain.

The result will be a layer of drought-prone soil over a layer of always-saturated soil, and no hummplant likes those conditions.

Sandy soils also present challenges for gardeners. Sand is easy to work with and drains rapidly, but it can quickly become very dry, and it retains nutrients poorly. Interestingly, the cure for a sandy soil is the same as the cure for a soil loaded with clay — add lots of organics. Organic matter is like a sponge in sand, helping to retain water and nutrients.

The organics in a soil slowly decompose, adding nutrients to the soil and supporting important microbial growth, but this process eventually destroys the organics. Therefore, adding extra organic matter is always a good idea when you are replanting.

I usually incorporate lots of organic matter into any soil I am tilling by spreading it on the soil surface before I dig. As I turn the soil, each shovelful includes some organic matter, and with a few extra turns here and there, I can mix the organic matter into the soil thoroughly as I turn over the garden.

Gardeners use many kinds of organic matter, and many of them can be obtained at no cost, including yard wastes, compost, and manure.

Yard wastes are fallen leaves, hedge clippings, lawn trimmings, pine needles, and similar stuff. Woody wastes should be avoided because they are very low in nutrients but high in carbon, and their decay can actually absorb nutrients from your soil, competing with your plants. Peat moss can be purchased and used in place of yard wastes.

I find that more is better with the organic materials recommended above and often add as much as 8 to 10 inches of leaves to a new bed. Organic materials improve the texture of the soil, but it is important to understand that they add relatively few nutrients. Fertilizer may still be needed.

Compost is a great soil conditioner, with nutrients in varying but usually low levels, depending on what went into the compost heap. Compost can be made from any organic material, or it can be purchased. You can't add too much compost to a garden.

Manures from cows, horses, or poultry are much higher in nutrients than other organic materials. They both fertilize and improve the texture of your soil. However, cow and horse manures contain lots of weed seeds, and any manure can "burn" plants if they are not added to the soil at least a couple of weeks before planting. Composting manures is a way to eliminate weed seeds and prevent burns while keeping the good qualities of manure.

Like most gardeners, I recommend **using mulch in gardens** to control weeds, reduce erosion, beautify the garden, and stabilize the soil environment under plants. Mulching between your plants isn't likely to kill existing weeds in your garden, however. You should remove any weeds and then mulch before a new crop gets started.

There are many mulches to choose from. I prefer organic mulches — the same yard wastes, such as lawn clippings, recommended for improving your soil. Organic mulches are inexpensive (often free), lightweight, decompose to enrich the soil, and they can be easily mixed with the soil when the time comes to replant your garden. The largest disadvantage is that they must periodically be replaced.

Lawn clippings should be added in layers no more than 2 inches thick at a time because deeper layers (or clippings stored more than about 24 hours) begin to rot and can really stink for several days. The other mulches can be layered as thickly as necessary to cover the ground and prevent weed growth, usually 4 inches or so deep.

To improve their appearance and help keep them from blowing around, leaves or pine needles can be chopped with a lawn mower before they are placed on the soil. However, if they are used to cover plants over winter, they should be left whole.

Wood chips (such as shredded tree trimmings obtained from an arborist) and sawdust may be used for mulch, but only if they have been stockpiled for a year or two and decayed sufficiently that they won't absorb nutrients from the soil, as described previously. Shredded bark or bark chips decay much slower than wood chips and so are not a danger to your soil. They make a suitable and attractive mulch but should be removed before tilling rather than worked into the soil like other yard wastes.

Organic mulches can be added at any time to a garden, and because they decay, they must periodically be replenished. The decaying mulch provides a supply of organics that worms, insects, and other creatures continually work into the soil.

The alternative to organic mulch is inorganic mulch. Gravel is often used, particularly in desert landscapes and dry (xeriscape) gardens. The downside of gravel is that it doesn't decompose when mixed with soil. You can't rework a gravel-covered bed without first removing the gravel. Limestone chips used as mulch can be helpful if you are trying to grow lime-loving plants in a region of acid soils.

Weed-control plastics and fabrics are often sold for use as mulch, but I don't recommend them. Once weeds become established in them (and weeds always do), they greatly complicate weed removal or replanting of the bed. Plastics also retard oxygen transfer between soil and air, creating unhealthy soil conditions. Newspapers, which are sometimes recommended as garden mulch, have the same effect.

Most garden plants respond to moderate fertilizing, and there are several ways of **providing fertilizer for your plants.**

Man-made fertilizers are available in granular and water-soluble forms. Water-soluble forms are easy to apply and are immediately available to plants, but are generally a little more expensive than granular fertilizers. Granular fertilizers are available uncoated or coated. The coated forms release their nutrients slowly and thus provide continual feeding. Uncoated forms release their nutrients much more rapidly and are usually the least expensive.

Natural fertilizers are derived from natural sources. They include manure and compost, which are used primarily to improve soil texture but also provide some nutrients. Although natural fertilizers are often referred to as organic fertilizers, the term *organic* is also used to describe the chemical form of a nutrient. Thus there are organic and inorganic forms of nitrogen, and both may be found in a single fertilizer, be it man-made or natural.

Natural fertilizers are typically less convenient and contain much lower concentrations of the three nutrients — nitrogen, phosphorous, and potassium — that plants need in large dosages. They may, however, contain a wider variety of trace nutrients than man-made fertilizers. Chemically, the nutrients that man-made fertilizers contain are identical to those in natural fertilizers.

Slow growth and yellow or off-color leaves can be signs that your plants need fertilizing. If you are not sure whether your plants will benefit from fertilizer, you can have your soil tested, or you can start fertilizing by applying a low dose to your beds.

Annual plants, which must produce a lot of growth in a single season, and fast-growing plants of all types generally benefit from fertilization. The exceptions are wildflowers, especially dry-climate wildflowers. They should be fertilized lightly if at all, since they are adapted for the low-nutrient concentrations typical of uncultivated soils. Potted plants, which have their roots restricted to a small volume of soil, rely on fertilization to obtain their nutrients and should be fertilized lightly at least every two weeks.

Most gardeners apply a balanced fertilizer of nitrogen, phosphorous, and potassium according to the package directions. Gardeners often prefer to apply low doses of a fertilizer more frequently, as opposed to high doses less frequently, to avoid "burning" plants with excessive fertilizer.

In addition to nitrogen, phosphorous, and potassium, there are many trace nutrients needed by plants, including iron, calcium, and magnesium. These nutrients are supplied to the soil by natural processes, including the slow breakdown of rocks. Gardeners who use compost find that the decaying mixture of plant materials helps to supply a wide variety of trace nutrients. Those who have rich soil or who use a balanced fertilizer regularly may never have to worry about trace nutrients. Some gardeners who need to provide trace nutrients apply rock powders to the soil.

The procedure for **growing plants in containers** is different from that for growing plants in the ground. Most plants can be grown in a good-sized pot or similar container, but they require more attention because the soil conditions in a pot — moisture content, temperature, amount of nutrients — fluctuate much more rapidly than do ground conditions.

Many potted plants require daily watering during the hot summer months, and missing a couple of days may kill the plants. If you won't be able to water regularly, select plants that tolerate drying out, such as red yucca (p. 75), fountain plant (p. 85), Mexican honeysuckle (p. 65), flame acanthus (p. 96), autumn sage (p. 80), soap aloe (p. 79), medicinal aloe (p. 93), and tree tobacco (p. 95).

You may want to consider an automatic watering system if you have, or want to have, many potted plants. These systems are not expensive, can be easily installed, will deliver water to each pot, and will enable you to take vacations and still have potted outdoor plants.

With the exception of the above listed plants, all of which will tolerate full sun while planted in a pot, plants should usually be placed in somewhat shadier conditions when grown in a pot than they would prefer in the ground. Potted plants also require more frequent fertilization than plants in the ground. I use liquid fertilizer at one-half the recommended strength, and apply it every week or so.

The size of your pots is important. Choose containers as large as you can manage. Large containers will have more stable soil conditions than smaller pots, and most of the hummplants listed in this book grow too large for a small pot. If you choose to grow in small pots, check the list of plants for hanging baskets and the list of houseplants for ideas.

Select light-colored pots, particularly if you will be placing them in the sun, to reduce the absorp-

Soil testing is available from agricultural extension services of the state, county, or state university or from private labs. Some tests can also be performed with purchased do-it-yourself test kits.

Fertilizer raises the salt concentration in the soil (fertilizer nutrients are chemically categorized as salts but are not the same as sodium chloride, the salt we eat). Too high a salt concentration draws water from a plant's roots or leaves, turning the leaves brown and potentially killing the plant.

A potted garden requires frequent care. Consider how much time you can devote to potted plants before selecting which ones to grow.

tion of heat into the soil. I generally use plastic pots because they are durable, lightweight, and inexpensive. Clay pots are an alternative, but they are heavy and break more easily than plastic.

Many pots come equipped with trays or saucers to sit in that catch and hold rain or water from a sprinkler. These saucers can provide extra water to plants that need it, or they can just as easily keep the soil in a pot saturated and cause the plant to die.

Except in dry climates, I recommend that all but the most vigilant gardeners remove the saucers from under their pots, and that the vigilant ones temporarily remove them during rainy weather. If you prefer saucers under your pots, try filling them with a layer of gravel so that the pot stays above standing water in the saucer.

A plant that sits too long in standing water may suffer from root die-off due to the waterlogged soil. When this happens, the plant typically wilts as it would if the soil had dried out. You can try to save the plant by moving it out of full sun. Don't let the soil completely dry out; keep it moist. But even with care, many plants will not recover.

After you have cared for it all summer and enjoyed watching it bring hummers to your patio or deck, you'll probably have a strong urge to **keep your potted plant alive over winter.** If you have a greenhouse, you can keep it growing in winter, but it probably won't grow inside your house.

Most potted plants, even shade-tolerant ones,

require much brighter light than most indoor situations provide. And homes are generally too warm for outside plants. The combination of warmth and darkness results in weak, spindly growth that saps the energy of a plant and often kills it. Finally, outdoor plants moved indoors often bring with them insects that can attack houseplants.

If you do choose to move outdoor plants indoors for winter, you must have a bright spot for them, such as a large south-facing window. A sunroom or cool glassed-in porch is ideal. It is a good idea to quarantine outdoor plants for a week or two when you bring them in, until you are satisfied that no outdoor bugs are present.

Even if you can't keep your favorite potted plant growing over winter, you can probably maintain it in a dormant state. I have not tried to overwinter all of the plants in this book by keeping them dormant, but I find that most plants hardy in zone 8 will survive winter if kept in a cold place, such as a basement, shed, enclosed porch — anywhere that temperatures will remain cold or cool all winter without dropping below freezing.

I have constructed simple outdoor greenhouses with plastic sheeting and inexpensive lumber for this purpose, using a few light bulbs to maintain temperatures above freezing on cold nights.

Before you place a plant in cold storage, cut it back severely, leaving only a framework of the main stems to support the next year's growth. Some people prefer to remove all of the leaves and green stems; others choose to keep a few leaves.

A storage temperature of about 35° F is ideal. If the temperature is this cold constantly, plants can be kept in the dark. At slightly warmer temperatures, the plant will grow very slowly and will require some light. The soil should stay slightly moist during the winter and may require occasional watering, but do not overwater.

As spring approaches, reintroduce your plants to sunlight and warmer temperatures, returning them to their winter quarters on frosty nights. Once new growth appears, apply fertilizer and resume regular watering.

It is tempting to try to save garden plants by transplanting them into pots and letting them go dormant over winter. Rather than transplanting them at the end of the growing season, it is better to grow them in pots all summer. If you wish, you can sink the entire pot in the ground — the inexpensive black plastic containers used by nurseries are ideal for this.

Many roots will grow out through the drainage holes, giving the plant access to much more soil than the pot can hold and allowing it to enjoy some of the benefits of growing in the ground. In the fall, simply lift the entire pot out of the ground and cut off any roots that are outside the pot before you move your plant to winter storage.

Soil-less soil

Potting soil, more specifically called potting mix, typically contains no soil. It is made up of materials like peat moss, vermiculite and perlite (minerals that are mined and processed to become a lightweight, porous rooting media), composted bark, lime, and often fertilizer. Coarse-grained mixes are sold for large containers. Potting soil is much lighter than real soil, making the pots easier to handle, and unlike garden soil, it remains loose and porous after repeated watering. If you choose to grow potted plants using soil from your garden, be sure to add lots of organic matter to help keep it loose and permeable to water, air, and plant roots.

Meet the BIRDS

of Summer

by Jack Griggs

A female ruby-throated hummingbird approaches the blossom of a trumpet creeper vine.

A pair of broad-tailed hummingbird eggs (shown twice actual size) rests in a downy nest. North American hummingbirds usually lay two eggs. Although tiny, each egg is a larger proportion of a hummer's mass than in other birds. While other birds generally lay eggs on consecutive days, a female hummer needs two days to produce her second egg.

The Lives of Hummingbirds — Tiny Tempests Living Large

Among nature's most improbable creatures, you would have to place hummingbirds right up there with kangaroos, meerkats, and the giant panda. If they weren't an observable fact, few people would believe that hummingbirds could exist. And only those with an off-the-wall sense of humor would imagine them being fearless, ferocious little beasts. Hummingbirds are more reasonably an exquisite, impossible fantasy.

However, with numerous real-world examples to study, ornithologists have explained away many of the mysteries of these birds, their co-evolution with flowers, the mechanics of their flight, their hyper metabolism. Scientists can tell us how their gorget feathers reflect such a brilliant spectrum of colors. They even know the exact total number of feathers a ruby-throated hummer has, 940 when counted back in the 1930s.

But if we want to know something about a hummingbird that can't be counted, dissected, or scrutinized under a microscope, we are probably still confronted with a mystery. We know very little about hummer migration patterns. No one has determined what role feeders play in maintaining or expanding the ranges or populations of hummers. And how in the world does a hummer find its way back in spring to the exact place where its feeder hung the previous fall?

Scientists may endeavor to explain the existence of a hummingbird, but I wonder if they aren't just obscuring the miracle. For instance, it's a fact that most North American hummers weigh in the neighborhood of 3 to 3.5 grams. How much is that? It's about the weight of half this page. Can you imagine cutting off the left half of this page, folding it into an origami hummer, and tossing it into the air? How does any trifle that vaporous fly to Mexico and back?

Most of the eight widespread North American hummers do migrate back and forth across the border between the U.S. and Mexico. They come north in the spring to nest and replenish their species, the most important event in their yearly routine.

A Bump on a Branch

Hummingbird nests vary from species to species but are usually artfully camouflaged with bits of bark, lichen, and moss to resemble a small bump on a tree branch. It takes the female about a week to complete her nest; less if the weather is good and she is able to scavenge material from an old nest; more if conditions are difficult. Sometimes the construction process continues during incubation. Females begin by building a platform of downy materials, gluing them together and to the tree branch with spider webs. The sides and rim are then added to the platform using the same downy material — plants, hair, and small feathers — bound with spider webs. The female sits in the nest to shape it, turning frequently and pushing the sides with her breast. To shape the rim, she holds it between her chin and breast and moves from side to side.

Males migrate several days ahead of females and select territories. When the females arrive, they don't pair up with males. The sexes associate only long enough to mate. Females select sites separate from the males for their nests, often near a previous nest site.

Females do all the incubating and caring for the young. Many may raise two broods, but this has not been observed in all North American species. In some, an occasional third nesting has been noted.

The most fascinating details of the unique lifestyle and character of hummers are explored in the following descriptions of the eight widespread North American species. Each account contains information that pertains to all hummers, so even if the ruby-throat is the only hummer you see, you will want to read the accounts of the other seven.

The description of each hummingbird includes a section on identification. Identifying an adult male is usually as easy as looking at pictures of hummer gorgets (throat feathers) and selecting the one that matches the bird being identified — but not always. The hue reflected by the brilliantly iridescent feathers can vary considerably. Note the different colors reflected by the gorget of the rufous hummingbird pictured on p. 6. All gorgets will appear black if light does not reflect off them at a favorable angle.

Females and young hummingbirds (young males resemble females) lack the distinctive gorgets of adult males and can be much more difficult to identify. The females and young of one species often resemble those of other species. In some instances, positive identification can be accomplished only by an expert observer.

Females and young may have clear throats, but more often they show vertical rows of dark stipling or small iridescent spangles. In some species, females commonly have a small patch of male-like gorget feathers at the bottom center of the throat. These feathers can be quite useful in identification since they are the same color as the male's gorget.

Hummers are usually quite vocal. Calls are difficult to describe, but at the Cornell Lab of Ornithology Web site (see Resources), you can click on a sound file of hummingbird vocalizations and compare the calls of different species.

Ruby-throated Hummingbird
Archilochus colubris

Each mid-September, the adjoining communities of Rockport and Fulton on the Texas Gulf Coast host the "Hummer/Bird Celebration!" It coincides with an extraordinary massing of ruby-throated hummers and other neotropical migrants as they prepare to cross the Gulf of Mexico on their return home to Mexico and Central America.

"The first ruby-throats show up in the middle of August, and I'll put out four feeders for them,"

A male ruby-throated hummingbird displays its ruby-red gorget and forked tail while hovering in front of a cigar plant (p. 73) blossom. Note the narrow black line bordering the upper edge of the red gorget and the white neck below.

says Susan Beree, of Rockport. "As the hummers increase, I set out more feeders, then all of a sudden it's like somebody opened the door and everybody left the party."

The birds leave with a weather front, Susan explains. "We start having our first winds out of the north in early September. All summer the winds are out of the south." When the birds sense that they have a reliable tailwind, they disappear en masse, and the next group begins to assemble.

The migration peaks in mid-September with hummers continually assembling and then leaving as a group. To serve them, Susan says, "I gradually increase my feeders to 25." Two feeder visitors that she was able to reliably identify each stayed exactly one week before disappearing, she says, adding, "Some of them get so plump!

"They typically leave during the day," Susan states. "The feeders will be really busy the evening before, then they have breakfast the next morning, and they take off. There'll only be a few hummingbirds still around by evening."

No other hummer faces any obstacle to migration even remotely comparable to the Gulf. The rufous hummer travels a longer distance in many cases, but it is all overland.

Some ruby-throats also travel overland, and others island-hop down the Caribbean, but the large concentrations each year at Rockport-Fulton and the lack of such concentrations farther south along the Texas coast indicate that a huge number gather to wait for the right tailwind to help them cross to the Yucatan Peninsula.

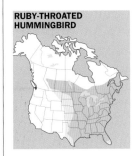

**RUBY-THROATED
HUMMINGBIRD**

SUMMER
WINTER
ALL YEAR
MIGRATION

A female black-chinned hummingbird (left) and female ruby-throated hummingbird (right) display their nearly identical underparts while sipping nectar. The small difference in color is due to lighting, and the slight variation in the amount of white on the outer tail feathers is a characteristic of individuals, not species. The right-side tail feathers of the ruby-throat seem a little shorter than those of the black-chin only because they are foreshortened in the photo. One diagnostic difference is the slightly more pointed outer tail feathers of the black-chin. What the picture can't show is that the female black-chin regularly pumps her tail while feeding and the ruby-throat seldom does.

For adult ruby-throats, the fall flight across the Gulf means that their long visit to North America is at an end. Home is just beyond the horizon. Many of them left their tropical homes in January or February. By the end of February, the earliest migrants were congregating on the northern shores of the Yucatan Peninsula, fattening up for the northward flight over the Gulf. They add fat reserves about equal to their normal weight before departing.

Northward crossings typically start at dusk, and birds don't make landfall in North America until the following day. If the weather is good and the breezes friendly, many birds will overshoot the coast by up to a hundred miles before stopping to rest and recover. If the weather is bad, they can struggle just to reach the beach, and many may fail.

The first birds to head north are mature males. The earliest females and many of the young males lag behind the first males by a week or 10 days. Migration continues over several months. The early birds don't reach their northernmost nesting territories until the middle of May.

Ruby-throats are remarkably faithful to their nesting and feeding sites, and it doesn't take a banding study to prove it. Anyone who has failed to get a feeder out on time in spring has seen the evidence — a perplexed hummer hovering right where the feeder hung the previous year. Birds also appear to repeat their migration routes from year to year, which explains why traffic often builds from one year to the next at yards that start providing for ruby-throats. The old birds keep coming back, and young ones join them each year.

Overland, ruby-throats migrate in daytime. Hot-air balloonists regularly report the curious birds checking them out at altitudes up to 200 feet or more. They average around 20 miles each day, less than an hour's flying time at a nominal 30 miles per hour.

Researchers and writers often attempt to tie the advance of migration to the blooming of a particular flower, but ruby-throat expert Bob Sargent suspects that the arrival dates anywhere in their range are governed first by the calendar date. "The timing was almost certainly established genetically by successful ancestors that hit the timing of blooming flowers and hatching insects," Sargent says.

Weather has an influence, however. Lanny Chambers, who for years has collected the dates that ruby-throats are first observed at locations throughout the East, says, "While the first birds cross the Gulf very reliably in the last few days of February each year, my sense is that their progress northward is affected by their food supply and the local weather conditions that influence it." He goes on to note that in his hometown of St. Louis, Missouri, the first arriving ruby-throats have been observed as early as April 8 and as late as April 23 in different years.

In the northern portion of their nesting range, ruby-throats arrive up to a month before flowers bloom and provide nectar. In these regions, the birds get their sugar from the sap wells that yellow-bellied

A female black-chinned hummingbird feeds her babies. The location of the nest, Arizona, ensures that the bird is not a ruby-throat. Identification is confirmed by the tail, which barely extends beyond the wingtips. Female ruby-throats have longer tails.

sapsuckers drill in trees. Ruby-throats aren't the only birds to filch sap from sapsuckers' wells, but they are the most persistent. Research shows that they visit the oozing holes even more often than the sapsuckers that drill them! In some areas, the birds apparently continue feeding primarily from sap wells even after nectar-filled blossoms become available.

Female ruby-throats usually build their nests (picture, p. 26) in woodlands, often near or over water. They may choose an orchard but rarely a backyard garden unless it has a stand of mature trees. The nest can be in a pine or a hardwood tree, usually on the outer portion of a branch but with a canopy of leaves over it to provide some cover. The nest may be within a few feet of the ground but often is too far above one's head to be viewed.

Males lead the parade home in fall, too. Some males leave as early as mid-July. Many hummer hosts in the East think that the last hummer they see at their feeders in fall is one of the summer visitors waiting until the last moment to leave. Banding studies show that visitors to a feeder or flowers late in the season are almost always migrants stopping to refuel.

Most ruby-throats have left the U.S. by the end of September. Some remain in south Florida over the winter. A few linger along the Gulf until winter, and a very few, presumed unfit to migrate, attempt to overwinter along the Gulf. Ruby-throats are not as hardy as Anna's or rufous hummingbirds, although they can go into torpor (p. 116).

Identification

East of the Mississippi, the only nesting hummer is the ruby-throated. Any hummer seen in the East in summer is presumed to be a ruby-throat, even if the distinctive marks can't be observed. The only confusion is with hummingbird moths.

Male ruby-throats are easily distinguished from females by either their gorgets or tail feathers. The red gorget is typically a rich ruby color. The tail is deeply notched, and the outer feathers are pointed.

Females and young ruby-throats have much fuller tails than males, and the outer feathers are tipped with white. Adult females may have a few iridescent spots at the center of the throat, but often the throat is clear white or lightly stippled with gray. By fall, young males can show widespread spotting on the throat.

Female and young ruby-throats strongly resemble female and young black-chinned hummers (picture, p. 110). Fortunately, the nesting ranges of the two species are separate, overlapping only slightly in Texas, so very few people have to deal with distinguishing them from each other.

Black-chinned Hummingbird
Archilochus alexandri

Black-chinned hummingbirds occupy much of the West in summer. They are very adaptable hummers, nesting from Mexico into Canada in a wide variety of habitats at elevations from low deserts to halfway up many mountain slopes. They are at home in cities and suburbs and common at feeders and garden flowers.

After nesting, some black-chins overwinter in south Texas and along the Gulf Coast but most retire to Mexico and don't return to the U.S. until late March or early April. The northernmost nesters reach British Columbia's Okanagan Valley in early May.

Like other hummers, the black-chinned defends feeding territories, but the only western hummer it encounters that it can usually dominate is the smaller Costa's. Faced with competition from Anna's, broad-tailed, or rufous hummers, the black-chin must often scramble for food sources.

The winter hummgardeners along the Gulf Coast have the opportunity to observe black-chinned hummingbirds compete for backyard feeders and flowers with a wide variety of other hummers. Longtime hummgardener, bander, and author Nancy L. Newfield, of Metarie, Louisiana, says that until 1978 she usually hosted more black-chins in winter than any other species, and that they successfully claimed and held territories. "But the tide changed in December 1978 when I hosted a major influx of rufous hummers," says Nancy. "They made life difficult for all the others. Still, I think that some black-chinneds managed to hold territories against the onslaught of the rusty demons."

BLACK-CHINNED HUMMINGBIRD

A male black-chinned hummingbird displays its most prominent field marks, a dark head and chin bordered with a band of violet on the throat and contrasting with a band of white on the upper breast and neck.

In the winter of 1985–86, Nancy says that buff-bellied hummers, another particularly pugnacious species, arrived in her yard in force. "Black-chinneds really got squeezed that winter, and I never had a lot of them after that," she says. "Since the winter of 1995–96, I've had no territorial black-chinneds."

Instead of holding a territory, a black-chinned hummer may visit a succession of food sources. Some may be marginal patches of flowers that are not defended; in other cases, the black-chin will try to sneak into defended territories. Other hummingbird species, faced with competition, may also adopt this feeding technique, called trap-lining for its similarity to checking traps in a sequence.

Dennis Demcheck reports that a female black-chinned hummer was overwintering in his yard until a young male rufous bullied her off her favorite perch over a patch of winter-blooming salvia. The black-chinned left the yard, but Dennis says she still sneaks back to the feeders. "Her behavior has definitely changed," he notes. "She used to be a constant vocalizer, especially in the mornings. Now she is quiet as a mouse, trying to avoid the notice of the mighty male rufous."

Identification

Male black-chins have a black gorget with a seldom-seen band of violet at the bottom that usually appears black. Because its face and head are also dark, the male black-chin often appears to have an entirely black head and neck contrasting with a bright band of white on the upper breast and neck.

Because the gorgets of other hummers often appear black, caution is needed when identifying a black-chinned male.

Female and young black-chinned hummers closely resemble female and young ruby-throats.

Rufous Hummingbird
Selasphorus rufous

The rufous hummingbird has no doubt about its proper rank among North American hummers. It's the baddest dude in the garden, even if it's not the biggest. It shares nesting range with the calliope and encounters several other species during migration, but it usually succeeds in commandeering any patch of flowers it wants. The blossoms it prefers are often the highest ones above the ground.

Even in migration, rufous hummingbirds are fiercely territorial and may stand guard for a week or more over productive patches of flowers, refreshing themselves and restoring fat reserves. When they migrate through the nesting range of the broad-tailed, black-chinned, or Costa's hummingbird, they consume many of the resources those species depend on. Studies of Costa's hummingbirds in southern California and Arizona show that their territories shrink and their body weight is impacted when the dominant rufous hummers are migrating through.

Rufous hummers don't tolerate each other any better than they do other species. Adult males claim the best feeding spots, and in fall, males often migrate on a different route than females and immature birds, one that promises the best flowers. Hummingbird flower expert and co-author Ron Rovansek relates his experience in Reno, Nevada, as rufous hummers migrated south in 2001. "I saw at least a couple of hundred rufous hummingbirds in

A male rufous hummingbird displays his diagnostic rufous markings, which include the entire back. The rufous color is not iridescent.

my yard but not even one adult male. I saw plenty of immature males, plus females both young and old."

One of the reasons the rufous has such an attitude is that it has the flying skills to back it up. Not only does it appear particularly speedy and agile, but it has the endurance to fly farther in migration than any other hummer does. Individuals that nest in Alaska and the Yukon may travel 4,000 miles or more one way from their winter range in Mexico.

Spring migration is up the West Coast. After passing through California, some rufous hummers head inland as far as the Rockies to nest; others continue north. They are forest birds, feeding in clearings, meadows, and brushy areas.

Rufous hummers usually build their nests on the outer portions of the lower branches of trees, either conifers or hardwoods, but they also use shrubs, ferns, and vines. Some scientists suspect that females may raise more than one brood per season, but so far no one has been able to document double-brooding in this species. Rufous expert William Calder suspects that in the northern part of their range, the short flowering season probably limits them to one brood.

After nesting, some rufous hummers fly south along the coast; others loop through the Rockies. Because of the riskiness of finding food during migration, rufous hummers lay on fat — as much as 72 percent of their normal body weight — before embarking. The fat reserves are precious, containing twice as much energy as an equal weight of sugar. As much as possible, a rufous hummer will fuel itself with sugar from nectar rather than dip

into its fat reserves. At night, it even goes into torpor (p. 116) to avoid burning fat.

Not all rufous hummingbirds return to Mexico and the borderlands of California and Arizona. An increasing number are showing up in winter in the East, particularly along the Gulf of Mexico. The birds first reported many years ago were assumed to be lost or to have scrambled brain circuits. However, lost and confused birds don't return winter after winter to the same yard and feeder, as do many of the adult rufous hummers that winter along the Gulf today. These birds have made their winter home in the eastern U.S. Are we watching the beginning of a major winter range expansion? Will it continue? Does it have anything to do with global warming? Time and research will tell.

Identification

You don't need to see the gorget on a male rufous hummingbird to identify it. If the bird is sitting, you only need to catch a glimpse of his rufous back to clinch an identification. All North American hummingbirds other than the adult male rufous hummer have green backs.

The rufous color extends to the sides, face, and tail on adult males. The gorget is orange-red to golden or greenish. The only green on most adult male rufous hummers occurs as iridescent patches on the crown and shoulders and perhaps a few random green spangles on the back. A very few may have extensive green on the back and be difficult or impossible to distinguish from adult male Allen's hummingbirds without an in-hand view.

RUFOUS HUMMINGBIRD

A female rufous hummer displays her rufous sides and the prominent rufous in her tail. Her back is iridescent green, although barely evident in this lighting. The female Allen's hummer is virtually identical.

The green back on an adult male Allen's hummingbird distinguishes it from the otherwise nearly identical rufous hummer. The paler look of the rufous hummer shown on p. 112 is a result of lighting differences.

ALLEN'S HUMMINGBIRD

Both rufous and Allen's males announce their presence with a distinctive metallic whine produced by small notches in several of the wing feathers.

Female and young rufous hummingbirds are indistinguishable from female and young Allen's hummingbirds in the field. When seen away from their separate nesting ranges, they are commonly referred to as rufous/Allen's hummingbirds.

Female and young rufous/Allen's hummers can be separated from most other female and young hummingbirds by the rufous wash on their sides and the bright rufous in their tails. The only other hummingbirds that share these characteristics are female and young broad-tails (picture, p. 14) and calliopes (picture, p. 19).

The rufous in the tails of female and young calliope hummers is all but invisible, and their tails are so short — usually not reaching the wingtips when at rest — that an observer with a good look can reliably distinguish them from rufous hummers, whose tails extend well beyond their wingtips.

Tails are also a good way to separate female and young rufous/Allen's hummers from their broad-tailed counterparts. The broad-tails, as their name implies, have particularly large tails. With experience and a good look, the difference in tail size can be recognized. And while the coverts under the tails of rufous hummers are washed with rufous (picture, title page), those on broad-tailed hummers are creamy white.

Mature female rufous hummers often show a few coppery iridescent feathers at the center of their throats. Old females can sport extensive displays.

Allen's Hummingbird
Selasphorus sasin

Allen's is the very slightly smaller, shorter-winged, and better-behaved cousin of the rufous hummingbird. Its nesting range hugs the California coast, extending just into southern Oregon, where it overlaps that of the rufous.

Even though it has the smallest range of any hummer that nests in North America, Allen's has two subspecies, a migratory race that nests from the Oregon border to Ventura County in California, and a resident race on California's Channel Islands and the Palos Verdes Peninsula. The resident subspecies is expanding its inland range from the Palos Verdes Peninsula and now nests throughout much of the Los Angeles basin and southern Orange County.

The vast majority of Allen's are migratory, and spring migration begins very early. Some males are in California by December, and by mid-January, migration is well underway. Fall migration is also early, with some males starting the trip back to Mexico in late spring, even before females are through raising their young. Females exit next, and young birds are last, most of them getting underway in late June or July, just ahead of the rufous hummers returning from the north. The resident subspecies may nest any time of the year.

Identification

Male Allen's hummingbirds are distinguished from male rufous hummers by their green backs, but there is a slight uncertainty because a few rufous hummers may show extensive green on

A male broad-tailed hummer hovers to feed at a scarlet gilia (p. 76) blossom. Broad-tailed hummers are the largest of the eight widespread North American hummingbirds.

An immature rufous hummingbird (left) and an immature broad-tailed hummingbird (right) reveal their similarities and one major difference — tail length. When tails are spread, the difference in size is even more noticeable. The rufous on the sides of a female or young broad-tailed is typically paler than in female or young rufous hummers, but these unretouched photos show how similar the colors can appear.

their backs. Seen in Allen's range, a green-backed male is safely identified as an Allen's, but seen elsewhere during fall migration or in winter in the East, the chance that it might be a green-backed rufous must be considered. The shape of the outer tail feathers, narrow and pointed in Allen's hummingbird, can be used to clinch the identification.

Female and young Allen's hummingbirds are inseparable in the field from their rufous counterparts except by range.

Broad-tailed Hummingbird
Selasphorus platycercus

Only a portion of the broad-tailed hummingbirds that live in Mexico and Guatemala migrate to the U.S. to nest. The ones that stay year-round in Central America live a life subordinate to larger and more aggressive hummingbirds. They scrape by on what the local dominant hummingbirds don't claim, including nectar from many plants that are primarily pollinated by insects rather than hummers.

The many broad-tails that migrate each year to the high slopes of the central and southern Rockies have little or no competition for the abundant hummingbird flowers that bloom there. Where their breeding range overlaps with that of another species, it is always a smaller or less aggressive hummingbird. Most broad-tails have already fledged their young by the time the disruptive and dominating rufous hummers migrate south from their nesting range in the northern Rockies.

The first broad-tail males reach southern Arizona by late February or early March and proceed north with the warming weather. By late April, they reach Colorado, and by the last week in May, they are at the northern limit of their range, Idaho.

The final leg of the journey is a slow, deliberate climb up a mountainside to their summer territory.

Birds make short-distance scouting trips up a slope at midday even before flowers on the high slopes are in bloom. Males look for the best feeding territories to claim; females scout out nesting sites. They return to blooming flowers or feeders at lower elevations before nightfall.

Throughout the summer season, males may shuttle up and down a mountainside seeking food or to find a warm place to roost. Females, however, must stay at their nest to incubate and brood their young at night, and it can get quite cold in the western mountains on a summer night. Hummingbird researcher William Calder reports a broad-tailed female that continued incubating during a June night when temperatures dropped into the low 20s and nearly an inch of snow fell.

Identification

The sparkling rose-red gorget and long tail of the male broad-tailed hummingbird are easy identifying marks. The green back is also a distinctively cooler shade of green than that of other North American hummers (picture, p. 76), but you can easily identify male broad-tails with your eyes closed. Just listen for the shimmering wing trill. The outer pair of wing feathers on the male broad-tail are modified to produce a 6 kHz tone. That tone is modulated by the wing beat, approximately 50 Hz when hovering, to produce the characteristic trill.

Female and young broad-tails also have the distinctive large tails and back color, but they don't have the wing whistle, and of course, they don't have gorgets. Their throats are often marked with rows of stipples or spangles, but they seldom have

**BROAD-TAILED
HUMMINGBIRD**

A male Anna's hummingbird guards a red-hot poker plant from the top of one of its spires. Iridescent red feathers flare to the sides of his gorget and cover his forehead.

A female Anna's hummingbird tends to nestlings about to outgrow their nest. Like many females, she has a lot of iridescent throat feathers. She also displays Anna's characteristic dingy gray breast.

the central cluster of male-like gorget feathers characteristic of female rufous and Anna's hummers.

Because of their rufous sides and the bright rufous in their tails, female and young broad-tailed hummingbirds can be difficult to separate from female and young rufous hummers. The differences are discussed under rufous identification.

ANNA'S HUMMINGBIRD

Anna's Hummingbird
Calypte anna

When other North American hummers head south to escape the onset of winter, Anna's hummingbirds remain behind. They live year-round as far north as Vancouver Island, British Columbia. Although often thought of as too delicate to survive freezing weather, Anna's are as tough as they are cantankerous. A succession of hard nighttime freezes will not harm them if they can find food during the day.

But freezing temperatures wither plant blooms and suppress insects. Anna's are reputed to eat more insects each day than other North American hummers, and in freezing weather, it takes resourcefulness to find them. Judy Walker, of Charlotte, North

Carolina, reports that an Anna's wintering out of range in her yard in 2001 foraged for insects in leaf litter during cold snaps. "The bird flew right above the ground. The air from his wings moved the leaves around and exposed insects that he picked up."

In Victoria, on the southern tip of Vancouver Island, Cam Finlay describes an Anna's gleaning bugs from a tree branch on a rainy, near-freezing day. "He was acting just like a chickadee, moving along a branch and pecking." Finlay reports that up to 750 Anna's winter around Victoria and that their numbers are growing and their range expanding.

Anna's in Victoria are all thought to depend on nectar feeders in winter, at least part of the time. In very cold weather, people try many things to keep feeders from freezing, Finlay says. "Everything from replacing them every hour or two, to thawing them out, to putting a light beside the feeder to keep it warm, to making a quasi-cave around the feeder with a box, open at one end. All methods work."

At nighttime temperatures below about 50° F, an Anna's hummingbird may drop its body temperature and reduce its breathing rate to conserve energy and maintain reserves that will last it through the night. Body temperature, as high as 109° F in daytime, has been measured as low as 43° F at night. Breathing can be suspended for minutes. In that state of torpor, birds can appear to be frozen. They are immobile, with eyes closed, bill pointed skyward, and feathers all puffed out into a ball. They do not respond to touch and can take 20 minutes or more to gradually awaken.

All North American hummers can go into torpor to survive cold nights. Anna's aren't the only

Anna's Makes Music or Tries to

In some southern California neighborhoods, the short, sharp chip of Anna's hummingbird is the most prevalent birdcall heard. Anna's not only calls but is one of the few North American hummingbirds considered to have a song. Some observers think it is a stretch to call the squeaky vocalization of the male Anna's a song, but there is no question that he intends to sing, no matter how unmelodic his voice. A male typically perches on an exposed branch to sing, just as a warbler would. While singing — and the male sings year-round — he typically swings his bill from side to side to display the brilliant glints from his head and gorget.

ones with this remarkable ability, but they are the only ones that, amazingly, choose the depths of a northern winter to nest and raise a family. It may seem like a case of evolution gone awry, but it makes sense when you consider the recent history of Anna's hummingbirds.

In the early 20th century, their normal range was limited to the Pacific slope from the San Francisco Peninsula south through the northern portion of Baja California. In this region, the season of abundance begins in December, when the first rains end the long annual drought. Flowers bloom; insects abound. The following months are the perfect time for Anna's hummers to bring young into the world.

Anna's started occupying range beyond their homeland in the mid-1900s. Gardens made it possible. Perhaps more than any other hummer, Anna's has accepted feeders and gardens and has flourished with the onrush of civilization. Today resident nesting populations extend east through the southern part of Arizona, as well as north to British Columbia. After nesting, many individuals disperse farther east and some wander as far north as Alaska.

The "winter-nesting gene" limits their potential range, but the hardiness of Anna's hummers permits them to utilize large stretches of the western coasts and river valleys where temperatures never fall very far below freezing. Finlay hasn't seen any evidence of a change in their nesting period in Victoria. "They continue to set up territory in November and December and nest from January into May, just like in California." He cites several records of young successfully fledged in March.

Before nesting, the female locates a nectar source she can defend. Since the Anna's hummer is as comfortable in yards as it is in the wild, many make their nests and raise their young in backyards. Note that if a male Anna's claims a yard or portion of it first, a female is unlikely to contest it.

Anna's usually builds her nest on a tree branch, although nests are also regularly found in shrubs and vines. Conifers are rarely used. Two clutches are usual, and a female may start building a second nest near the first one while still tending to the nestlings in the first nest. Nests are seldom reused, but materials are often scavenged from old nests for reuse. Although many Anna's wander after the nesting season, banding studies indicate that females often return to the same vicinity to nest year after year.

Identification

The Anna's hummingbird is average-sized but bulky. The male has a patch of iridescent red feathers on his forehead and another behind the eye, as well as red gorget feathers. The gorget flares at the corners. The only other North American hummer with this pattern of iridescence is the much smaller Costa's. However, the Costa's gorget is purple and flares much more dramatically.

Female and young Anna's have a distinctive bulky look and dingy gray underparts. Tails resemble those of the ruby-throated or black-chinned hummingbird (picture, p. 110). Most adult females have a small triangular patch of male-like iridescent feathers on their throats, and many have extensive patches.

Costa's Hummingbird
Calypte costae

Costa's hummingbirds have not accepted feeders and gardens as readily as the closely related Anna's hummers have. They mostly stick to their wild haunts — the sage scrub and dry chaparral along

COSTA'S HUMMINGBIRD

The exaggerated flare of the gorget of the male Costa's hummingbird is recognizable even when the violet color is not reflected. Not as obvious in this photograph are the violet patches on the crown and behind the eye.

A female Costa's hummingbird sits on her nest in a jojoba tree. Both the large head and short tail are apparent in this photograph. Note how the tail does not extend beyond the wing tips.

A tiny male calliope hummingbird displays his streaming-patterned, wine-red gorget.

the coast of California and the low desert scrub of western Mexico, southern California, and southern Arizona. Individuals show up sporadically in the Pacific Northwest.

The bulk of the population winters in western Mexico and Baja California. The few that winter in the U.S. live mostly among chuparosa plants in the Sonoran Desert. Their numbers increase throughout the winter and peak in March and April. By summer, they have finished nesting, and nearly all of them have disappeared. Nesting averages about one month later in the Mojave Desert, and the first birds arrive in February.

There is some evidence that the desert-nesting birds migrate to coastal California and join the coastal breeders rather than traveling directly back to Mexico. The birds that nest on the California coast start showing up in March. The population peaks in early summer and then declines as males leave, followed by females and juveniles. By the end of September, only a few overwintering birds remain.

Like other North American hummers, the male Costa's performs a courtship flight display to attract females. His looping dives and whistles are particularly impressive. When a male Costa's sees a female visiting his territory, he buzzes or circles her. While she sits, he climbs steeply to perhaps 100 feet or more and begins a series of dramatic high-speed loops that exhibit his skill and fitness. It is a performance that requires much practice to do well.

At the top of the loop, the male dives powerfully and begins a high-pitched whistle. Still whistling

loudly, he pulls out of his daredevil descent near the object of his passion and only a few feet above the ground. But he doesn't stop; he loops up to repeat the dive. Near the top of his ascent, he slows down, gathering his energy for another headlong rush to the ground. The loops are continuous and are accompanied by a wing noise at the bottom varying from a soft humming to a harsh wing ruffling.

It takes the male about six seconds to complete a loop, and he may performs dozens or only a few before beginning the final phase of his display, a rapid flight away from the twittering female, zigzagging sharply from side to side as he disappears. It is only a matter of seconds, less than a half minute, before the male usually reappears. The female may stay or go, but copulation has never been noted to directly follow the display.

Identification

Costa's is a small hummer with a short tail, short bill, and large head (pictures, pp. 16, 117). The violet gorget of the male flares distinctively at the corners, and as in Anna's, the iridesence on Costa's extends onto the head.

Females can be recognized by their shape, particularly the short tail. The only other North American hummer with such a short tail is the calliope hummer. Female and young calliopes have rufous sides; Costa's has no rufous color on its sides or elsewhere. The pattern of the tails of female and young Costa's resembles that of the female black-chinned hummingbird (picture, p. 110).

Calliope Hummingbird
Stella calliope

Calliope hummingbirds accompany the much more numerous and larger rufous hummers in their spring migration up the coast of California. As soon as flowers start to bloom in the western mountains, the calliopes head up the slopes, some following the parade of blossoms all the way to the timberline.

Feeding on flowers in alpine meadows, the calliopes mate, and females nest and raise their young. They manage to coexist with the dominant rufous hummers in much of their range, partly by feeding close to the ground and behaving inconspicuously.

The fall trip home, as far as is known, is also at high elevation along the western mountain ranges. Calliopes don't encounter many backyards in the remote regions they nest in and migrate through, although some do visit gardens and feeders, including those in lowland areas.

The calliope is the smallest nesting hummer (which is to say, the smallest bird) in North America. Weighing about 2.7 grams, it is some 20 percent lighter than the rufous hummingbird. It is so small that it exists at the very edge of possibility for a warm-blooded vertebrate animal.

CALLIOPE HUMMINGBIRD

The male broad-billed hummingbird has a gaudy red bill to accentuate his glittering costume. The broad-billed is one of several hummers that, within the U.S., nest only in a few parts of Arizona, New Mexico, or Texas near the Mexican border.

Being warm-blooded means that a body has to generate heat to keep warm. The larger the animal, the more food it burns (metabolizes), and the more heat it generates. A large animal is like a large campfire; it needs only occasional refueling to stay alive. Fueling a hummingbird is like keeping a tiny fire burning with a succession of twigs.

Bodies lose heat through their surface. The larger the surface area, the more heat is lost to the surroundings. The tiny calliope has more surface area for its weight than any bird in North America. It and other hummers also lack the insulating down of larger birds. So a calliope not only generates less heat than larger birds but also loses the heat faster. The only way it can stay warm and alive is to eat often and metabolize food extremely rapidly. It takes about 10 minutes, for instance, for a calliope to digest a fruit fly and excrete the hard parts.

If it were significantly smaller, the calliope simply couldn't cope to stay alive. Only cold-blooded creatures, insects, can exist at sizes much smaller than the calliope hummingbird.

Identification

Male calliope hummingbirds have their own distinctive gorget variation. Instead of being a solid mass of overlapping iridescent feathers, the gorget of the calliope flows in wine-colored streamers.

Females and young calliopes are distinguished by their small size, short tail, and the pale rufous on their underparts (picture, p. 19). There is some rufous at the base of the tail, but it is not obvious.

The Lives of Summer Songbirds — Raising a Family

Numerous songbirds from several different families make the journey from Central and South America to the U.S. and Canada to nest. Although they are all larger than hummingbirds, many are much harder to see. One of the most visible of the summer songbirds are **the orioles.**

Orioles like to feed and nest in scattered tall trees and consequently are well adapted to urban parks and mature suburbs. They commonly return to the same nesting site each year while young birds disperse to new territories.

The Baltimore oriole (picture, p. 23) is the most common backyard oriole of the East; Bullock's (pictures, p. 22 and below) holds that distinction in the West. Orchard orioles (picture, p. 9) inhabit much of the East but prefer to nest in rural areas, especially near water. Scott's and hooded orioles are found in parts of the Southwest and California.

In the two common backyard orioles, Baltimore and Bullock's, males arrive in spring a few days before females and yearling birds. They waste no time staking out a small territory. Males sing to attract females and display to those that pass through their domain. A female that accepts a male's overtures will start building her nest in his territory, and together the two birds will defend it.

Yearling males have less success attracting mates than older males. They often have to wait a year until they have their adult male plumage to successfully mate. As yearlings, they resemble females.

The nests of Baltimore and Bullock's orioles are sack-like structures that hang from the small outer limbs of large deciduous trees and are concealed by foliage. The female generally does the nest building, although the male sometimes brings her materials

A female Bullock's oriole feeds on an orange. Female and young Bullock's orioles may be a little paler or brighter than this specimen, but the brightest yellow-orange is always on the head. Female Baltimore orioles may be nearly as colorful as males (picture, p. 47) or they may be drab. On drab female and young Baltimores, the brightest color is on the breast rather than the face.

A male summer tanager feeds a cowbird chick while two baby tanagers beg for food. Summer tanagers aggressively defend their territory from any cowbirds they see, but cowbirds are able to approach and deposit their egg when the tanagers are temporarily away.

The female scarlet tanager has not a hint of scarlet on her. Like the females of other tanager species, she is greenish olive above and greenish yellow below. This female scarlet tanager has darker wings than the female summer tanager, and she lacks the white wingbar of the female western tanager.

and assists. The female weaves the nest using long blades of grasses or similar vegetable fibers. She also uses hair, twine, and synthetic fibers if available, and lines the nest with soft, downy materials.

The nests of orchard, Scott's, and hooded orioles are smaller and not as deep as those of Bullock's and Baltimore orioles. The Scott's oriole often attaches her nest to yucca plants, and the hooded oriole frequently hangs hers on the underside of a palm leaf.

Female Baltimore and Bullock's orioles commonly lay four or five eggs, but smaller and larger clutches are also reported. Females incubate the eggs for approximately 12 days and then brood the nestlings for several more days. The male will sometimes bring her food while she is on the nest, and he helps feed the nestlings, which grow rapidly and fledge in about two weeks.

Baltimore and Bullock's orioles raise one brood per season but will often nest a second time if the first nest fails.

Oriole-Watching by Ear

The songs of Baltimore and Bullock's orioles are strong and clear, occurring at a midfrequency range that even damaged older human ears can hear. Baltimore oriole songs have a pure whistled quality; Bullock's are more nasal. There is much individual variation in the songs, which leads scientists to suspect that males learn them rather than knowing them through genetic encoding. Some Baltimore males regularly sing songs that last less than a second and contain six notes or less; others sing a dozen or more notes that last for two seconds or more. Bullock's songs contain more and shorter notes on average and never have the repetition of tones characteristic of the Baltimore oriole. Female Baltimore and Bullock's orioles also sing, but the songs are usually only a few short whistled notes.

The brilliant tanagers are as eye-catching as orioles, but they generally stay in the canopy of large trees and are less often seen. Their presence is usually revealed by their songs.

Three tanager species are widespread in the U.S. Scarlet tanagers (pictures, p. 31 and above) nest in deciduous and mixed deciduous-coniferous forests in the East from the Appalachians north to southern Canada. The appropriately named western tanager inhabits western deciduous and mixed forests (picture, p. 22). Ranging across the South from Florida to California is the summer tanager (picture, above).

The mating and nesting habits of tanagers are similar to those of the orioles previously described. Males claim a territory and sing to attract females, which build nests and raise a single brood. Some summer tanagers may raise two broods.

Tanager nests are not the tightly woven, hanging type created by orioles. Instead, they are loosely woven, cup-like structures resting on branches. Sometimes the nests are so flimsy that the eggs can be seen through the bottom.

One of the major differences in the lives of orioles and tanagers is that tanagers in many areas have their nests parasitized by brown-headed cowbirds. Orioles recognize and will remove a cowbird egg, but tanagers don't. Cowbirds replace a tanager egg with one of their own to be cared for by the tanager. Sometimes two or more tanager eggs are replaced.

The scarlet tanager is also threatened by forest fragmentation. It nests in the forest interior, and when the forest fragment is too small, the eggs or nestlings are often lost to predators or cowbirds.

Not all summer songbirds have the dramatic colors of male orioles and tanagers. The thrushes that migrate from the tropics are plain brownish-backed birds with brown spots on their white breasts. Males and females look alike.

There are six species of **spot-breasted thrushes,** and one of them, the hermit thrush, remains in the southern and western U.S. in large numbers over winter. The others are all summer visitors from the tropics. Without experience, a person may have difficulty distinguishing one species from another.

In much of the U.S., the spot-breasted thrushes are migrants on their way to or from their northern or mountain forest nesting grounds, but the veery and the wood, Swainson's, Bicknell's, and hermit thrushes breed in some regions of the U.S.

The thrushes also differ from the colorful orioles and tanagers in that they are primarily birds of the forest floor. They gather insects and fruit from leaf litter on the ground and from the low understory.

Nests vary from species to species, but all are simple cups woven from vegetation. In some species, they are built in low vegetation, shrubs, or the crotch or lower limbs of a tree. In others, the nest is often built directly on the ground, concealed in shrubs or similar understory.

For all their differences, spot-breasted thrushes follow a nesting routine very much like that of the orioles or tanagers. Females build the nests, incubate the eggs, and brood the young. Males assist with the feeding. One brood per season is the norm.

Like tanagers, many spot-breasted thrushes are threatened by forest fragmentation and by cowbirds.

The wood thrush (picture, p. 35) has become the poster child for declining summer songbirds because of its losses and continued vulnerability.

The plain, shy spot-breasted thrushes make their biggest impression with their flute-like songs. Speaking of the wood thrush, Thoreau wrote of the "ethereal quality that sets the thrush apart from all others." The name of the veery, one of the spot-breasted thrushes, is derived from its *vee-ur* song, given in a series of cascading tones.

There are several warblers, such as the water-thrushes and the ovenbird, that have dull plumages and live like thrushes on the forest floor, but most of **the numerous warblers** that arrive each spring are very colorful arboreal birds.

One of the earliest to arrive is the northern parula, a tiny bundle of bright colors. Many parulas winter on islands in the Carribbean, and some nest in the southern U.S. By early May, some parulas already have fledglings to witness the many other warblers still en route north to begin nesting.

The 50-plus North American species of warblers live very different lives. There is a species for almost every habitat and many species that occupy a variety of habitats.

Black-and-white warblers are one of the specialists. They forage ike a nuthatch or brown creeper for insect matter on a tree's trunk and large limbs, the only warbler to do so.

The American redstart (a warbler) often forages like a flycatcher, males flashing bright salmon patches in the wings and tail as they hawk flying insects.

Quite a few warblers, including the common yellowthroat (picture, p. 29) and orange-crowned warbler, nest on or near the ground. Many others,

The Cornell Lab of Ornithology, in a citizen-science program dubbed Project Tanager, monitored numerous scarlet tanager nests and was able to put numbers to the birds' acreage requirements. Using the data, the scientists at Cornell prepared forest management guidelines for birds of the forest interior.

This veery nest with eggs is on the ground, hidden deep in a dense stand of ferns. Veeries often nest in moist or swampy areas. The nests are frequently a few feet above the ground in a shrub or small tree.

A red-eyed vireo feeds a nestling. Red-eyed vireos are one of the most abundant summer songbirds, but they are heard much more often than they are seen. Their nests, like this one, are regularly built in the fork of a small tree branch.

such as the yellow and chestnut-sided warblers, prefer shrubs or other low growth. Cerulean and Cape May warblers (picture, p. 23) are two of many that regularly nest 50 feet or higher in trees. Prothonotary warblers nest in cavities.

Warbler nests, wherever they are and whatever they are constructed with, are usually built by females, and the eggs are incubated only by females. Both parents care for the nestlings, and unless there is a nest failure, they usually attempt only a single brood per season.

Among the most abundant and likely warblers to visit a backyard are the yellow warbler, the yellow-rumped warbler, the magnolia warbler (in the East), and the orange-crowned warbler (in the West).

Some of the summer migrants are **birds with stout conical bills** for cracking seeds. These birds migrate to North America for the same reason the others do — to raise their young where there is an abundance of insects. During the spring and summer, birds such as the black-headed grosbeak and rose-breasted grosbeak (picture, p. 24) eat more animal matter than seeds or other vegetable matter, and they feed insects to their young.

The two grosbeaks like open woodlands and areas with scattered trees. They commonly visit and nest in parks and yards, choosing a shrub or small tree in which to build their loosely constructed, cup-shaped nests. Females do the nest construction, but males share in incubation and brooding duties.

The brood patch in males is just a bare patch of skin on the belly. In females, the brood patch is much more developed. Several days before laying her first egg, a female songbird will molt the downy feathers from a large area of her belly. The skin of this area thickens and the blood vessels in it grow larger and more numerous. The area becomes puffy and loose so that it will drape over the eggs and heat them to the body temperature of the mother.

At night, it is the female grosbeak that sits on the nest to keep the eggs warm. During the day, male and female spend about equal time incubating.

The smaller conically billed birds of summer, the buntings, are as colorful as the orioles, tanagers, or warblers. In the East, the widespread species is the indigo bunting (picture, p. 25), which inhabits overgrown fields, hedgerows, and scrub. The lazuli bunting (picture, p. 42) occupies similar habitat in much of the West, and the two share range in the Southwest. Painted buntings (picture, p. 24) are found in parts of the South.

The buntings often raise two broods or more during a nesting season. When that occurs, the female may start her second nest before the nestlings in the first brood have fledged. The male then assumes full care for the first brood.

This handsome male black-headed grosbeak is displaying as he would to a female. The nuptial flight is preceded by loud singing from an exposed perch. The male continues to sing as he flies toward the female with wings and tail fully spread, displaying the striking pattern of his plumage. He gradually climbs a few feet in stiff winged flight and then glides back to a perch. The whole flight takes 8 to 10 seconds.

CORNELL LAB OF ORNITHOLOGY
Cornell Lab of Ornithology
159 Sapsucker Woods Rd.
Ithaca, NY 14850
800-843-BIRD (2473)
(outside U.S.) 607 254-2473
http://birds.cornell.edu

NATIONAL WILDLIFE FEDERATION
Backyard Wildlife Habitat
   Program
11100 Wildlife Center Dr.
Reston, VA 20190-5362
703-438-6000
www.nwf.org/backyard
   wildlifehabitat/

MANUFACTURERS
Aspects, Inc.
245 Child Street
P.O. Box 408
Warren, RI 02885
888-ASPECTS
www.aspectsinc.com

Avian Aquatics, Inc.
312 Walnut Street
Milton, DE 19968
800-788-6478
www.avianaquatics.com

Droll Yankees
27 Mill Road
Foster, RI 02825
800-352-9164
www.drollyankees.com

Duncraft
102 Fisherville Road
Concord, NH 03303
800-593-5656
www.duncraft.com

Nature Products
P.O. Box 6950
Warwick, RI 02887
800-556-7670
www.natureproducts.com

Opus
P.O. Box 525
Bellingham, MA 02019
508-966-3182
www.opususa.com

Perky-Pet Products, Inc.
2201 S. Wabash Street
Denver, CO 80231
303-751-9000
www.perky-pet.com

Plasticraft Nature Line
800-239-4105
   (for catalog)
www.plasticraftmfg.com

Tejas Hummingbird
   Feeders
P.O. Box 85
Rio Frio, TX 78879
210-735-1696
830-232-5167
www.tejashummer.com

Wild Birds Unlimited
800-326-4928
   (for locations)
www.wbu.com

ORGANIZATIONS
American Bird Conservancy
1250 24th Street NW,
   Suite 400
Washington, DC 20037
202-778-9966
www.abcbirds.org

Hummer/Bird Study Group
P.O. Box 250
Clay, AL 35048-0250
205-681-2888
www.hummingbirdsplus.org

The Hummingbird Society
P.O. Box 394
Newark, DE 19715
800-529-3699
www.hummingbird.org

Lady Bird Johnson
   Wildflower Center
(information on native
   plants and nurseries)
4801 La Crosse Avenue
Austin, TX 78739-1702
512-292-4200
www.wildflower.org

National Audubon Society
700 Broadway
New York, NY 10003
212-979-3000
www.audubon.org

National Fish and Wildlife
   Foundation
1120 Connecticut Avenue,
   NW, Suite 900
Washington, DC 20036
202-857-0166
Fax 202-857-0162
http://www.nfwf.org/

North American Native
   Plant Society (NANPS)
P.O. Box 84, Station D
Etobicoke, ON M9A 4X1
416-680-6280
www.nanps.org

Operation RubyThroat:
   The Hummingbird Project
Hilton Pond Center for
   Piedmont Natural History
1432 DeVinney Rd.
York, SC 29745
803-684-5852
www.rubythroat.org

Partners In Flight
Terry Rich, National
   Coordinator
208-378-5347
Terry_Rich@fws.gov
www.PartnersInFlight.org

Southeastern Arizona Bird
   Observatory (SABO)
P.O. Box 5521
Bisbee, AZ 85603-5521
520-432-1388
www.sabo.org

WEBSITE
Hummingbirds!
(migration charts and more)
www.hummingbirds.net

Application for Certification

**BACKYARD WILDLIFE
HABITAT™**
NATIONAL WILDLIFE FEDERATION®

Take heart, you needn't be a zoologist or botanist to fill out this application. The National Wildlife Federation looks forward to acknowledging your efforts in providing habitat for wildlife where you live or work. Do your best to fill out this application, and if there are problems, we'll get back to you with some suggestions. Within 6-8 weeks of receiving your application, we'll send you a beautiful personalized certificate suitable for framing and you have the option of purchasing a yard sign to educate others about your project.

CONTACT INFORMATION *(Please TYPE or PRINT legibly)*

Applicant Name _____

Organization Name (if applicable) _____

Name(s) to Appear on Certificate _____

Address of Habitat _____

City _____ County _____

State/Province _____ Country _____ Zip/Postal Code _____

Telephone _____ E-mail Address _____

Mailing Address (if different from above) _____

Office Use:
Habitat # _____
Fee Rcvd. _____
Certified _____
Cert. Sent _____
BWH Type _____

If you are applying for someone else, please provide your contact information:

Contact Name _____

Telephone _____ E-mail Address _____

PROPERTY INFORMATION

Property Size (approx. acres) _____

Have you ever applied for certification before? ☐ Yes ☐ No   If yes, list Habitat # _____
If yes, is this application for ☐ New Property ($15 fee waived if you are certifying a new property) ☐ Second Property

Is your property ☐ Urban ☐ Suburban ☐ Rural

How long have you been gardening for wildlife at this property? _____

Did a Habitat Steward or Host assist you? ☐ No ☐ Yes - Name of Steward or Host _____

PROCESSING INFORMATION *(Allow 6-8 Weeks for Processing)*

☐ $15 Application Fee enclosed

This fee covers our processing and handling costs and is non-refundable. Make checks out to:

**National Wildlife Federation
Backyard Wildlife Habitat Applications
11100 Wildlife Center Drive
Reston, VA 20190-5362
(703) 438-6434**

**NATIONAL
WILDLIFE
FEDERATION®**
www.nwf.org™

☐ I want an additional certificate. I've included an additional $5 for each extra copy of the certificate.

Please keep a copy of this application for your records.

HABITAT INFORMATION

1. Plant List:
Plant communities form the foundation of habitat for all wildlife. Plants that are native to your region are best. Please try to list the trees, shrubs, grasses, perennials, annuals, ferns, cacti, etc. that grow in your habitat. Also indicate an approximate quantity of each species. (Attachments welcome – see #8.)

_____   _____   _____   _____

_____   _____   _____   _____

_____   _____   _____   _____

_____   _____   _____   _____

2. Food:
Plants are the best food source for wildlife. Feeders can be used as a supplemental source of food. Remember some creatures will become food for others in a balanced habitat. Be sure to encourage a diversity of wildlife in your yard to ensure a healthy ecosystem. Tell us how you provide food:

Plant Foods: ☐ Seeds   ☐ Nuts   ☐ Berries   ☐ Fruits   ☐ Nectar   ☐ Foliage/Twigs   ☐ Sap   ☐ Pollen
Feeder Type: ☐ Tube   ☐ Platform   ☐ Suet   ☐ Hummingbird   ☐ Other _____

3. Water:
Wildlife needs a clean water source for drinking and bathing. Tell us how you provide water:

☐ Birdbath   ☐ Water Garden/Pond   ☐ Lakefront   ☐ Riverfront   ☐ Stream   ☐ Wetland   ☐ Vernal Pool
☐ Puddling Area   ☐ Coastal   ☐ Spring/Seep   ☐ Other_____

4. Cover:
Wildlife needs places to find shelter from the weather and predators. Tell us how you provide cover:

☐ Wooded Area   ☐ Dense Shrubs/Thicket   ☐ Bramble Patch   ☐ Evergreens   ☐ Ground Cover   ☐ Brush Pile
☐ Log Pile   ☐ Rock Pile/Wall   ☐ Meadow/Scrub/Prairie   ☐ Other_____

5. Places to Raise Young:
In order to provide complete habitat, you must provide places for wildlife to raise young. Tell us how you provide a place to raise young for nesting birds, denning mammals, egg-laying amphibians, reptiles, fish, butterflies, and other insects and invertebrates:

☐ Mature Trees   ☐ Dense Shrubs/Thicket   ☐ Meadow/Scrub/Prairie   ☐ Water Garden/Wetland
☐ Trees with Cavities   ☐ Dens in the Ground   ☐ Plants for Caterpillars to Eat   ☐ Other_____

6. Resource Conservation:
Tell us how you are conserving resources for people and wildlife:

☐ Establishing a rain garden or buffer to filter storm water   ☐ Capturing roof rain water   ☐ Mulching
☐ Xeriscape   ☐ Using drip soaker hose instead of sprinkler   ☐ Removing invasive exotics   ☐ Composting
☐ Planting native plants suited to the area   ☐ Reducing or eliminating pesticide and chemical fertilizer use
☐ Reducing or eliminating lawn areas   ☐ Keeping your cat indoors

7. Wildlife:
Please list the wildlife that your habitat supports.

☐ Insects/invertebrates   ☐ Fish   ☐ Amphibians   ☐ Reptiles   ☐ Birds   ☐ Mammals
Share specific species: _____

_____

8. Attachments:
Along with this application, please send us a simple sketch and/or photos of your habitat since we cannot visit it in person. Good quality photos and sketches may be selected for our website, but cannot be returned. Feel free to include other attachments to share additions to your plant and wildlife list or wildlife stories. All attachments must be no larger than 11" x 17." **Be sure to include your name and address on the back of all attachments, including each photo.**

☐ Photos enclosed (no more than five, please)
☐ Sketch enclosed